Nick Lyford
===========

Thanks for the support, and enjoy the reading!!

signature

Emmanuel S. Kirunda.

BEYOND THE FOURTH HERITAGE

A Personal View on How to
Transcend Our Heritages of Birth

Emmanuel S. Kirunda

authorHOUSE®

AuthorHouse™
1663 Liberty Drive
Bloomington, IN 47403
www.authorhouse.com
Phone: 1 (800) 839-8640

© 2016 Emmanuel Kirunda. All rights reserved.

No part of this book may be reproduced, stored in a retrieval system, or transmitted by any means without the written permission of the author.

Published by AuthorHouse 07/22/2016

ISBN: 978-1-5246-1704-2 (sc)
ISBN: 978-1-5246-1705-9 (hc)
ISBN: 978-1-5246-1703-5 (e)

Library of Congress Control Number: 2016910881

Print information available on the last page.

Any people depicted in stock imagery provided by Thinkstock are models, and such images are being used for illustrative purposes only.
Certain stock imagery © Thinkstock.

This book is printed on acid-free paper.

Because of the dynamic nature of the Internet, any web addresses or links contained in this book may have changed since publication and may no longer be valid. The views expressed in this work are solely those of the author and do not necessarily reflect the views of the publisher, and the publisher hereby disclaims any responsibility for them.

Table of Contents

Dedication ix
Acknowledgements xi
Foreword xiii
Preface xv

PART 1: BEING HUMAN 1
    1. Origin of Mankind 3
    2. Collective Unconscious 6
    3. Collective Consciousness 12

PART 2: RISE AND FALL OF CIVILIZATIONS 19
    4. Lost Ancient Civilizations 21
    5. The Six Cradle Civilizations 28
    6. European Classical Civilization 46
    7. Islamic Civilization 54
    8. European Western Civilization 66
       Origin of Consciousness and the Modern Mind 72
       A Brief History of Christianity 90
       Western Civilization is Not Dead, but Hurting 105
    9. The Three Sins Of Islamic
       and Western Dominance 113
    10. Africa In The Modern World 119
       The African's eternal dilemma 121

PART 3: TOWARD A HUMAN CIVILIZATION 131
    11. Thesis: The Heri of Kesa 137
       Definition 143
       Explanation 150
       A Fundamental Concept in Mathematics 156

The Limit of the Tribal Heritage 161
The Limit of the Religious Heritage 166
The Limit of the Western Heritage 183
Convergence of Consciousness & Rationality 187
A Brief Discussion About God: 195
The Tyranny of Experience: 210
How the Heri solves the African's
Eternal Dilemma 213
12. A Case For Doubt 222
End Notes 255

Appendix
Africa And Modern Civilization 257
   A. Africa In The Modern World 259
   B. Africa And The Pre-Modern Mindsets 262
      1. A Porous Mind 268
      2. Religion is Largely Bicameral 274
      3. The Herd Mentality 281
      4. Everything is Supernatural 291
      5. The Lack of Spatialization of Time 294
      6. The Lack of Agency 298
   C. Our Psyche Was Dismembered 307
      The Four Psychological Ills 308
      1: The Victim Mentality 314
      2: Inferiority Complex 318
      3. Our Eagerness to Consume Foreign Things 328
      4. The African's Eternal Dilemma 331
   D. Social Development Was Sabotaged 332
   E. Solving The Psychological Dismemberment 341
      The Cure for The Four Ills 345
   F. Solving The Social Sabotage 353

Table of Figures

Figure 1: The Spectrum of Mindsets 77
Figure 2: The Kamp Diagram Due to The Dilemma 128
Figure 3: My Family Lineage 144
Figure 4: The General Heri of Kesa 148
Figure 5: The Specific Heri of Kesa 149
Figure 6: Convergence Model of Understanding Life 193
Figure 7: The Heri Discussion of God 201
Figure 8: The Kamp Diagram Due to The Heri of Kesa 219

Dedication

To the uneducated Africans: So much to know, yet so little I know.

Acknowledgements

From the bottom of my heart, I would like to thank all those people who devoted their time to reading my first book and gave me enormous encouragement and feedback. This final book in my trilogy would not have happened without you. The list of such people is long, but I'd like to mention a few. Lynn Gilbert, your recommendation for me to read Julius Jaynes filled the big gap I had in my thinking and the result is a central theme of this book. Dickson Wasake, Kwame Rugunda, Daniel Kawuma, Christopher Bond, Jehanzeb Noor, Justas Staisiunas, Irene S. Kwaga, Nicholas Twinamatsiko, Andrew Othieno, Dauda Mawanda, Jaffar Tendo, Daniel Makubuya, Loyola Karobwa, Chip Herlocher, Jayson Post, Daniel Yanez, Stig Aune, James Jones, you each know your contributions and I thank you very much from the depth of my heart.

Also, let me send a big thank you to the groups of people, both friends and strangers, who came to my book signing events. More specifically, those people (mainly the Huns rugby club players) who came to Nasty's Bar in Austin, Texas, for my first book launch party, those who came out to the book signing at Monkey Wrench bookstore in Austin, the students and professors who attended my event at Lafayette College (special thanks to Prof. Ziolkowski and Prof. Veshosky), all those who attended my presentation at the Uganda North American Association in Chicago 2009 (special thanks to Erin Minckley Chlagmo), the people who attended my first Uganda presentation in December 2011 at Basoga Twekobaino in Jinja, and the students who attended my book signing at Makerere University in May 2012 (special thanks to Emmanuel Kitamirike, Professor Muzaale who was the chief guest, and Olavi Ndawula (RIP)).

Specifically I would like to also thank these four groups of people: 1) Irene S. Kwaga and Dauda Mawanda, thank you so much for the work you put into organizing the Retreat on The Fourth Heritage at Serena Hotel, Kampala in December 2015. As you know, the outcome of that retreat greatly shaped my approach to this book. 2) My two editors John Murdock and Irene S. Kwaga, I am greatly indebted to you for making my writing standard enough for the audience. And my proofreader Stefan Abrutat, thank you for sparing a week out of your busy schedule to show the world that rugby players can also read a 500-page book in seven days. 3) The writer of my foreword, Gordon Montgomery. Your understanding of my work truly touched my heart and in fact opened my eyes to realize that an Irish person also has a triple heritage just like me. This work, in a big way, is courtesy of your encouragement.4) The good people of Authoright. The final touches you put on this book and all the professional work you have put into bringing this book to a global market, are greatly appreciated.

More generally, I want to thank all the people I have ever come in contact with. Our relationships, whether good or bad, have enriched my life and helped me develop to a point where I can write a clear proposal regarding how I think as an African and, most importantly, do so in a simple framework that I believe any boy or girl from any part of the world will be able to adopt and use to transcend their heritages of birth.

Foreword

When my dear friend Emmanuel S. Kirunda, author of *The Fourth Heritage* and *The Fourth Republic*, asked me to write the foreword I was at once honored and shocked. He has really created a masterpiece with this, his bravest and most personal work to date, one which I am sure will have a deeply reverberating global impact for those who can perceive its profound message. He explained to me, in his inimitably polite and matter-of-fact way, that I actually understood what he was trying to convey and in our several discussions back and forth, I actually do believe he may be on to something. That's the nature of the brilliance of this man's writing and indeed his being. He thrusts others into the limelight, eschewing such center stage and having others believe that we are greater than we know ourselves to be. And that, essentially, is the thrust of this book that I'd like to congratulate you on getting into your hands by whichever means: physically or digitally. With any luck he'll have quite a bit of time in the well-deserved limelight with this latest book. Having been to an early reading of the first book I can attest to his being even more compelling "live."

The book deals with no less than humanity: where it came from to develop what we call civilizations and where the author suspects (and I concur) it is going. This is a brave book like no other I've read. It is constantly personal, sometimes very personal, as with the Chile incident. There are many subtle touches of humor along the way that keep the reader engaged, the energy light, while still allowing us to delve deeper into what is essentially a treatise on an entire new future for humanity. It's deeply educational, especially for those with only a cursory knowledge of the entire breadth of human history. It's even, dare I say it, controversial in its exposition of a dozen well-crafted steps, or hypotheses, that lead the reader into the depths of not only history, or indeed the future, but also into the delicious dimensions of human consciousness – collective or otherwise.

In my work as a coach, especially in the area of energetic healing, I support my clients in gaining clarity about who they are regarding their life's purpose and then guide them to live from that true source. Aligning what I have seen from working with hundreds of human beings, I found myself nodding vociferously throughout the book. It's clear this planet and all of us on it are evolving right in front of our own eyes. Will everybody wake up in time and see what the author here lays out for us? We, the entire universe, all of humanity, are energy on some level. So given that premise, what if we stopped looking outside of ourselves at the given socio-economic and cultural structures and instead looked inside at our true selves - the selves we know in our souls to have always been and energetically operated according to. What if that true self within us never left us, but has been waiting since the dawn of time in Africa to finally emerge as a new guiding light for humanity?

Gordon Montgomery BA MSc
Healing Coach
Austin, Texas
March 2016

PREFACE

I used to doubt myself and my abilities. I used to doubt how great I could be. My recollection is that these seeds of doubt were planted when I was about seven years old. In my first book I wrote about how at the age of five or six I used to feel invincible around the house and in the neighborhood. The neighborhood men used to give me immeasurable compliments, and at home I felt like the king as I would act out the part of Baba Omuto – The Little Father. I lost that childhood invincibility when I started school and the other kids began making fun of my given name. Looking back, this is the earliest time I recall starting to doubt myself as the all-powerful Baba Omuto. I think psychologically it was around this time that I began drawing inwards, questioning whom and how good I was. When kids would tease me about my name I would go back home crying and feeling sad. During those episodes I started thinking that if I could cry and I needed the protection of the real father, then maybe my being "Little Father" wasn't enough. This was the earliest seed of doubt planted in my mind.

Over the first four years of primary school which I spent at Iganga Town Council Primary, I mostly did well in school and that kept my confidence high. But there were also low points where I experienced some hardships on the playground, and didn't have enough money for a decent snack at break time. So doubt came into my mind in intermittent stages. When I did well in school I was super confident in my abilities. I specifically remember the first time I got the best grades in class (during my third term of Primary Two) and feeling that great sense of invincibility again. But as I mentioned in my first book, my grandmother died shortly thereafter and the next year of Primary Three was a total disaster. During the first term I was almost last in my class, and despite improving somewhat in the second term, I ended the year performing very poorly again in the third term. Primary Three (third grade) was a watershed period in my primary school career, a total disaster. I only understood better what happened that year when I was an adult and came to the realization that the loss of my dear grandmother affected me in ways no one ever considered. So that year was disastrous for my confidence, especially with regards to my abilities in the classroom and beliefs about my general level of intelligence.

Then suddenly in Primary Four I bounced back to being in the top ten of my class. Just like that my confidence shot up once again. I remember dancing and running home with my third term report card which declared me sixth overall in the class that year.

I bring all this up to illustrate the fact that I can pretty much point out stages in my life where I have seesawed between confidence and doubt. This has also manifested itself in other life challenges such as applying to universities, applying for jobs, performing well at work, and even socially in dating girls. It has also extended to my religious faith, resulting in periods when I doubted the very tenets of my religion of birth and periods when I had complete confidence that Jesus was the best thing to ever happen to mankind. All in all, I can point out when I was confident in a situation and when doubt took me over. I have now ingrained it in my psyche that maybe that is just the way life is; sometime you are high and sometimes you are low.

The last time I felt doubt about how great I can be was on January 30th, 2003. On that day I said, "To hell with it!" I took it to heart that I could do whatever I wanted to do, and be whoever I wanted to be. I was playing rugby for my school and loving it, I started concentrating on what I wanted out of my education and not what the school wanted to teach me - the feeling was great! I had a very happy, fun-filled social life and I began writing what has become these three books. I really felt like no one out there could tell my story for me. With a personal sense of confidence in how to articulate what I believe about who I am and how society should be, I started writing without a shred of doubt in my mind.

The people who have read my books (both in Uganda and in other parts of the world) have given me very heartfelt feedback about the impact the books have had on them. Some of this feedback has even included stories of life transformations. I had one grown man (a white American) tell me through tears about how my first book put into perspective a sad chapter of his life that involved a failed interracial romance. I have had teenagers tell me how they have been transformed to truly embrace the objective knowledge of science as opposed to superstitious traditional beliefs. I even had two Ugandan men tell me that my first book had an impact on them the way the Bible did. I have had many African friends agree with me that our problems are not political or economic, but rather they are psychological, and that we as a society should be talking more about the issues I raise in my first book. So much positive feedback from readers has inspired me to write this final book to my maiden writing adventure.

With this final book, I have no doubt that even more people will be impacted by its ideas, and in even more forceful ways. This third book is bigger in scope than the first two books combined and the reason for this is that I no longer doubt myself, or my abilities, or how great I can be in this life. I am ready for whatever.

I remember this feeling became very clear when I returned from the US to Uganda in late 2011 after going 11 straight years without returning home. My youngest sister, who was about 13 when I left, was now a grown woman. She conjured up some memories about me and in her excitement she called me "daddy." That is when it dawned on me that she had no recollection of our late father, and that I was the only fatherly figure she had ever known. This episode took me back to my infant days when I wanted to be "The Little Father." The sense of responsibility bestowed upon me as "the male" member of the family was exacerbated when my only brother passed away in 2013. At that time, my elder sister said to me very seriously, "Little brother ... what a pity. You are now the only man in the family, you have to look after your mother and all six of us." So just like that, I could not keep thinking that I was just a little brother to my three elder sisters – they all began looking up to me for guidance as their fatherly figure. This responsibility was compounded even more when you realize that my mother practically treats me like an old member of the family or clan; I am not just her young and only son now.

When Freud said religion is man's psychological yearning for a fatherly figure – I know this yearning first hand from the intimate relationship I have with my family. With such societal expectations, I have no choice but to rise up and act like the man of the family to my mother and my six sisters. And for the most part it is going okay, except on those increasingly frequent occasions when the old woman mentions that she wants to see her daughter-in-law and several grandchildren (my mother once told me that I should aim to have at least five children, and she says I can't argue with her because if she hadn't aimed for a whopping eight children I wouldn't have been born).

I am telling this personal story so that while reading these three books you will understand that I am writing them from a practical point of view. When I write about culture or religion or world affairs, it is not because I studied these things extensively or I am an authority on them. It is because they have a direct effect on me and how I relate to my family as well as my community; they also affect how my family and community relate to me. So when I say in my writing that I am coming from the vantage point of seeing the world in the way my illiterate family members see the world, please keep in mind that that is because my perspective is not that of a typical person born in the West, raised speaking English and knowing about modern civilization from a point of view that takes for granted most aspects of modern life. There are members of my immediate family who cannot comprehend the fact that the earth is round, and if you think I'm joking, rest assured that my only brother died at age 40 unable to comprehend that the earth is round and that it goes around the sun.

As I've mentioned, this is the last book in the trilogy that starts with *The Fourth Heritage* and then *The Fourth Republic*. I started writing the ideas that became the three books back in January of 2003. I remember sharing the core conclusions that are now the foundations of these books with my Delta Upsilon fraternity brothers at Lafayette College, and as the only black and African brother in the fraternity at the time it was very special for me to have had such privileged white American students as my audience. The first draft I wrote was one massive rambling treatise on the ideas now distilled throughout the trilogy. It took me over six years just to write out the first topic that now constitutes the core idea in my first book; the topic of who we are as Africans born within the triple heritages of tribe, religion and European influence. It then took me another two years to write the second book, a standalone piece about the kind of society I envision within my country of Uganda that could best enable the people to attain their own personal Fourth Heritage.

So as I publish this final book about the topic I started in the first book – the point that the developed peoples of the modern world have something I call a "Heri" which propels them to development – the reader should know that it took over 13 years from the time this general idea came into my mind until these words went to print. Since 2003, I have been distilling it in my mind. During this distillation time I moved from the US back to Uganda and am now living in London, UK. I have changed careers three times – from civil engineer to working in an investment bank to working in my current position as a project controls professional in the oil & gas industry. Socially, I have taken on the new hobbies of playing golf and tennis, and stopped playing rugby altogether because I lost interest – I still watch, though.

One element that has enabled me to write three books easily while having a full-time job and also a fully-fledged social and sport life is that in high school, I taught myself how to type on the keyboard very fast. The average person types about 40 words per minute, while a good secretary types about 60 words per minute. I have timed myself and on average I type 55 words per minute. That has given me a lot of efficiency and productivity when it comes to writing my books.

Throughout most of my time writing this third book, I was calling it *The Heri of Kesa* – because the thesis chapter bears that name. However, for branding purposes, it became necessary that I use the phrase "Fourth Heritage" somewhere in the title, simply because this book is a specific detailed discussion of the general "Heri" issue I introduced in the first book. For those of you who haven't read the first book, in it I discussed how the word "Kesa" came about ... it is the nickname I took up in Primary Four (fourth grade) when I moved from my home town of Iganga to study at Nkumba Primary which was in another part of the country. My move to a new town where no one knew me gave me a chance to recreate myself, and since I had been psychologically tortured in Iganga where many people made fun of my last name, I coined the acronym Kesa as my first act of personal reinvention. With that name, I attained a new identity. Up until now, whenever long lost schoolmates from Nkumba or even from my Ugandan high school call me Kesa, it conjures up good memories in me because it was the first creation I made in this life that forever changed my destiny. However, as we all know, sometimes we outgrow nicknames. I am now more used to going by the other nicknames of "Sonny" or "Sunny" which are not of my own choosing, but that of my friends in the US.

The breadth of the scope of this book came to me after I recalled my first days at Nkumba Primary School. Starting in Primary Five (fifth grade), we were taught by Mr. Dan Badebye about the ancient civilizations of Mesopotamia and Egypt. I was really intrigued by the things we were taught, and on many occasions I remember immersing myself in imitating ancient Egyptian writing by scribbling rudimentary hieroglyphics or Sumerian cuneiform writings. When I finally got the inspiration to broaden my scope of this book and cover ancient cradle civilizations, in a way it became my outward pouring of the things I imagined during those days at Nkumba Primary – it dawned on me that maybe this book is my only chance to make use of the knowledge I got in Primary Five. One such thing I used to imagine and ponder was what ancient civilizations took root in what is present day Uganda, especially since it was the source of the Nile upon which ancient Egyptian civilization relied on for its life support.

I mentioned in the first book that in 2003 I started writing my thoughts about how I wish to see my world, out of a great deal of frustration I was feeling. While studying in the US, I was reading about a lot of problems back home in Africa: witch doctors kidnapping children for human sacrifices, Christian leaders bamboozling the general public (the worst incident of which was the burning of over

900 people in a church in 2000), political instability from competing dictatorships, infrastructure decay with no culture of safety (boarding schools burning down regularly due to arson or bad electrical wiring), rampant poverty among relatives and throughout society, and the weirdest one for me was a period of time when different parts of Uganda were struck randomly by lightning, resulting in the loss of life and property. Feeling the immensity of these problems, I wanted to help by doing the thing that would have the most impact from my vantage point. There are millions of dollars being donated by other people, thousands of volunteers helping out with diseases and poverty, hundreds of consultants and foreign attaches helping out with political and economic problems. As one Ugandan and African, I felt that I had been blessed with a vast breadth of experience insomuch that I received the strong conviction that sharing my point of view through writing would do a great deal of good for so many people with backgrounds like mine.

I am not unique – okay, every human is unique – what I mean is that I am not much different from other people. I am very sure that my efforts to analyze the core problems in our society and offer a resolution is not a new thing. Furthermore, the desire to understand what keeps Africa and people of African descent occupying the lowest levels of human development in Western civilization is shared by many. Take, for example, Frantz Fanon – the black Caribbean-turned-Algerian freedom fighter – who was maybe the greatest anti-colonialism writer from the pre-independence Africa of the 1950s and 1960s. In his book *Black Skin White Masks*, while lamenting the state of colonialism in Africa and the suffering of his fellow black man in Africa, America, Europe and the Caribbean, Fanon said:

My unreason was countered with reason. My reason with "more reason." Every hand was a losing hand for me. I analyzed my heredity. I made a complete audit of my ailment. I wanted to be typically Negro – it was no longer possible. I wanted to be white – that was a joke. And, when I tried, on the level of ideas and intellectual activity, to reclaim my negritude, it was snatched away from me. Proof was presented that my effort was only a term in the dialectic. (Fanon, p.101).

Fanon further adds: "I should constantly remind myself that the real leap consists in introducing invention into existence." (Fanon,p.179). Picking cue from Fanon, at the onset of my writing, I realized that the only way to move forward and genuinely tackle the mountains of problems I faced as an African, or as a black person, was to use my brain more for creating the world I wanted to see and less for analyzing the problems that were abound. The task of analyzing is already done by so many people, including the countless political scientists and lawyers who can analyze any political system far better than I could ever do. Nonetheless, I have yet to read a simple yet holistic account of an African social structure as the one in *The Fourth Republic*. I decided to diagnose the problems in our society and offer specific creative solutions in written form. Let the experts (lawyers, politicians, economists, professors, etc.) do the analysis and critique of what I have written.

In my three books, I have devoted more than 80% of my efforts to "creating," because of the very many qualified people who can do the analyzing. I know there are a multitude of PhDs who can analyze all the issues I am writing about in more refined ways than I have time to. Take, for example, religion. There are so many religious preachers and writers who can analyze the Bible inside and out, but none of them have presented me or my fellow Africans with a creative device that can be used to stand on to help us appreciate life – or religion – without also feeling like we have very little agency and that we are somehow inferior, as all the revelations from God come to non-Africans, despite us being the first people on the planet. As a young person, I never came across any tools or analytical devices that could help me fight all the negative psychological complexities I felt while internalizing religion as it was preached to us by our "well-read" preachers.

I started my writings with a lot of anger; anger toward my society, anger toward my leaders, anger toward my teachers, and anger toward my forefathers. But over the last 13 years I have cooled down, sobered up, and done so much thinking that I now feel sympathetic toward our leaders, teachers and forefathers. It is not that they deliberately put me on the short end of the stick of history, but rather, they did not and do not have the necessary tools to put me out of the misery I found myself in – both psychologically and socially. So I took it upon myself to create my existence (to borrow Fanon's words) and forgive the shortcomings of my forefathers and current leaders. I have done so much "creating" in my three books that I really deeply feel I have exhausted myself regarding the three topics of "Who we are," "How should our society be," and "How can we develop modern mindsets."

In my mind I have really gone beyond the three heritages of my birth (tribe, religion and Western heritage). While visiting Uganda in 2013, I remember two separate occasions where groups of people who knew my tribal heritage tried using tribalism to insult me by speaking negative stereotypes about "my people," but I totally ignored them and just bore a big smile on my face. In my new transcendent mind, I don't represent my tribe and the generalizations they spoke have zero psychological impact on me. On the religious side, lately I have come across so many Muslim colleagues who go out of their way to defend their religions due to the havoc of terrorism that is unfolding all over the world. In my mind I keep trying to remember if I used to defend Christianity as a young man, but nowadays whatever evil people may do in the name of Christianity has no bearing at all on my identity or my religiosity. In fact, I have a whole list of crimes and evils that were committed by Christians in the name of their religion, but it doesn't rattle me at all to reject them because in my mind I have gone beyond being identified by my Christian heritage. I don't deny my Christian heritage, but it does not define my deepest sense of who I am. On the Western colonial heritage side, I am currently devoting a lot of energy to studying languages other than English and I am finding more joy in learning about Asian and South American cultures than I ever did drilling my mind with all the glorious details of the mighty British Empire. Actually, for a while I remember wanting to go live in Japan because I fell in love with its non-Christian ways of looking at life, which is very similar to my tribal view, except that they are now a modern society while my people are still engulfed in oral tradition.

My current mindset is so much about hard work, contentment, joy and a general relaxation about life that I feel, by sharing these final ideas in this book, more people might be inspired to change mindsets and live a more optimistic and joyous life so that together we can embark on recreating our wonderful world. This is the only planet we know of that has life – can we make it one full of more happiness and less misery? I have bottomed out so much in my thinking about the issues I write about that sometimes I don't have the energy to argue about them at all. Sometimes I feel like the whole world is missing the point; we are busy debating politics and entertainment or sports, yet I think we should be discussing issues like the ones I write about here. So as you read this book, bear in mind that more than anything, I would love to interact with you and I welcome your critique or opinion on these matters (www.4thheritage.com).

In *The Fourth Heritage*, I talked about the lack of a Heri being one of the two cardinal problems that hinder our development in Uganda, Africa. In this book I want to explain my personal Heri, which I have used to develop intellectually and otherwise. I ended *The Fourth Heritage* with a quote from the late Professor Ali Mazrui which reads, "It can be said that Africa invented man, the Semites invented God and the Europeans invented the world or at least the idea of the world."

This book is organized in three parts. In the first part I discuss how "Africa inventing man" means that when you look at the creature "man" there is no dispute that its origin is in Africa and its essence, whether in Africa, Europe, America or Asia, is similar in the most fundamental way that is human. The fact that modern civilization has been created by non-Africans, and has many centers that are in other places but Africa, is among the reasons I believe the modern human soul is facing so much trauma and hopelessness. For example, wouldn't you expect to run into psychological non-alignment if you were to artificially build a way of thinking that puts the beginning of mankind in some Asiatic desert, when all the universal knowledge (science) points to the irrefutable fact that Africa is the cradle of mankind? Regarding this point, my favorite writer, Jacob Bronowski, says that, "If an understanding of man's origins, his evolution, his history, and his progress is not the commonplace of the school books [worldwide], we shall not exist." I take the idea of Africa being the cradle of the human species to be more than an intellectual exercise; it has spiritual meaning to me, and it should to every human being.

In the second part of this book I discuss the second part of Mazrui's quote, which says "the Semites invented God and the Europeans invented the world." I show the fact that even if man and the first civilizations arose in Africa, the current modern civilization has been made by non-Africans, specifically the Arabs with regards to Islamic civilization and the Europeans with regards to Western civilization. I go through the history of the rise and fall of the six ancient cradle civilizations before the current modern one, and end by mentioning that the current Western civilization has not yet fallen, but it is hurting.

After the first two parts, which explain the extent of how Africans are similar to other humans (through the collective unconscious), and the way Africans have been left behind in modern civilization, in the third and final part of the book I discuss my proposed solution on how I changed my mindset and how it can be used by Africans and others to fit and thrive in the current modern world. I use the device of the Heri of Kesa for my analysis and proposed solution. Lastly, I extrapolate from that analysis my solution for the whole of humanity by elaborating on the fact that our species' ability to develop and find peace depends directly on Africa's ability to develop and find peace.

Emmanuel S. Kirunda
London, England
February 2016

*****

<u>Summary of *The Fourth Heritage*</u>

Introduction

I write about how my 20 years of education have primarily been in the sciences. That education was meant to lead me into an engineering career so that I could solve technical problems. However, after five years of practicing civil engineering, I wanted to use my intellectual capital to write something that could solve problems in my home society of Uganda and Africa.

Chapter 1: Our Triple Heritages

I write about how the triple heritages of tribes, religions and European colonialism permeate all facets of our Ugandan / African society. I got the idea of a triple heritage from reading the Ugandan-educated Kenyan academic Prof. Ali Mazrui whose ground-breaking book *The Africans: A triple heritage* was turned into a BBC TV series in the 1980s.

Chapter 2: Our Need

Our need as Ugandans or Africans is to develop economically and intellectually. I write about the objective fact that there are two regions of the world that are developed: the Western world and where Europeans migrated, and the Far East countries of Japan and the four Asian tigers (Taiwan, Hong Kong, South Korea and Singapore). I use four specific groups as examples from the developed world to illustrate what leads to development: Americans, Germans, Japanese and "The Scientists." I write about the fact that each of those four groups has developed intellectually because of something I have called a "heri." Unlike Richard Dawkins' idea of the selfish gene or meme, the heri is a cooperation-based phenomenon inherent in a group of people and it defines their identity and way of life, which they use as a springboard to create value within their societies. I write about the heris for the four specific groups and conclude the chapter by showing that Ugandans specifically, and Africans generally, don't have a heri, hence our lack of development.

Chapter 3: Our Problems

I write about the fact that we Africans have two types of problems: 1) the visible problems e.g. underdevelopment, wars, and poverty, which the world sees and tries to help Africa with (though with debatable outcomes), and 2) the invisible problems that are the real cardinal problems we need to be talking about in our societies. The invisible problems are a result of the lack of a heri and our indigenous cultures being dominated by the religious and western cultures. The visible problems are just the tip of the iceberg – mere symptoms. Only we as Ugandans / Africans can solve the actual fundamental problems – the real diseases, which manifest in the form of backward psychological mindsets.

Chapter 4: Solutions That Don't Work

I write about the fact that all our solutions since gaining independence from colonialism have been geared towards the visible problems, and no one has come up with an intellectually analyzed solution to solve the invisible psychological problems that I present. Politics and the education systems in Africa have not come up with an original solution to tackle our invisible problems. The failure to solve our problems leads us into internalizing an inferiority complex and a mentality of victimhood because it becomes easy to blame the outside world and history for our predicament.

Chapter 5: Thesis – The Fourth Heritage/ Integrating Our Triple Heritages

I write about the need for us as a people to come up with an original framework of identity that affords people the freedom to choose only what is beneficial for them from the triple heritages. I describe this mental framework and go on to show how it can solve those cardinal problems that are invisible to the outside world. Society's adherence to the forces of groupthink, be it tribal or religious, is the main cause of our lack of advancement and higher consciousness. I write about how the idea of a Fourth Heritage is intended to address the invisible problems and not the visible ones. However, in due time, the benefits of the Fourth Heritage can lead to a self-sufficient society that can tackle the visible problems as well. Furthermore, I write about how the Fourth Heritage addresses the problems that Prof. Mazrui wrote about; namely cultural confusion, nation-building, language problems, religious and indigenous conflicts, et cetera.

Chapter 6: Morality and The Fourth Heritage

I write about the history of western moral philosophies and give a brief structure of the major theories of morality. I end on the note that the most widely accepted ideals of morality in today's modern world are Kant's ideas of duty-based moral theories (categorical imperative and respect of persons). I show how this Kantian morality is very much identical to the tribal moral principle of Obuntu Bulaamu. Indeed, both Kant's moral principles and Obuntu Bulaamu are in line with the golden rule, "Treat others as you would have them treat you." The Fourth Heritage is in line with the main tenets of

Kantian philosophy and is fully in agreement with each of us seeing the humanity in one another in order to guide our good moral actions.

Conclusion

I conclude the main ideas of the book by quoting from Prof. Ali Mazrui: "It could be said that Africa invented man, that the Semites invented God and that Europe invented the world, or rather the concept of the world." I call upon my fellow Ugandans and Africans to embrace the idea that we should not be proud of just one of the three heritages, but rather, we should aim to celebrate the synthesis of the triple heritages based on our individual interpretations.

Appendix

This is a more detailed discussion about the heri of the scientists. In the main part of the book I briefly write about how the heri of the scientists is skepticism. In the appendix I go into details to show how skepticism has led to paradigm shifts in the history of science, beginning with Nicolas Copernicus all the way up to Albert Einstein.

*****

Summary of *The Fourth Republic*

In this second book I propose an original paper-based model for Ugandan nation-building that offers each citizen a personal "Ugandan dream." It is divided into eight chapters:

Chapter 1: The Assumptions

The ten 'ifs' that can render this model a failure, or in other words, the conditions and circumstances that could hinder the achievement of the much needed nation-building and self-realization.

Chapter 2: The Fundamental Pillars

The five initial conditions I believe the vast majority of citizens can agree upon and which can act as a cornerstone for our national society.

Chapter 3: The Fourth Republic

The new general framework on how our society and nation could be re-organized.

Chapter 4: The Non-Political Branches

The two branches of national authority (human heritage and judiciary branches) that should be the entities which facilitate each citizen's embrace of the new post-tribal nation. They serve every citizen independent from politics.

Chapter 5: The Political Branches

This chapter is about the two arms of government, namely the legislature and executive arms.

Chapter 6: Inter-Branch Offices

The chapter proposes several impartial national offices that function independent of the four national authority branches.

Chapter 7: Local Government Administration

The two tiers of local administration (local councils and districts).

Chapter 8: What Next

A generalization on how this Fourth Republic model could be adopted in Uganda and eventually in the East African Federation initiative that is being worked on by the five countries of Burundi, Kenya, Rwanda, Tanzania and Uganda.

PART 1

BEING HUMAN

Whether you are a blind man in an African village, a one-legged Chinese girl in China, or a high flying German lawyer, all humans share the true story of originating in Africa and having not only similar physical features, but also the same bedrock of the human soul – their unconsciousness.

1

ORIGIN OF MANKIND

As a species of creatures, the human being or *Homo sapiens* – as we are scientifically called – lives on this planet called Earth that revolves around the Sun once every 365 days. Since time immemorial humans have grappled with the question of where we came from. Each community of people has come up with very creative stories called "myths" that explain the origin of humankind. My tribe has one; all indigenous peoples have their stories. The most popular mythological story of the origin of man is that of the ancient Hebrew people, whose story is written in the Bible. As I wrote in the first book, each mythological story (written or oral) tells of the first man and his wife, and how it is that "community" came to be. I also quoted Prof. Mazrui, saying that, "All these ethnocentric traditions of the origin of mankind are variations of the image that the village is the world and the social group is the human race." I also mentioned in the first book how the creation story of the Dogon people of Mali seems to be even more compelling than the Biblical story, in that it has astronomical references.

All of those traditional accounts are mere creative stories that cannot be objectively verified. The only objectively verifiable explanation of the origin of mankind is what science has come up with. You cannot use any mythical story to arrive at an objective explanation of the origin of man. For example, when you use the Bible, even if it does not explicitly say when the Earth or man was created, traditional Christians believe what a European monk who lived in the Middle Ages came up with: that the Earth is 6,000 years old. You cannot make a leap from such an assertion to the evidence given by science that the Earth is in fact about 4.5 billion years old. Unlike the ethnocentric stories about the origin of the world and man, which put the particular tribe telling the story at the center of creation, science is the only explanation whereby people in Europe, Asia, America and elsewhere have all agreed beyond any reasonable doubt that the first human beings were in Africa, specifically Eastern Africa.

In the appendix of my first book I wrote a very elaborate account of the scientific explanation regarding the origin of man. But in a nutshell, let me retell it here again.

The first hominid that was our ancestor arose in Africa about 7 million years BC, but our actual species, *Homo sapiens*, evolved from *Homo erectus* between 200,000 and 500,000 years ago. Through a scientific dating method, e.g. using carbon, modern scientists can know the exact age of any bones or fossil they find anywhere. Through analysis of the blueprint of all living creatures, DNA, scientists have shown that all humans are 100% similar and equal in their biology, while we are 99.6% similar to chimpanzees, 98.2% similar to gorillas, and 93% similar to regular monkeys.

Science has also been able to tell us the story of the beginning of time itself and everything that has happened since then. You have to understand that time is an arbitrary concept. It is not a real, tangible thing or one of the fundamental elements in nature. Time is just the measure of events. For example, a day is the measure of how long the earth rotates on its axis (24 hours), and an hour is just a number representing 3,600 seconds, and a second is just the measure of the number of oscillations / vibrations of quartz crystals (32,768 vibrations to be exact). Even the most modern method of keeping time, the atomic clock, is just a means to measure the event of the nucleus of the Cesium-133 atoms remaining in a specific spin state (it stays in one state when 9,192,631,770 electromagnetic waves pass through it). In the macro world, one year is just a measure of how long the earth takes to go around the sun and return to its initial position. So when science says that the universe is 13.7 billion years old, all they are saying is that all events that have ever happened and everything that has ever existed did so within the past 13.7 billion years. There were no events, no time, no nothing before 13.7 billion years ago. As far as the human mind has progressed, we cannot know or even comprehend the reality of more than 13.7 billion years. It is possible that people in the future will be able to, but currently nature spans from 13.7 billion years ago to NOW. Period!

The main take away is that as we grapple with all the problems of the world, it is extremely important that at least we agree and start teaching our children the universal fact that humans have a common origin and it was in Africa. This is in line with that Ali Mazrui quote, "It can be said that Africa invented man…" and Jacob Bronowski's quote that, "If an understanding of man's origins, his evolution, his history, his progress is not the commonplace of the school books [worldwide], we shall not exist."

In this chapter, I have discussed my first hypothesis of how to transcend our heritages of birth.

<u>Hypothesis 1</u>: The origin of all humans is in Africa.

2

COLLECTIVE UNCONSCIOUS

As a species of creatures, the human being or *Homo sapiens* has things that are shared by all its members. There are physical things, e.g. all normal humans have two eyes and one mouth, but there are also non-physical things, e.g. normal humans dream while asleep (not all the time of course). In this chapter I want to talk about one such fundamental attribute of humanity that sets the stage for the rest of this book. This attribute is that of unconsciousness. According to the dictionary, unconsciousness is defined as "not knowing or perceiving, or lacking self-awareness." Africans and all non-Africans share a common state of being when they are unconscious. This is the second fundamental vantage point I want to share with everyone. Aside from our common origin in Africa, we also have a fundamental attribute that binds us all as humans. Even if humans come in different cultures and have belonged to different civilizations over the ages, at least we have some *ab initio* mental state we all share.

Being unconscious is the most rudimentary characteristic of being a human being. It is the *ab initio* way of existing because we are not alert or awake or thinking. This state is the same across all races and cultures of humanity. When you are asleep, the unconscious state of your mind is identical whether you are a woman or man, a black person or white person, Ugandan or Japanese. I cannot venture too deeply into this subject as it is as wide and complex as the ocean, and I am not qualified to discuss it in academic terms, but I do want to scratch the surface a little bit, as it has pertained to my experience.

This passive state of being is exhibited by each individual person differently. However, for the purpose of this book, I want to talk about elements of the unconscious mind that are not confined to one person, but are universal to all human beings. For those interested in the subjective nature and structure of the personal unconsciousness, you have to start with reading the twentieth century German psychoanalyst Sigmund Freud, "the father of modern psychology," who explores in great depth the personal unconsciousness and its implications in regards to personal dreams, sexuality, fantasies, cultural taboos, etc. From Freud's work, we now understand that one's mind is constituted largely by the unconscious part, and people are guided more by their unconsciousness than their consciousness, even when fully conscious and alert.

In Sigmund Freud's theory about taboos that he wrote in the early part of the twentieth century, he refers to my tribe (the Basoga) as a savage tribe that inhabits the northern shores of Lake Victoria. He rightfully says that we have a strong taboo about incest. Despite his somewhat harsh words, in kind of a German way, I understood what he was writing, because I have lived among my tribe and I know what we believe. A good example of what Freud was referring to is the fact that mothers can't touch or be close to their sons-in-law. I know this because I have witnessed how my mother can't even sit in the same room as my sister's husband. Since I started reading books as a means of soul-searching, from an early age I developed a sense of not being offended just because of something written or uttered by someone. I just can't get offended by other people's views of me, however negative. Many of my friends have regularly urged me to be "offended" because of some insults or whatever, but somehow I think God created me without that emotional sense. So I couldn't get offended by statements like my tribe being called "savages." Instead, stumbling on such statements only led me to more intellectual inquiry. For example, I wondered why can't I, a native African, ever say a statement like that about Freud who is a German? Furthermore, why is it that even if I said it, most likely he himself would not get offended?

Back to the subject of unconsciousness, I stumbled upon it in the form of "the collective unconscious" during my first year of university in one of my elective classes outside the engineering curriculum. The formulation of this term is most attributable to Freud's peer and counterpart, the Swiss psychoanalyst Carl Jung. According to Jung, the collective unconscious is the structure of the unconscious mind that is universal to all human beings of every race or culture, and indeed is the soul of all humanity. The idea of collective unconscious suggests that there exists a psychic system of an impersonal and universal nature which does not develop individually in people but is inherited as a member of the human species. The reader has to bear with me; it is true that both Freud and Jung might have tackled such a universal human theme with a Eurocentric bias. Nonetheless, I would be guilty of bad intellectual ingenuity if I didn't reference such titans of the human intellectual enterprise just because they were Europeans or had a Eurocentric bias. Don't forget that you can't read my books without reflecting on what Ali Mazrui said: "It can be said that Africa invented man, the Semites invited God and the Europeans invented the world or at least the idea of the world."

The collective unconscious consists of two main building blocks: 1) natural instincts and 2) primordial structures that Jung called "archetypes." Instincts like wanting to have sex, or protecting your child at any cost, or wanting to eat when you are hungry, are universal to all humans in all cultures. The second part of Jung's theory, i.e. that of "archetypes," is the one more pertinent to the subject at hand. Archetypes are pre-existing forms of our psyche that we have inherited from all our ancestors and are part of who we are even if we don't know it or are not conscious of it. They are universal themes found in each mythology of every culture on Earth. Some of the major archetypes that are common to each and every group of people are: the theme of life after death, sacred objects or places, the theme of the wisdom of the elders, and the yearning for order and pattern in the universe as opposed to chaos or randomness. This last example is very pertinent to the subject at hand, because all groups of people go to great lengths to create ethnocentric myths about the origin of mankind with their group as the central race or tribe, with the sole purpose of creating "order" about the story of life on Earth. We are too scared to entertain the thought that life could have arisen here on Earth randomly.

Let's look at the archetype of "life after death" to illustrate the similarity of our collective unconscious across all humanity. All our human civilizations over time believed, and still believe, that a human life still exists even after someone dies. Even if there are some people who throughout history have not believed in this theme, their numbers are very few and they don't represent the traditional collective groupings I am discussing here. In ancient Egypt, when someone died, the community believed that that person continued existing, so they came up with a system whereby they buried people with lots of food, belongings, and sometimes dead men would even be entombed in pyramids with their living wives. In African tribal traditions, when someone dies, we universally believed, and still believe, that their spirit stays around the community with family members and it can interfere and guide affairs in the real world. I was born into such a belief system, and trust me, it has its practical benefit of keeping people's psyches intact after the rupture of losing a loved one. In Japan they believed, and still believe, that when one dies, that person becomes a "kami" (spirit) who lives around the community and can be worshiped in special shrines – this is 100% the same as African traditional beliefs. In ancient Greece, thousands of years before Christianity, people believed that after death the spirit went to a place underground called "Hades." It is interesting that when European Christianity was born in the first year AD, Christianity took on the Greek belief that a dead person goes to a place underground called "Hell" (derivation of Hades). If Christianity had arisen in Africa, maybe the belief in a place called "Hades" or "Hell" would not have slipped into the conscious beliefs of the religion. But I don't know! Lastly, in Papua New Guinea, some tribes still believe that when someone dies, they still are alive and will continue to live forever but without the ability to move, so to activate the positive attributes of the dead within the living, the living people eat the dead person.

All the beliefs of these different people may take on different rituals and Earthly practices, but they all come from the same unconscious archetype we have as human beings; the dead are really not dead, they merely transition to some other place. I have met many people who no longer believe in this archetype, but they are the exception, not the rule.

To conclude this chapter, I have briefly discussed the second fundamental subject that sets the stage for the rest of the book. That is, all humans are similar in as far as the most rudimentary state of mind – that of the collective unconscious – is concerned. In the next chapter, I discuss one of the major factors that leads to the differences in the way people think and act.

In this chapter, I have discussed my second hypothesis of how to transcend our heritages of birth.

Hypothesis 1: The origin of all humans is in Africa.

Hypothesis 2: Even if the origin of all humans is in Africa, the Semites created the idea of one God as it is known to most of us and the Europeans created the modern world as we know it; the most important similarity shared by all humans is the collective unconscious.

3

COLLECTIVE CONSCIOUSNESS

In the first chapter I discussed our common ancestry as human beings, one that every child in the world needs to be taught – if we really want to unite the world – which is that all stories of man's origin are ethnocentric except the scientific theory that man was created in Africa. Then in the previous chapter I discussed a very important aspect of being a human being, which is that all people have a similar collective unconscious. In this chapter I want to discuss the fact that different groups of people think and act differently because of the differences in the collective consciousness. Collective consciousness is the social milieu or "something in the societal air" that makes people think and act in a particular way. The different ways could be moral, political, and religious or in any other way that is in the communal social arena.

Human consciousness is a very broad and difficult topic – even more so than that of the unconsciousness (for a more in-depth discussion of the attributes and development of consciousness itself, see the sub-chapter under Western civilization). Although only psychologists study and are interested in the unconscious, all kinds of peoples are interested in the subject of collective consciousness, e.g. religious people, politicians, and celebrities. These people are interested in our general collective consciousness and many go on to define, influence and try all kinds of ways to control it.

I define collective consciousness as bubbles of mindsets and expected behaviors in a community. The social bubbles start with a collective grouping beyond the family or blood relation, and end with the societal grouping called "civilization." So while I cannot talk about a collective consciousness of my family or of my clan (both these groupings are based on blood relation), I can talk about a collective consciousness of a tribe (grouping of clans which are not blood-related; that's why people within a tribe can marry each other without it being incest), a nation (grouping of different tribes or ethnicities), a religion (grouping of different peoples from any part of the world who believe in a specific traditional way of relating to their idea of God), and a civilization (which is the largest collective grouping of a segment of humanity).

Collective consciousness cannot come about based on the idea of the true eternal God, the source of everything. By this I mean the God that Spinoza called the Infinite Substance, or the sum total of all the laws of nature. This source God operates in the realm of the collective unconsciousness and the subjective consciousness. The only way the idea of God can be used to create a collective consciousness is if, by God, you mean the one created by countless different cultures. So when I talk about a religious collective consciousness based on God it is based on the created God, not the source God. If this were not the case, it would be common to find many people switching religions freely with their respective family's full support. So it is important to understand that the only way people truly reach out to know the source God is if they escape the bubble of their religious collective consciousness and use their subjective consciousness. God or the source is 100% in the realm of personal consciousness, and when it goes beyond the personal it is universal (concerning all humans and all things in the known world, without favoring one ethnic group or culture of people). Therefore, when people talk about God of "this or that" religion, it is a gross misrepresentation of the objective reality of life or the working of the universe, as it is merely an ethnocentric social discourse which equates religions to ethnocentric groupings; and as I said in chapter one, all ethnocentric dialogues are a misconstrued belief that "the group is a universal entity representing all mankind" – see the sub-chapter about "the limit of religious heritage" for details of an in-depth discussion about this point.

Bearing in mind my discussion above, religions have everything to do with the collective consciousness. In fact, the role of religion is to create a specific collective consciousness. And religious books are the main culprits used to create and sustain a collective consciousness. That explains why, when individual people have a subjective consciousness different from the prevailing religious consciousness, those people rebel against the status quo religion and the extreme case is that they go on to create new religions or new collective consciousness based on new holy books. Examples are Jesus and Paul regarding the creation of Christianity from Judaism, Mohammad and the creation of Islam from Judeo-Christianity, Martin Luther and the creation of Protestantism from Catholicism, Joseph Smith and the creation of Mormonism from mainstream Protestantism, to mention just a few. That is why, while the creators of religions do so after a genuine encounter with the divine, the people who follow them (the religious follower) usually do so without any encounter with the divine, and rarely do those people live spiritual lives the way the creators of the religions do. As the German scholar Max Muller said, "He who knows one religion, knows none." If one is comforted in, and knows, only one religious collective consciousness, that person in many ways is religiously ignorant.

The origin of the collective consciousness for a group of people is the environment they are in. Depending on the social or natural environment that abounds, people will start looking at other peoples, or things happening in the community, or hear stories about events and times and consequently, a people will start thinking in a certain way, start expecting a certain behavior, and indeed develop customs and traditions to live by. So there is a different collective consciousness that comes up among people who live in a desert versus those who live in the jungle, or those who have an abundance of food versus those with near famine conditions, or those who experience winter versus those with the sun year-round, etc. From the myriad origins of the collective consciousness, we end up with myriad groupings of people. These groupings go on to create societal expectations for their peoples – taboos, norms, customs and traditions. These are specific bubbles of collective consciousness. Like change that inevitably comes over time, collective consciousness within a group can also change with time. In fact, some people who know this can go a step further and influence or create collective consciousness for their group – look at the way nationalism has worked over history and how some leaders are able to change the social atmosphere of their countries. They do this by preaching a certain narrative or sense of belonging that people want to associate with.

A very vivid example of collective consciousness is the issue I discussed in my first book concerning societies that have shame or guilt as their benchmark for morality. In the Western world, if people don't act as expected, they develop guilt – a personal conscience and feeling that one has done something wrong. On the other hand, in other non-western societies like traditional African societies, people feel shamed – a personal conscience and feeling that one has wronged their society, not necessarily that the act was wrong in and of itself, independent of the society. For example, someone from a guilt-based society might never understand or appreciate why a girl from a shame-based society could commit suicide upon learning of her pregnancy due to her feeling of betraying the family honor.

A very good modern example is the taboo against the use of derogatory words in society. In the US, use of the N-word was okay before the 1960s, but since the civil rights movement no one in the US can use it in normal social dialogue without getting a backlash or being outright penalized by society. That is in the US. Now compare the fact that when I went to Chile in 2003, I got out of the airport to get a cab, and a driver ran up to me shouting, "Hey my N$%#&@, do you want to ride with me?" By then I had already formulated my thinking about collective consciousness being a bubble within a particular society, so I understood where he was coming from. In fact, I understood also because as someone born in Uganda (a country where we never had slave trade the way we read about West Africa or the East African coast), I had never internalized the negativity and sensitivity associated with the word the way American people have. In a way, the experience of slavery has created a specific collective consciousness within the American society that a foreigner like me found hard to internalize.

In ancient times, peoples used to have different collective consciousness from what we have now. In ancient Egypt, when important people died they would be buried with their worldly possessions, which included wives and servants. The modern person finds this hard to comprehend, and in fact there is no moral compass you can use today to judge such a social practice. However, when you understand that those people had a totally different belief system regarding right, wrong, God, and the idea of the afterlife, you get to appreciate that their collective consciousness bubble was grossly different from what we have today.

An important thing I would like to mention is the fact that people from one collective consciousness find it hard to understand or appreciate or have the social ear to hear what is going on in a different society with a different collective consciousness. You'll find that someone from a shame-based society is flabbergasted when they go to a guilt-based society and sees that no matter how badly people act, society does not ostracize them.

The bubbles of collective consciousness are geared toward the members of the group, not those outside it. The current Western modern civilization is the first human civilization that is enabling people to have a universal collective consciousness that cuts across ethnicities and religions. As I will discuss in later chapters, because the modern civilization is based less on blood relation, there are numerous examples of people with a modern mental disposition who look at others not as tribes or nations or religions, but rather as all of humanity, all one race of human beings.

Collective consciousness has also gone through cycles during human history. There is evidence that when another civilization comes up where an older one has been, traces of the old civilization can be wiped out completely. Starting from the fifteenth century, we have evidence that when the Europeans came to the Americas, they systematically destroyed and wiped out most traces of the ancient native civilizations and the collective consciousness that used to be in the social air of the land we now call the Americas. If it weren't for the pyramids as remnants of these ancient civilizations, it is possible that a visitor to the Americas today would believe that it always looked like an extension of Europe. Another very good example is what is happening in Iraq and Syria. If the extremist terrorists take over and rule that part of the world, it is possible that in 100 years, no one would know anything about classical Greek or Christian civilization ever setting foot in Syria or Iraq. This would be achieved by their systematic destruction of all monuments and the burning of all books from the non-Islamic civilizations.

In this chapter I have discussed my third hypothesis of how to transcend our heritages of birth.

Hypothesis 1: The origin of all humans is in Africa.

Hypothesis 2: Even if the origin of all humans is in Africa, the Semites created the idea of one God as it is known to most of us and the Europeans created the modern world as we know it; the most important similarity shared by all humans is the collective unconscious.

Hypothesis 3: Even if all humans are similar, there are real differences and inequalities among peoples due to the differences in collective consciousness.

PART 2

RISE AND FALL OF CIVILIZATIONS

Since *Homo sapiens* emerged on this planet called Earth between 200,000 and 500,000 years ago, we have been growing and developing from simpletons to more complex forms, and with each stage our societies have also been growing in complexity. The general stages of social development have been as follows: first, people organized themselves as families, then clans (groups of families), then tribes, and lastly, as post-tribal groupings (e.g. city-states, nation-states, religious kingdoms, empires, etc.). The post-tribal groupings are what built the highest formal groupings of human social organization, "civilizations." We all need to keep in mind that the idea of "tribes" is not a static state of existence but rather a transient stage in social development. Civilizations have their beginnings and their ends. The first civilizations in Africa rose and fell thousands of years ago. The current civilization we are in, "the Western European Civilization," started after 1200 AD and it has not yet fallen.

4

LOST ANCIENT CIVILIZATIONS

Carl Sagan is once quoted to have said, "Absence of evidence is not evidence of absence." He said this statement in regard to people who were arguing that there is other intelligent life anywhere in the Universe. Given the fact that our Milky Way galaxy has billions of planets and suns, and yet there are over 400 billion galaxies that we have been able to observe / detect, Sagan's line of reason was to caution skeptics of intelligent life in other parts of the universe by reminding them that just because we humans have not seen the evidence of intelligent life elsewhere, does not give us an absolute belief that there can't be any life anywhere else. If indeed there was no other life at all out of the billions and billions of planets in the universe, then indeed it is a big waste of space!

Similarly, modern historians have argued about which ones were the first civilizations on Earth, and there isn't one absolutely agreed-upon verdict. They don't agree sometimes for self-importance reasons, but realistically it is because of the lack of concrete evidence.

I was taught in Primary Four and Primary Five (fourth and fifth grades) at Nkumba Primary School, and later on I also researched that there were six different cradle civilizations for mankind. This does not mean that indeed there were only these six and they were the first ones, it just means that the majority of historians have agreed upon these six. If they had agreed upon three, it would have been three. Indeed, if historians come across evidence pointing to ten cradle civilizations, then the school books will change and students will be taught about ten cradle civilizations. In the next chapter I will go into details about each of these agreed-upon six civilizations. For this chapter, I want to discuss an alternative line of argument which forms the basis of my fourth hypothesis on how to transcend our heritages of birth – which is the reason I have written this book.

*** A general word on civilization ***

The Webster dictionary gives the following definition for the word "civilization:" It is a relatively high level of cultural and technological development; specifically it is the stage of cultural development at which writing and the keeping of written records is attained. Another definition is, "civilization is the condition that exists when people have developed effective ways of organizing a society and care about art, science, etc." With this definition in mind, it becomes possible for us to conclude that there were civilizations before the cradle civilizations, but due to lack of evidence, we are not taught about them.

To date civilizations or the general history of man, historians use four main categorizations of periods based on the source of tools people used in their everyday life. The first is prehistory or the Stone Age, for which we don't know when the start was, but it ended about 3300 BC. It could be argued that the Prehistory era started at the time of the formation of the planet Earth around 4.5 billion years ago, or some million years after that. It is just that historians look at the past with man in mind, and since we have a lot of evidence starting about 10,000 BC of man using stones, most people erroneously think that prehistory started at that time. More scientifically authoritatively, the Stone Age (or Paleolithic Era) started around 2.5 million years ago, though there are recent flint tool discoveries in Kenya dating back 3.3 million years. Different cultures transitioned from the Stone Age at different times; there are still Stone Age tribes today, for example, in the Amazon, Africa, and Indonesia. In this chapter I am discussing only the Prehistory age.

The second age is what is called the Ancient Era or the Bronze Age, which lasted from about 3300 BC to various times in various parts of the world – in Europe it ended between 1200 BC and 600 BC, depending on the region. It is the age we have evidence of the six cradle civilizations (see next chapter) and the start of classical Greco-Roman civilization.

The third period is the Middle Age or roughly the Iron Age, which started between 1200 BC and 600 BC in different areas, and ended between 1 BC and 500 AD in Europe. In some parts of Africa it lasted up to 800 AD. This Age included the Dark Ages in Europe, the rise of Christianity and Islam, and the Mongol conquests of Asia and Europe.

The fourth and final period is the Modern Era in which we live today. The Modern Era also started at different times in different parts of the world, e.g. in Europe it started with the Renaissance of Italy, in some parts of Africa it started with colonialism. The Modern Era is where we have evidence of man starting to use alloys like steel and plastic and everything in today's world, including cotton, rubber, etc. Some of the highlights of the Modern Era are the age of enlightenment, the industrial revolution, the space age and the digital age.

My contemplation about civilization has led me to conclude that civilizations rise and they are maintained due to two factors that define the people's collective consciousness. I call these factors "concentrating agents." Concentrating agents are attributes that lead to the development of "concentrated minds" – the actual type of mental structures needed to actually build and maintain the civilization. The first concentrating agent is the post-tribal grouping of people. The second one is the writing system. The post-tribal grouping helps to concentrate the collective consciousness of diverse people around the ruler (e.g. emperor) and the symbols of the group (e.g. the anthem, flag and concepts like citizenry). The writing system enables the people to write down and communicate across an immense geographical area and over long stretches of time, their ideas, stories, religions and general way of life. Over hundreds of years, each new generation's collective consciousness gets concentrated by way of reading from prior generations. This happens to the point where a person within a given civilization can have mental references that stretch across thousands of years.

~

Given that we don't have much evidence about the prehistory age, between 4.5 billion and 10,000 BC, we are left with imagining what makes sense to fill in that big gap of no data. One of the tools that can help us fill in this gap is the concrete evidence from science that Planet Earth has undergone several ice ages. There is scientific geological evidence that since about 2.4 billion years ago, Earth has been covered by ice five times, each time lasting about 100,000 years. The last ice age recorded lasted from 70,000 BC to 10,000 BC. So, while all the evidence historians agree upon is only from 10,000 BC to now, there is a whole lot of time that is just not known, but actually has a lot of significance for life here on Earth.

Isn't it possible that for the tens of thousands of years before the last ice age, there might have been civilizations of people or other creatures, e.g. dinosaurs, but then their civilization was wiped out by the ice, never for us to have any evidence for? Given that our current civilization is barely 3,000 years old, it is totally possible that for 5,000 years between 300,000 and 200,000 there could have been a civilization as sophisticated as ours, but it was destroyed beyond recognition by the ice that covered the planet for hundreds of thousands of years.

The periodic eradication of life or civilization on Earth over the millions of years past cannot be talked about in any human method other than scientific research. No cultural or religious narrative talks about these very important events on our planet. Scientific research now has shown that about 99% of all life that has ever lived on this planet was wiped out at one time or another in the previous five cataclysmic events. Scientists talk about these five cataclysmic events by finding evidence of the five geological eras: the End Ordovician, Late Devonian, End Permian, End Triassic and End Cretaceous. It is a humbling fact that of all the life that has ever lived on this planet, over 99% of it became extinct millions of years ago. When scientists say that the dinosaurs existed for millions of years, and were dominant over life on Earth until about 60 million years ago, what a massive gap we are left with, since now we can hardly see any practical evidence of "life under the dinosaurs."

This gap period is very telling when you consider that there are ancient stone monuments found all around the world, e.g. Stonehenge in England, stone head monuments on the Easter Islands in the Pacific, stone circle remnants in southern Africa, etc. Since archaeology cannot date stone structures the way they can accurately date fossil remains, no one knows for sure how old these stone structures are. If they are from 100,000 years ago, that begs the question: what kind of civilization constructed them? In fact, since modern science teaches us that man evolved in Africa only less than 200,000 years ago, it is quite possible that there were non-humans who evolved between 1,000,000 and 800,000 years ago, whose civilizations were wiped out by an ice age. In my deep meditations about life on this planet, since there are ancient cultures, e.g. the Sumerians and others in other parts of the world who talk of a great flood wiping away life on Earth, I often wonder whether those cultural stories are referencing the same events that science has uncovered as ice ages.

As I said, the above line of reasoning does not have majority backing due to lack of enough evidence, but in my struggle to rationalize how I can transcend the limiting aspects of my tribal heritage of birth, when I ponder the big stage of history stretching up to the beginning of this planet 4.5 billion years ago, it is not out of the realm of possibility that the time between the creation of the earth and 10,000 BC had several advanced civilizations of people, or other creatures, whose evidence of existence is no longer here for us to see due to natural calamity. If not for natural calamity, it could also be due to the successive civilizations purposefully destroying evidence of the preceding civilizations, the way ISIS now is destroying all evidence of the existence of pre-Islamic civilizations in the areas of Syria and Iraq that it has conquered.

In this chapter, I have discussed my fourth hypothesis of how to transcend our heritages of birth.

Hypothesis 1: The origin of all humans is in Africa.

Hypothesis 2: Even if the origin of all humans is in Africa, the Semites created the idea of one God as it is known to most of us and the Europeans created the modern world as we know it; the most important similarity shared by all humans is the collective unconscious.

Hypothesis 3: Even if all humans are similar, there are real differences and inequalities among peoples due to the differences in collective consciousness.

Hypothesis 4: Absence of evidence is not evidence of absence. Just because we don't have undisputed scientific evidence of civilizations before 10,000 BC does not mean that for certain periods between the creation of the earth 4.5 billion years ago and 10,000 BC, there were no advanced civilizations (humans or other creatures) that inhabited Africa and other parts of the planet.

5

THE SIX CRADLE CIVILIZATIONS

Each of the six cradle civilizations that historians agree on started independent of one another. Though sometimes they existed at the same time, they did not have any contact with one another. One was in Africa (Ancient Egypt civilization), another was in the Mideast between the Euphrates and Tigris rivers (Mesopotamia civilization), another was in ancient India (Indus Valley civilization), another was along the Yellow River (Ancient China civilization), another was in North and Central America (Mesoamerica civilization) and another was in South America (the Andean civilization).

Each of these six cradle civilizations arose and flourished without borrowing anything from one another, and any similarities they happen to share are because humans are similar. So when you see that the civilizations in the Americas had humongous pyramids just like the Egyptians, the only connection is that during that particular time in man's evolution, people tended to have a view about the after-life that was shared between those in Africa and those in the Americas – even if these two groups of people never interacted. According to my personal analysis, I think the source of such similarities is from the fact that all Earthlings are plugged into the same collective unconscious, whether in our mother's womb or when we are asleep or when we create myths about our different societies.

Unfortunately, not all the six cradle civilizations have as much archeological evidence left behind, due to erosion over the thousands of years that have passed since their collapse. And in some instances, later civilizations purposefully destroyed any evidence from the previous civilizations - exactly like ISIS is doing to Mesopotamian and Christian civilizations in the areas it has conquered in Iraq and Syria. For this reason, I will also briefly discuss the post-cradle civilizations that arose in the areas of the respective cradle civilizations, since some of them have more tangible evidence to discuss than their preceding cradle civilizations. A good example is how the Mayan and Aztec civilizations in Mesoamerica have more archeological remains compared to their cradle Olmec civilization.

Cradle Civilization in Africa/Ancient Egypt:

The cradle civilization in Africa has the most significance for us as present day humans because, as I mentioned in the first chapter, mankind started in Africa. Most of the evidence points to the fact that the cradle civilization in Africa stretched along the Nile River from Nubia in the south (present day Northern Uganda and South Sudan), through Upper Egypt in the middle (present day Sudan), all the way to Lower Egypt where Alexandria sits today. The Nile is the longest river in the world and because it has several tributaries, it has several sources. However, the source of one of the major sections of the river that flows out of Lake Victoria on its journey to Egypt is about 30 minutes from Iganga, the small town where I was born. I remember after being taught about this civilization at Nkumba Primary School, every time on my way home during school holidays, as we would pass the bridge at Jinja I always imagined the point in Lake Victoria where the river starts. I always imagined the great Ancient Egyptians sailing down the Nile till that point of the source. I identified with the Ancient Egyptians because they were Africans like me and the lifeblood of their civilization was the Nile, whose source is a sacred place for my tribe.

Archeologists point to the fact that even if people lived in the area that came to be called "Ancient Egypt" during the Pleistocene age (more than 100,000 years ago), the days of glory for the civilization as we know it existed between just before 3000 BC up to its fall around 300 BC. The first concentrating agent or post-tribal grouping was characterized by a multi-ethnic multi-racial state, with one ruler called the Pharaoh. There was also a complex system of temples and a religious belief system about "the way of the soul". Their burial system utilized pyramids as a method of guiding the souls of the deceased to Heaven. The second concentrating agent, or the writing system, was by way of animal-based symbols called hieroglyphics. By studying hieroglyphics, we understand that Ancient Egyptians had complex systems of irrigation, advanced medicine, mathematics and measurement systems (they pioneered works in arithmetic, geometry, number theory, etc.), and they had elaborate burial customs of mummifying their dead people and burying them within pyramids in receptive chambers called sarcophagi. The dead were also entombed with a copy of *The Book of the Dead* which documented much of the culture's very complex religious belief system, built around a pantheon of different gods.

According to the great American historian Will Durant, the creation of the Egyptian calendar in 4241 BC is one of the most important creations of human civilization, as it set Egyptians on the course to studying astronomy; it mapped the year into 12 months of 30 days each plus one additional five day short month, mapped the course of the Sun, and guided a social fabric for more than 4,000 years. When Christians say that the world was created 6,000 years ago, actually they mean 4,004 BC; the year Bishop Ussher calculated as being that of the creation in the Bible ... this means these ancient

Africans created a calendar 237 years before the God of the Bible supposedly created the world.

From *The Book of the Dead*, we learn that Ancient Egyptians believed that a person has both a physical side and also a spiritual side to their existence. Upon dying, the spiritual side would go through a series of trials and encounters with a variety of gods until it could be judged by the main god Osiris. If one passes judgment he unites with Osiris and other gods and lives in a place similar to the physical Egypt (a place with animals, the river, reeds and garden tools to do manual labor, etc.). Judgment was by way of a negative confession about the 42 sins prescribed by the gods. The negative confession was in the form of "I did not do ..." as opposed to our present Judeo-Christian divine commands which are positive prohibitions of bad deeds, "Thou shall not do ..." It was not clear how long people would go through the trials before judgment, and if one failed judgment it was not clear what happened to him – this is quite different from the Judeo-Christian idea where the sinners go to a place called Hell. One account is that if people failed judgment in the afterlife they would be killed again terribly by some mean gods – a textbook case of double jeopardy.

After more than 3,000 years (way longer than the current European Christian civilization has been around), Ancient Egypt ran out of gas around 300 BC. It was conquered first by the Persians and then the final blow was from Alexander the Great, who became the first Greek pharaoh of Ancient Egypt.

A note about the people of Ancient Egypt: Because the state was a multi-ethnic grouping, Ancient Egyptians came in all colors and races. There were citizens and pharaohs who were dark-skinned and others who were lighter-skinned. Back then issues of race and color were not as political as they are today. On the same token, there were dark-skinned slaves and light-skinned slaves. The coming of the Arabs into Egypt and the introduction of Islam happened very recently in the grand scheme of things, it happened around 640 AD, so we are 100% sure that the Ancient Egyptians were not Arabs. Non-Arab dark-skinned and light-skinned people had been the natives of the land we call Egypt for thousands of years before the land was conquered by the Islamic Arabs to the point that now most people think it has always been Arabic and Islamic.

Mesoamerica Civilization:

This was the civilization in what are now the Mexican states of Veracruz and Tabasco. It occupied vast areas of Mexico and its influence stretched down to Nicaragua in Central America. Its main city centers were San Lorenzo, and later, La Venta. The civilization was built by people whom we don't really know much about, but the later civilization of the Aztecs called these people the Olmecs. According to the Encyclopedia Britannica, the Olmec civilization is the oldest in the Americas and from it sprung later civilizations like the Zapotec, Totonac, Teotihuacan, Mayan, Toltec, and lastly, the Aztec.

There is evidence that the Olmecs reached the peak of their cultural prowess between 2000 BC and 400 BC. However, they could have been civilized from as early as 12000–8000 BC, as there is evidence that the domestication of growing maize dates back to earlier than 7500 BC.

The most striking evidence of this civilization is the remnants of the colossal stone heads. Modern historians think that these heads might have been those of their leaders. Some of them weigh as much as eight tons and rise up to three meters tall. These rulers were evidently of negro race, akin to native Africans. It is not clear if all the people were black like Africans or just the rulers. There are also remnants of smaller sculptures that show people of Chinese descent probably from the Xia dynasty of 2000 to 1500 BC China.

The Olmecs ruled supreme in this part of the world and had no known contact with other civilizations in the Andean region of South America or in Egypt, Mesopotamia, China or India. They left complex inventions which were eventually adopted by later civilizations such as the Mayans of southern Mexico and Guatemala, the Teotihuacan of central Mexico (200–900 AD) and the Aztecs of central and southern Mexico (who were the ruling civilization by the time the Europeans encountered North America in the sixteenth century AD).

In 2007, I was fortunate enough to visit several remnants of these great civilizations of ancient America. I climbed up to the top of one of the most amazing pyramids from the Teotihuacan civilization, "The Pyramid of the Sun," which is an enormous stone structure over 70 meters tall and more than 200 meters wide and 200 meters long. I also visited the Grand Cholula pyramid in Puebla, Mexico with its amazing mazes of tunnels. Cholula is the biggest architectural building of the ancient world, as its base is 400 meters by 400 meters (the great pyramid of Giza is taller but has a much smaller base). But my favorite of them all was the pristine-looking and amazingly preserved Chichen Itza pyramid of El Castillo. When it was voted in 2007 as one of the seven wonders of the Modern World, I totally concurred. At a small foot print of a 50-meter base and 30-meter height, climbing up the steep steps of that ancient temple makes you feel like you are truly walking in the footsteps of time and you experience a union with departed civilizations. What a treasure the ancients left us!

The Olmec calendar was made famous by the Mayan civilization. The calendar has elaborate demarcation of short and long counts of time divided into several cycles including the Tzolkin cycle which has 260 days (from 20 days grouped in 13 divisions), the Haab solar cycle of 18 months each divided into 20 days plus a five-day-long special month, and the Calendar Round which is 52 Haab, or roughly one generation of a person's life. It also has a longer count system that reached up to 63-million-year calendar periods divided into major cycles.

Civilization in the Americas before Europeans arrived also points to advanced mathematics. We even have evidence that they may have been the first peoples to use the number zero (this was a great achievement, as even the almighty civilization of the Romans did not have the concept of a zero). Their numeral system consisted of using a base-20 counting method (unlike the base-10 system we use now wherein the movement of a decimal from a number like 1.5 to 15 requires it be multiplied by 10, for their base-20 system you had to multiply by 20).

Mesopotamia Civilization

This was the civilization of the pre-Arab lands around the Tigris and Euphrates rivers in modern day Iraq, Syria and Kuwait. This area was called the Fertile Crescent because thousands of years ago it was a very conducive area for agriculture and that largely explains why this great civilization arose there. The civilization started at the beginning of the Bronze Age (around 3300 BC) among the pre-Arab peoples called the Sumerians, Assyrians and Babylonians. Over time it grew and engulfed other peoples until it morphed into the Persian Empire between 550 BC and 300 BC, which in turn was conquered by the Greek classical empire under Alexander the Great in 330 BC.

Mesopotamia left us one of the most advanced writing systems we have encountered from the ancient world. The earliest Sumerian writing was in an intricate system called cuneiform, which was based on triangle shapes. In Primary Five / fifth grade, our social studies teacher used to have us practice writing in the cuneiform language. I remember feeling a sense of wonder at how neat a way people would construct whole meaningful sentences by arranging and rearranging triangle shaped letters. During my holidays back home in Iganga, I used to jealously guard my notebooks and many times I would lose myself in writing long paragraphs in cuneiform sentences. I could not share this information with anyone in my family as my parents were illiterate and my only brother had stopped schooling in Primary Four so he could not be bothered with anything related to books. I remember it was a lonely period of day dreaming and abstract imaginations of me straddling the Mesopotamian world in my head.

In mathematics and counting, unlike the modern era where we use the base-10 counting system, or the Olmec / Mayan civilizations which used base-20, the Mesopotamians used base-60. It is from this civilization that we get the time system of 60 minutes, 360 degrees and 24 hours (24 is a really a way of saying 1440 minutes divided by 60 minutes).

This civilization also brought us *The Epic of Gilgamesh*, which is regarded as the oldest great poem ever written. It was written in the Babylonian city state of Ur circa 2200 BC, but according to American scholar Julius Jaynes there were several versions of it and the one from the Assyrians of 650 BC is as prominent as the Babylonian one. Many historians regard many of the parallelism between the Bible and *The Epic of Gilgamesh* as a plagiarism by the Bible writers, as many parts of the Bible came more than 1,000 years after the great poem. The following are a just a few examples of the many parallel stories shared by *The Epic of Gilgamesh* and the Bible. 1) The epic tells a story of a "great flood" which is very similar to the story of Noah – the Hebrew story seems to have been adopted during their enslavement by the mighty Mesopotamian Babylon Empire. 2) The Hebrew ethnocentric story of Adam and Eve is close to the Gilgamesh story of Enkidu and Shamhat, a human couple placed in a perfect garden where the man is tempted by the woman, with a cunning snake also playing a sinister role. 3) The Kings of the Babylonian empire were often referred to as shepherds because they had to look after their subjects like a shepherd looks after sheep; similarly, the Bible is filled with stories of how God is the good shepherd.

To say the Mesopotamian civilization influenced the story of the Hebrew people is an understatement. Consider the following: 1) The Hebrew calendar was hugely shaped by adaptations of the Babylonian calendar, e.g. the names of each month, and having seven days in a week. While the Egyptian calendar system demarcated the month into three weeks of ten days each, the Babylonian civilization had a different calendar of seven days in a week. The writers of the Book of Genesis used a seven-day week because that was the calendar system used in the Mesopotamian civilization. It is quite possible that if they had used the Egyptian civilization calendar, we would now have weeks of ten days. 2) The cosmology of the Mesopotamian world consisted of a flat Earth surrounded by seas and God being above Earth sitting in a chair. It is the exact cosmology used by the writers of the first book of the Bible: "God created Earth from the waters around it," and God is up in a place called Heaven, where he sits on a mighty throne.

King Hammurabi of Babylon was the first recorded ruler to codify written law; everyone has read about the famous "An eye for an eye, a tooth for a tooth," statement. Written around 1800 BC, his law influenced many other laws, e.g. those attributed to the Hebrew, Moses, and those in the books of Exodus and Deuteronomy, parts of which modern scholars agree were written around 600 BC – again more than 1,000 years after the first Babylonian codified laws. There isn't much evidence that there was a man named Moses who wrote those books, but even if he did, he lived around 800–1400 BC at the earliest, which is still 400–1000 years after Hammurabi's laws had influenced the wider Mesopotamian world. In fact, some historians maintain that the figure of Moses as the law giver for the Ancient Israelites is very similar to other mythological figures from ancient civilizations, e.g. Manu in ancient India who was a law giver and first king of men, Menes who was the founder of the first dynasty of Ancient Egypt, and Minos as the first king of Crete, Greece.

Mesopotamia and its extension, Persia, brought us maybe the greatest religion of the ancient world, Zoroastrianism. Since the Arab conquest of Iran in 650 AD, the Islamic civilization has now systematically engaged in wiping this religion from the face of the Earth, but for thousands of years it was the heart and soul of Mesopotamian / Persian empires which once ruled the civilized world. The religion was started by a prophet called Zoroaster more than 3,500 years ago. It was the first monotheistic religion, having only one supreme God, Ahura Mazda.

According to the Encyclopedia Britannica, there is evidence that Zoroastrianism influenced Judaism and, by extension, Christianity and Islam. Most of the themes of Zoroastrianism were copied by the non-native Persians, especially in sixth century BC by the enslaved people known as the Hebrews. The most authoritative evidence regarding the writing of the latter parts of the book of Genesis comes from the Priestly cultish strain around the sixth century BC. This group greatly contributed to the Genesis story of the Yahwist and Elohist groups. The general Zoroastrian story goes like this:

> Around 1500 BC, a 30-year-old man called Zoroaster had a revelation wherein a shining figure from above, "an angel," takes him to the presence of Ahura Mazda or "God Almighty." Ahura Mazda then gave Zoroaster the message about the true religion, Zoroastrianism. The revelation mandated that he go preach to all peoples of the world the true religion. In this work he was helped by special heavenly personalities (angels). The aim of man was to worship the only true God Ahura Mazda. However, man encounters problems of living righteously and worshiping God because of the works of the evil being called Angra Mainyu, "Satan." But man, with the aid of Ahura Mazda, will defeat Angra Mainyu.

You can replace the names with Judaic, Christian or Islamic names and you have the same entities and themes. However, you need to note that these themes are different from religions that did not have contact with the influence of Zoroastrianism, e.g. Buddhism, Hinduism, Shintoism, Jainism and Taoism. One major theme absent from those non-Middle East religions is the evil being that prevents man from worshiping the true God. Buddhism specifically teaches that there is no devil or sin, but rather "absence of God" and "absence of good deeds." Absence of God does not equate to the existence of an evil being.

Other specific themes of Zoroastrianism are the golden rule, angels and demons, a heaven and a hell, a reward or punishment after death, the theme of a messiah or savior for mankind – Zoroaster returning to Earth in the future to save mankind. The main difference between Zoroastrianism and the other Middle Eastern religions is its idea of God as a unity of human spirit, hence God has both masculine and feminine attributes, "an" – god, and "ki" – goddess.

Ancient China Civilization

The Ancient China civilization is the predecessor of later East Asian civilizations (China, Japan, Korea, Taiwan, etc.). The civilization arose before the second millennium BC. With much debate, many believe the first ancient Chinese dynasty was the Xia dynasty around 2200 BC. The Xia dynasty is a mythic dynasty, so it is not very clear if it actually existed or was a figment of people's imaginations. It is similar to the Chwezi dynasty in Uganda and the Great Lakes region of Africa, where we suspect the semi-god people called the Bachwezi may not have actually existed, although different present-day tribes claim to be descendants from them. The real truth is somehow in the middle, in that these mythic stories combine real historical facts with "made up" tales. So the Xia dynasty was also inhabited by the mighty semi-god peoples.

However, there is real evidence that the Shang dynasty existed around 1800 BC. Archeologists have found several Bronze Age artifacts dated to that era.

Ancient China became a political and cultural unit in 221 BC with the rise and consolidation of all the small kingdoms by Emperor Qin, who started the Qin dynasty. There are several modern day Chinese movies depicting this glorious episode in the Chinese people's unique civilization. It was during the Qin dynasty that the famous Great Wall was built.

Ancient China brought us the two great non-theistic religions of Confucianism and Taoism. They really are not religions per se, which is why they are called non-theistic (no belief in a supreme divine being), and are really more of "a set of practical teachings." Anyone can learn about them and live according to their teachings without converting or being labeled an adherent believer of a religion.

Confucianism is an ethical and philosophical system of thought started by the great philosopher Confucius in the sixth century BC. It is about how to attain personal advancement and harmony with others and with the universe. Its closest doctrine of a "Heaven" is something to be achieved here on Earth; it's a worldly heaven referred to as Tian. Confucianism has no eschatological doctrine – teachings about the end of days or final judgment. It emphasizes hard work, harmony with family and society, and paying respect to the departed. In a way, it teaches purely humanistic virtues, not divine prerogatives, and treats secular or human creations as the things that are "sacred."

Taoism is similar to Confucianism except with a distinct addition of something called "a way" or "a path" that people and the universe take. This "path" is called a "tao." The tao is kind of a mystery that each person searches and tries to know, but in the end as it is written in the great Chinese classic *Tao Te Ching* "the tao that can be told is not the eternal tao." It is this school of thought that produced the ubiquitous East Asian motif of a Yin Yang (the symbol that represents opposites: bad and good, dark and light, female and male, cold and hot). The Yin Yang is the symbol on the South Korean national flag, and it is used by Chinese, Korean and Japanese peoples in so many facets of their iconography.

Buddhism was also prevalent in ancient China, but it actually has its origins in India – so I will discuss it in the context of the Ancient India civilization.

Ancient China produced a writing system not based on an alphabet of letters like the Western world, but rather a myriad of special inscriptions or characters. The oldest characters go back to the second millennium BC. The present characters, called Han characters, are the building block not only of the Chinese Mandarin language (used in China and Taiwan) and Chinese Cantonese language (used in Hong Kong), but also of the Korean and Japanese languages – though with a lot of modifications. While the English Latin alphabet has only 26 letters, which one needs to learn in order to understand words, the Chinese language has over 50,000 characters, and one just has to memorize them. An educated Chinese person needs to know about 3,000 characters in order to read a newspaper intelligently, and between 4,000 and 8,000 in order to read a book. Readers of the language have to memorize thousands of distinct characters, a rigorous and rote-based process, which is one of the main reasons that East Asian peoples are very good at mathematics and other subjects based on symbols.

Indus Valley Civilization

This civilization arose in the present day Indian sub-continent (Pakistan, India, Afghanistan, Bangladesh, Sri Lanka). It arose independent of its counterparts to the west (Mesopotamia) and to the east (Ancient China). There is evidence that this distinct civilization arose as early as 8000 BC in Haryana, present-day India. But it peaked in the Bronze Age between 3300 BC and 1300 BC, a period largely referred to as the Harappan period; that is why some people refer to it as the Harappan Civilization. From its peak, it faded over many years leading up to the Iron Age around 300 BC. There was another Civilization called the Vedic Civilization that arose at the tail end of the Harappan period. The Indus Valley Civilization encompasses both cultures.

In the Harappan period, major cities sprang up in the valleys of the Indus and the Sarasvati rivers. These urban centers were very sophisticated for their time in that they had sanitation systems with waste water drainage along roads, houses connected to central water systems, and general urban planning of the cities. People participated in advanced metallurgy to create tools out of bronze, copper, tin, etc. Socially, the inhabitants of this civilization were decentralized without a supreme king or ruler, and historians say this explains why this civilization did not have big citadels or monuments like the pyramids of the Americas and Egypt.

Written inscriptions have been found on ceramic pots, tablets, and seals, which suggest that the civilization had a widespread literary culture. It is in this ancient culture that cremation of dead bodies started, which would go on to become a central practice of Hinduism even up to today.

As the Harappan civilization was starting to decline, the Vedic civilization sprang up – there is still debate whether these civilizations were the same. The Vedic civilization is the direct precursor of Hinduism, Jainism and Buddhism. Vedic spirituality is based on the four books widely known as The Four Vedas: *Rigneda*, *Yajurveda*, *Samaveda* and the *Atharvaveda*, which were written in a language called Vedic Sanskrit in the second millennium BC. The Vedas set the bedrock of Hindu religious practices as they spell out the mantras, benedictions, the rituals and symbolic sacrifices that are hallmarks of Hinduism. The last chapters of the Vedas, called the Upanishads, are of greater importance as they have some of the greatest spiritual insights that non-Indians have come to learn about worldwide. The Upanishads teach life philosophies of how to achieve Brahman (ultimate reality), what Karma is (retributive action) and the doctrine of Moksa (human salvation through reincarnation).

Unlike the Abrahamic religions which have one holy text each, along with the Vedas and Upanishads, Hinduism has several sacred texts, two major ones being the *Bhagavad Gita* and the *Brahma Sutra*. In Hinduism, good and evil is not as clear as it is in Christianity. For example, the ultimate trinity of the Gods – Brahma, Vishnu and Shiva – play both good and evil parts. I first learned about Hinduism in my high school years at the United World College in New Mexico, but I really got to dive into the teachings of the Vedas and Upanishads through the works of the great American religious philosopher Joseph Campbell, who was a good friend of George Lucas and whose philosophy is the centerpiece of Lucas's *Star Wars* movies. I also learned about Hinduism and Buddhism through reading the Princeton professor Elaine Pagels' works on the origin of Satan in Christianity, and her finding that there are a lot of similarities between early Christianity, especially Gnostic Christianity, and Buddhist or Hindu teachings. In fact, some scholars have suggested that the theme of a solitary Christ, or a "living Christ," is very much in line with the "living Buddha" concept in Buddhism, and since the early Christians who went eastward came in contact with Hinduism and Buddhism, it is not farfetched to conclude that they could have borrowed themes from the East. Pagels also contends that the actual thematic details of the Devil in Christianity have their roots in Hindu themes as opposed to their vague Judaic counterpart.

Andean Civilization

This cradle civilization flourished around the Norte Chico area of present day Peru, South America. At its height it covered a big area stretching to Northern Chile and Bolivia. Some accounts claim it existed as early as 3200 BC. The civilization also built pyramids, massive ceremonial buildings, had advanced potato and cotton agriculture, and sophisticated animal husbandry with llamas, guinea pigs, etc. Spiritually, the people believed in Staff Gods, or gods who were pictured with big sticks in their hands that are believed to represent the source of their divine authority. Hallucinogenic drugs played a big part in their spiritual rituals, and this practice has survived until the present where you still find many Amazonian Indians using different forms of hallucinogenic drugs for journeys of enlightenment and medicinal practices.

In this same area, another society arose thousands of years later: the Inca Empire of 1100 to 1532 AD. It became the biggest Pre-Columbian civilization in the Americas. The word Inca referred both to the people and to the title of the king. At one time during the reign of Tupac Inca, it had more than 12 million people and occupied an area which spanned a distance equal to that of North America to Central America. The Incas are the ones who built Machu Picchu, the enormous ruins of a citadel, or small city, that is still one of the most visited sites of the ancient civilizations in the world. Machu Picchu is a UNESCO World Heritage Site, and was voted as one of the New Seven Wonders of the World; the other six include the Christ the Redeemer statue in Rio, the Taj Mahal in India, the Chichen Itza pyramid in Mexico, the Petra in Jordan, the Colosseum in Rome, and the Great Wall of China. Personally, I feel very lucky to have been to two of these Seven Wonders (Christ the Redeemer and Chichen Itza), with plans to visit Rome and the Colosseum this year. The Inca Empire was conquered by the Spaniards in 1532 AD during the reign of Tupac Amaru, the last Inca.

In this chapter, I have discussed my fifth hypothesis of how to transcend our heritages of birth.

<u>Hypothesis 1</u>: The origin of all humans is in Africa.

Hypothesis 2: Even if the origin of all humans is in Africa, the Semites created the idea of one God as it is known to most of us and the Europeans created the modern world as we know it; the most important similarity shared by all humans is the collective unconscious.

Hypothesis 3: Even if all humans are similar, there are real differences and inequalities among peoples due to the differences in collective consciousness.

Hypothesis 4: Absence of evidence is not evidence of absence. Just because we don't have undisputed scientific evidence of civilizations before 10,000 BC does not mean that for certain periods between the creation of the Earth 4.5 billion years ago and 10,000 BC, there were no advanced civilizations (humans or other creatures) that inhabited Africa and other parts of the planet.

Hypothesis 5: The six cradle civilizations, i.e. Ancient Egypt, the Olmecs of Central & North America, the Andean civilization in South America, the Mesopotamian civilization of the Middle East, the Indus Valley civilization of the Asian sub-continent, and the Ancient China civilization, were multi-ethnic, multi-racial civilizations that hold significance for all humans.

6

EUROPEAN CLASSICAL CIVILIZATION

European Classical Civilization is the civilization of ancient Greece and ancient Rome, which at their height covered the area around the Mediterranean Sea (eastern Mediterranean, the Middle East, and North Africa). During this civilization, present day North Africa was not populated by Arabs, and was considered very much a part of the Greek and Roman world.

This civilization lasted for about 1,500 years, from the eighth century BC to about the seventh century AD. Its earliest period is mostly remembered by the works of the Greek writer Homer in his epic poems *The Iliad* and *The Odyssey*. These two books are the first Western classics, and are so integral to the history of literature and story that it is a big disservice to your intellectual life if you have not read some portion of these two fundamental books of the Western canon. I consider myself lucky to have attended Lafayette College, which assigned us the reading of *The Odyssey* before we even reported for our first day of school.

The Iliad is a book primarily about the ten year Trojan War, a mythical Greek story about how the Greeks went to fight the city of Troy after its leader Paris captured Helen, the wife of the Greek king of Sparta. The end of the war is world famous as the Greeks, under Odysseus, disguised themselves in a Trojan Horse to gain access to the impregnable city and bring about its sacking. Achilles and Ajax are some of the other great protagonists in this Greek epic.

The Odyssey is a book about Odysseus' ten-year-long journey back home to Ithaca after the fall of Troy. It tells of his trials and challenges to sail home, as well as the different people and situations he encounters along the way. By the time he returns home, his son is more than 20 years old and his wife Penelope, who had been faithful to him all those years, has a long list of suitors, all of which he engages and manages to kill.

In these two books you get to learn the gist of Ancient Greece, its cultural customs, religious beliefs, names of major players and gods, important cities, and in general, the day to day life that men of the time lived.

The Greek civilization is known for a lot of things which still influence our world today. Greece is commonly credited as bringing about "the birth of democracy," because each Greek city state had a sophisticated system of rulers that were elected by the populace. The Olympic Games derive their origin from the ancient games at Olympia, where athletes from all over Greece used to compete in honor of Zeus – the Supreme God. The social religious life of Greece was centered on the Pantheon and a long list of gods and goddesses who resided on Mount Olympus, but would come down and interact with mortal people. This is how the mythical offspring of gods and mortals came about, such as Helen of Troy (the daughter of Zeus and a woman called Leda). Examples of the gods of the Greek Pantheon are: Zeus (god of the sky and king of the gods), Apollo (god of music), Aphrodite (goddess of love), Athena (goddess of wisdom), Poseidon (god of the sea), Hades (god of the dead and the underworld), Dionysius (god of the vine), and many more. The Pantheon building is still standing today.

Greece is also very much known for the Academy of Athens, which was the central place for teaching skeptical knowledge. From Greek skeptical knowledge, we get tremendous human achievements in mathematics (though heavily influenced by the Egyptians) such as:

1) Arithmetic (the math of natural numbers and integers, and methods of formal proofs by induction and deduction), 2) Geometry (the math of shapes epitomized by Euclid's works in the theory of elements and the Pythagorean theorem which explains the relationship between the sides of a right triangle), 3) Mathematical Analysis (measures and analytical functions), and 4) Trigonometry (which began as an application of geometry to astronomical studies), to name just a few.

In science, or what used to be called natural philosophy, we have the works of Archimedes (the math and science genius famously / infamously known for running in the street naked shouting, "Eureka! Eureka! I understand it, I understand it!" after having a "eureka experience" in the bathtub regarding a method of measuring the volume of irregular objects), and works by Ptolemy (creator of the first sophisticated model of the planets and stars).

In philosophy, who hasn't heard of Socrates, the man sentenced to death by drinking poison for teaching the people of Athens how to think and reason? This man is considered by many to be the greatest philosopher of all time and his famous doubts regarding God are still unmatched; "Does God command things because they are right or are things right because God commands them?" Then there is Plato, the man who brought us all Socrates' teachings and founded the Academy of Athens, though he is best known for his works *The Dialogues* and *The Republic*. Aristotle, who studied at Plato's Academy for over two decades and mastered everything there was to master, ended up teaching Alexander the Great.

Ancient Greece also brought us enormous achievements in logic, politics, music and the arts.

Greek culture came under Roman rule after the Roman conquest following the Battle of Corinth around 146 BC. From then on, the Latin-speaking people originating from Rome ruled over a vast area around the eastern and western Mediterranean coasts. The Roman people had established their kingdom back in 753 BC. As legend would have it, "Roma" was started as a small city kingdom by two brothers, Romulus and Remus, who descended from the Greek people of Troy, but were raised by a wolf. The kingdom lasted for 344 years before evolving into a republic in 509 BC. The republic lasted for 482 years (509–27 BC) and then the Roman Empire came about and lasted for about 500 years (27 BC to 476 AD). Note that it is not clear when the empire really fell as it declined over several centuries, but many historians consider the deposition of the last emperor, Romulus Augustus, in 476 AD as the official collapse.

What came to be known as the grandeur of Rome started with the founding of the Roman Republic. It ushered in a constitution which had the hallmark of the modern day checks and balances system whereby the leaders of the republic, two consuls who ruled interchangeably over a period of one year, were checked by a powerful senate. Beginning in the third century BC, Rome started conquering the nearby Italian cities in what came to be known as the Punic Wars, and by the first century BC had conquered much of the Mediterranean coast. One of the most innovative political positions that worked wonders for the republic was the office of the Dictator – the senate would give power to the consuls to choose one man to be above the law during very trying times, such as war and famine. For example, during the restless years in the mid-first century, Julius Caesar assumed several dictatorships and, after killing all his competitors, he ruled supreme over the republic. Caesar was killed in 44 BC on the Ides of March / 15th March (which event is known worldwide by its depiction in Shakespeare's play *Julius Caesar*).

After Caesar's death, the turmoil that ensued led to the rise of Octavian who defeated his fiercest rival Mark Antony, resulting in the joint suicides of Antony and his wife Cleopatra of Egypt. Thereafter Octavian became the first Roman Emperor in 27 BC, taking upon himself the title of Augustus. And that marked the beginning of the grandeur of the Roman Empire.

The Roman Empire ruled almost all of what we call Europe today (except Ireland, northern Britain, and parts of eastern Europe and Russia), along with the whole of the Middle East and northern Africa. Under Emperor Tiberius, it is historically true that a leader of the Roman province of Judea (modern day Israel) called Pontius Pilate was the Prefect of Judea from 26–36 AD; this is a central fact in the Biblical account of the death of Jesus. During the time of the Roman Empire, the Latin language, based on the alphabet (A, B, C, D... Z), was the means to write and communicate everywhere except for a few areas of the eastern Mediterranean which used the Greek alphabet (A – *alpha*, B – *beta*, Γ – *gamma*, Δ – *delta* ... Ω – *Omega*) whose form of Greek, Koine Greek, was used to write the New Testament of the Bible.

The empire grew very powerful and achieved enormous fetes in civil government, literacy, engineering, economic systems, military theory, and general quality of life, which were exemplified by the spectacles staged in the Roman Coliseum. Roman law was of such great achievement that up to now, other than England with its common law tradition, the rest of continental Europe and South America use forms of Roman codified laws. I once had a chat with a South American friend who was studying law. It is then that I comprehended that law students in Roman codified law countries have to memorize word for word long complicated codes of law, unlike our English-influenced common law countries where students study case law and merely understand precedence of historical judgments. Also high on the achievement ladder was the Latin alphabet, which is the foundation of most European languages and many African languages like my own Lusoga. In fact, the Latin language was so influential that for more than 1000 years it was the official language used by the Roman Catholic church in its religious services and publications, and it is still used by modern science for all names given to all species of life, e.g. the scientific name for human beings is the Latin name *Homo sapiens.*

In the third century AD, the Roman Empire was too big to govern so Emperor Diocletian divided it into two provinces which we call the Eastern Roman Empire, with Byzantium as the capital, until moving to Constantinople in modern day Turkey (and taking on the new name Istanbul), and the Western Roman Empire with Rome as the capital.

It is not possible to pinpoint when exactly the classical Greco-Roman civilization ended, but for sure it ended sometime between the fourth and seventh centuries AD. The Empire faced a lot of pressure from invading Germanic tribes from the north and the Huns from the east. Given the disconnect between east and west, military coordination and efficiency became a problem. It did not help that there was a lot of moral decay in the ruling class. This was epitomized by the emperor, Caligula, who used to have sexual orgies in the senate and made his horse a senator. Internal fighting finally led to a coup in which Odoacer deposed the last Western Roman emperor, Romulus Augustus, in 476 AD.

So this ended the incredible story of Rome which had existed in its three different forms for about 1,200 years. In its wake it left a variety of Latin peoples all over Europe who ended up forming different nations and languages known as romance languages (Spanish, Portuguese, French, Italian, and Romanian). Note that English also borrows a lot of Latin words, because England was under Roman rule for almost 400 years, but essentially English is more of a Germanic language than a Latin one.

The Eastern Roman Empire limped on for much longer. The final blow was the Muslim conquest of the Mediterranean world; this included Syria and Egypt in the late 630s, the rest of North Africa in the 660s, and finally Spain in 718. The first Arab siege of Constantinople in 674–678 and the second and final Arab siege of Constantinople in 717–718 did tremendous damage to what remained of Roman culture. The eventual capitulation of the city in 1453 at the hands of the victorious Muslims completed the Islamization of modern-day Turkey.

The Roman refugees fleeing Constantinople after the Muslim conquest took a lot of classical antiquities with them to the area that is now Italy, and that played a big role in the ignition of the Italian Renaissance which would bear forth the current glorious Western civilization.

The Greco-Roman civilization used the concentrating agents of a republic and then an empire as the post-tribal grouping of diverse peoples like Romans, Greeks, Jews, Arabs, North Africans and Europeans. The Greek and Latin alphabets were the cornerstone for a sort of universal code of communication throughout what was then the "known world." Still today we use the Greek alphabet in all our mathematics and Latin alphabet to write most of the world's languages (English being a prime example).

In this chapter, I have discussed my sixth hypothesis of how to transcend our heritages of birth.

Hypothesis 1: The origin of all humans is in Africa.

Hypothesis 2: Even if the origin of all humans is in Africa, the Semites created the idea of one God as it is known to most of us and the Europeans created the modern world as we know it; the most important similarity shared by all humans is the collective unconscious.

Hypothesis 3: Even if all humans are similar, there are real differences and inequalities among peoples due to the differences in collective consciousness.

Hypothesis 4: Absence of evidence is not evidence of absence. Just because we don't have undisputed scientific evidence of civilizations before 10,000 BC does not mean that for certain periods between the creation of the earth 4.5 billion years ago and 10,000 BC, there were no advanced civilizations (humans or other creatures) that inhabited Africa and other parts of the planet.

Hypothesis 5: The six cradle civilizations, i.e. Ancient Egypt, the Olmecs of Central & North America, the Andean civilization in South America, the Mesopotamian civilization of the Middle East, the Indus Valley civilization of the Asian sub-continent, and the Ancient China civilization were multi-ethnic, multi-racial civilizations that hold significance for all humans.

Hypothesis 6: After the collapse of the African cradle civilization of Ancient Egypt, the Greco-Roman civilization became the intellectual foundation to what we know now as the European Western civilization.

7

ISLAMIC CIVILIZATION

As the Roman Empire was crumbling under its own weight, beginning in the fourth century, and Europe was wallowing in the dark ages where life was characterized by backwardness, anarchy and lack of civilization – though current historical thinking is that this period was not as stagnant as previously thought – in the year 610, the seeds of what would become a distinct civilization for mankind were planted. That is the year Muslims believe God started revealing the Koran / Quran (the central divine scripture of Islam) to his messenger Mohammad Ibn Abdullah through the angel Gabriel. You cannot understand Islamic civilization unless you understand the origin and articles of faith of the religion.

Even though Uganda is less than 15% Muslim and the rest is Christian, as students we were taught C.R.E. and I.R.E. (Christian Religious Education and Islamic Religious Education), so everyone in Uganda grows up knowing the major beliefs of these two religions. Some people ask me why a country with such a minority Muslim population had a Muslim president (Idi Amin Dada), and I reply that while Muslims hold important political and social positions in the country, the real reason is that in Uganda, religion is largely an issue of identity, not theological divergence. As such, we Christians know what Muslims believe, but we don't believe it ourselves. For example, due to the very harmonious religious atmosphere in the country, we Christians grow up knowing that Muslims are the only ones who slaughter animals in society. This is because it is haram (forbidden) for Muslims to eat animals slaughtered by Christians, yet Christians can eat animals slaughtered by Muslims.

Mohammad was born in Mecca in 570 AD. Muslims believe that in 610 when Mohammad was 40 years old, while in a cave at Al-Hira, God started revealing the Koran to him. The revelation lasted the entirety of his life, until he died at age 62.

Mohammad's first follower was his first wife, Khadija. He married many more women after her death, but only 12 others are officially considered his wives, including Aisha whom he married when she was six, but did not consummate the marriage with until she reached the "acceptable age" of nine. Aisha went on to be one of the most important women in early Islam as she spread Mohammad's message for over 40 years. Soon after Khadija began believing Mohammad, his cousin Ali Talib and close friend Abr Bakr also began believing that he was receiving revelations from God.

By 613 he had a sizeable following and started preaching in public places. The local merchants and leaders were opposed to his new message and conflicts started developing. One of the major conflicts was Mohammad's preaching against the local polytheistic religious practices, whose focal point was the Ka'aba building. Ironically, this is the same structure that would later be turned into the holiest Islamic religious focal point on the eventual triumph of Islam. Equally ironic is the fact that it is now believed by Muslims that the Ka'aba was built by Adam and later rebuilt by Ibrahim and Ishmael. By 622, resistance in Mecca had reached a boiling point and it forced Mohammad to move with his followers to Medina. This migration is a special event in Islam called Hijra, and it marks the start of the Islamic calendar as year 1.

While in Medina, rivalry with Mecca intensified until a Meccan expedition in 624 by the Quraysh tribe came with 10,000 men to crush Mohammad and his band of 313 Muslim fighters. According to Encyclopedia Britannica, the battle was at a place called Badr and many Muslims regard it as the most significant battle of their religion because, according to them, angels fought on behalf of the Muslims to bring about their victory. Mohammad fought the second major battle against the invading Meccans at Uhud where he was gravely wounded and, thinking he was dead, the Meccans returned home. But he survived, and following recovery, he revealed more verses of the Koran.

Between 628 and 629, Mohammad led his Muslim followers on their first conquest of the town Khaybar. After taking the city, he instituted the religious tax Jizyah, which provided for Christians and Jews to live in the city so long as they paid this tax. This became the model for the treatment of Jews and Christians wherever Islam conquered. Even if their non-belief qualified them as infidels, at least they believed in the Bible from which Islam draws many of its themes. In 630, he sent a Muslim force of 10,000 that easily conquered Mecca. By 631, Mohammad and his Muslims had conquered most of Arabia, hence the title "Conqueror of Arabia" that some historians have bestowed on him. As more people pledged allegiance to the religion, he continued to reveal more verses of the Koran.

In 632, Mohammad and some of his followers made the first official "Hajj pilgrimage" from his home Medina to his town of birth, Mecca. In Mecca he performed all the rituals that became the standard for Muslims to perform on their pilgrimages to Mecca. He also decreed civil laws on how community should be governed and how marriages should work. More importantly he forbade all tribal rivalry and feuds, instilling a universal identity of Islamic community, the most famous of which was the multi-ethnic and multi-racial message he commanded his followers to embrace. He declared the end of "the age of ignorance" and from that time onward the Arabs were united for the first time in history, not by tribal bond but rather by the written word. With that he had accomplished the two concentrating agents for a civilization: 1) he had created a post-tribal grouping, and 2) he had created a written accord which would act as the undisputed source for guidance on life and man's place in the universe. When he died in the house of his third wife, Aisha, on June 8th, 632, he left behind several sons and daughters along with hundreds of thousands of followers.

Islamic civilization is based on the Koran and Mohammad and what they say about the oneness of God. The major critical distinction between the Koran and the Judeo-Christian Bible is that while the various books of the Bible were created and written by various men over hundreds of years, according to a fundamental article of faith for Muslims, the Koran was there at the beginning of creation itself but was only eventually written by Mohammad through a verbatim revelation from God. Hence, the overbearing resistance to alter the text in anyway.

Also, it is crucial to understand that, unlike Judaism and Christianity which evolved over hundreds of years without any specific beginning, Islam was specifically created piece by piece by Mohammad and the Koran actually says, "Today I have perfected your religion for you. I have approved Islam as your religion." That is why Islam can be very prescriptive (e.g. pray five times a day, fast during the holy month, make a pilgrimage to Mecca, don't eat pork, etc.), while Christianity tends to be more inspirational than prescriptive. It is an oxymoron to be a Muslim if you don't follow the five pillars of Islam, but other than my baptism when I was a week old (which is not even prescribed in the Bible, but was done out of tradition), there isn't much the Bible prescribes for me to do in a specific way every day or during a holy month in order to be Christian. The main reason for this is that Christianity was created by men like Paul and Mark starting about 30 years after the death of Jesus. Since Jesus, like Socrates, did not write his divine message, these people created Christianity out of inspiration they had concerning his life and teachings. So they used their deepest human consciousness to create a system of belief that can speak to very deep psychological archetypes in every person (see the next chapter for details of the Christian creation).

Together with the Koran, there are two other books that are central to the Islamic faith: the *Haddith* and the *Sunnah*. The *Haddith* is a collection of the sayings of Mohammad, while the *Sunnah* is an account of his physical actions in life. Muslims are supposed to emulate the life of Mohammad as much as possible.

Unlike Christianity which recognizes only the minor and major prophets of the Jewish tradition, Islam expands the term to consider people like Adam, Noah and Jesus as prophets. Islam holds that Jesus, or Isa, was a great prophet, but it does not hold that he was the son of God or that he rose from the dead. The combination of these last two beliefs act as the cornerstone of Christianity – that Jesus was the son of God, who lived on Earth as man; he was killed and rose from the dead after three days. Muslims believe that Jesus was just a prophet like many others. They believe that he never died, but that God took him directly to heaven and that it was a different man who was crucified that Friday at Golgotha. I remember how I used to argue with my Muslim friends in school in Uganda about the Jesus issue. I kept wondering how they could believe that for 600 years (between Jesus' death in 33 AD and Mohammad in 632 AD) Christians were wrong about Jesus being crucified and buried.

Central to Islam is the *Shahadah* (the Creed), which reads, "I testify that there is one God Allah and Mohammad is his messenger." Its counterpart in Christianity is the Nicene Creed or the Apostle Creed (see the next chapter for details). It is important to note that even if the word "Allah" was used by pre-Islamic Arabic speaking peoples (polytheists, Jews and Christians included) to refer to the creator deity, in modern usage it refers to the Muslim God – this is a classic example of the evolution of a word. The last phrase of the *Shahadah* is enormously sensitive to Muslims because they believe that Mohammad was the last prophet or messenger from God. Accordingly, no other prophets will come in the future. This creed is further fortified by the doctrine of Ismah, or infallibility of Mohammad and his protection from mistakes. The infallibility of Mohammad is one of the main reasons why there are Muslims who will kill other people deemed to be desecrating the name or the person of Mohammad. It is akin to the infallibility that is accorded the Pope by Catholics, which was one of the main causes of the Reformation in Christianity when the Protestants rebelled against the belief that it was not possible for the Pope to err. I am a product of this Protestant thinking (as codified in 1571 by the *39 Articles of Religion* of the Anglican Protestant Church), and growing up I used to have very interesting conversations with my Catholic friends at Nkumba Primary School, despite not actually even knowing what a doctrine was.

The word Islam means "submission"; total submission to the will of Allah. This has something to do with why Muslims regularly use phrases like "God willing" ("Insha Allah"), "All praises be to God" ("Alhamdulillah"), and of course, "God is great" ("Allahu Akbar"). Other religions seldom invoke the word of God in such passing ways.

The most fundamental concept of the *Shahadah* is the Tawhid – the belief in the oneness of God. Unlike Christianity which has the trinity (God the Father, God the Son and God the Holy Spirit), according to Tawhid, it is supremely important that you revere the oneness of God, hence the tendency for some Muslim countries to have blasphemy laws for punishing anyone who is found guilty of desecrating the oneness of God and / or the verbatim word of God as it is found in the Koran.

There are five pillars of Islam, which are obligatory to all believers: 1) the *Shahadah*, 2) praying five times a day, 3) giving alms to the poor, 4) fasting during the month of Ramadan, and 5) Hajj, or the pilgrimage to Mecca once in your lifetime if you can afford it financially and physically (upon the return from which, you are given the title of "Hajji" if a man, or "Hajat" if a woman).

After Mohammad died, there was dispute over who the real heir should be. Some followers wanted Abu Bakr, the prophet's friend and companion to be the caliph of all Muslims, while others wanted Ali Talib, his cousin and son-in-law, to be the heir. The present day Shia Muslims (accounting for 10–20% of the world's Muslim population, and predominantly found in Iran and Iraq) believe that Ali was the rightful heir, while the Sunni Muslims (accounting for more than 80% of world's Muslim population, and predominantly found in Saudi Arabia and the remaining Islamic countries) believe Abu Bakr was.

At the height of its golden age, the Islamic world was the beacon of light and knowledge for what has become the modern world. Central to this was the House of Wisdom in Baghdad which housed scholars from all over the known civilized world, and who translated classic Greco-Roman books into Arabic. As a result, the Islamic civilization made tremendous contributions to mathematics and the sciences. In fact, what we now call "the scientific method" was started by the great Persian scientist Alhazen. Modern day numerals (0, 1, 2 ... 9) were made universal after their adoption from India by Islam, hence we call them Arabic numbers. Algebra and algorithms were invented by this civilization. Their astronomy was world class to such a degree that most of the stars today have Arabic names. The world's oldest degree-granting school, the University of Alkaraouine, was founded by the Islamic civilization in 859. These are just a few examples of this society's contributions to the world.

The civilization came under tremendous strain starting in the eleventh century when a resurgent Christian Europe started a series of invasions known as "The Crusades," intended to take back territories that had been captured by the Arabs in the seventh century, central of which was the Holy Land near Jerusalem. Its decline was further exacerbated in the thirteenth century with the destruction of the House of Wisdom and the sacking of Baghdad by the invading Mongols. Also, the Reconquista started by Christian monarchs in Spain and Portugal in 1482 gave a devastating blow to the Islamic civilization with the total expulsion of the Arabs from the Iberian Peninsula in 1492 – after 700 years of Arab rule over Spain and Portugal.

The great Turkish Ottoman Empire placed the entire Arab Middle East under its mammoth Islamic caliphate in the early sixteenth century for over 400 years. However, in the early twentieth century, while under internal pressure from the Young Turks agitating for nationalism and external pressure from the Europeans during the First World War, the Ottoman Empire was dissolved in 1922 when the last Sultan was deposed and the modern day Republic of Turkey was born. That marked the end of the last strong Islamic political entity.

The Islamic intellectual prowess that was the beacon of human knowledge during the days of the House of Wisdom is no longer with us. While researching this sub-chapter, I stumbled upon a video of the American physicist Neil deGrasse Tyson, director of the Hayden Planetarium in New York City and considered one of the most popular astrophysicists in America. In the video he was talking about who in history has had "the naming rights" of the natural world. He mentioned that between 800 AD and 1100 AD, the Arabs and Islam in general had the naming rights of the natural world and science as they were the center of the civilized world back then. The Arabs / Muslims named most of the stars in the heavens (he showed long lists of stars that have Arabic names). Great men like Alhazen and Abd Al-Sufi did pioneering works in physics, optics, mathematics and astronomy, including the discovery of new galaxies like the Andromeda galaxy near our own Milky Way galaxy. In short, human civilization and investigative inquiry using natural science was based in the Muslim world, specifically in Baghdad, between the years of 800 and 1100 AD.

However, something happened in the twelfth century that precipitated the decline of the Arab / Islamic civilization. He ascribed the decline and collapse to religious scholar Abu Hamid Al Ghazali, who preached that mathematics and science were un-Koranic. Upon further research, I discovered that other writers also ascribe the blame partly to another scholar, Nizim al Mulk. Long story short, from around the twelfth century, communities all over the Muslim world started putting more importance on religious studies than mathematics / science and investigative inquiry. They emphasized religious schools, called "Madrasas", over secular schools. Social mobility started being based on religious studies, and leaders were picked based on religious education as opposed to investigative knowledge. As a result, studies in mathematics / sciences were stifled.

It just so happened that around that time, Christian western Europe was starting to recover from its slumber of more than 500 years of the Middle Ages (see the next chapter on how Europe took on the charge of progressing mathematics and the sciences starting with the Italian Renaissance).

Flash forward about 1000 years to now, and the evidence is very clear that western Europe, and its extension of North America, now has "the naming rights" over much of our current human civilization. A few examples for this reality are: the modern Arab borders were created by European colonialists; most of the countries of the world have been created, mapped and colonized by Europeans / Americans; nearly all the cutting-edge findings in the sciences are documented in European languages (primarily English); the computer, the internet, and the majority of current inventions are primarily taking place within western universities, and the best students from around the world flock to universities in Europe or North America.

Mr. Tyson was discussing the idea of "naming rights" by alluding to the fact that, unlike the age of 800 to 1100, there have not been any major original scientific ideas in the Arabic language for over 1000 years now. He also mentioned that since the inception of the Nobel prizes in 1901, there have been a mere three Muslims to win the prize in the sciences (one Pakistani, one Turk and one American Egyptian) and a grand total of 12 Muslims out of an overall 855 recipients who have won the prize in all categories for the more than 100 years of the prize's existence. So even if Muslims number 1.6 billion people (23% of the world population), they have won only 1.4% of the overall Nobel prizes ever given. Yet, just for Nobel prizes in the sciences alone, Jews have won over 25% of all prizes given out. With a population of about 15 million people worldwide (0.2% of world population), that is a staggering percentage. In fact, according to the Jewish Virtual Library, Jews have won more than 20% of all Nobel prizes since the program's inception, which is 193 out of 855 laureates. It goes without saying that the majority of the winners in any category belong to Christians, because since the twelfth century, Christian Western Europe has had "the naming rights" to human world knowledge. More than 65% of Nobel winners have been Christians, yet Christians account for only 33% of the world population. To understand the preeminence of the Jewish–Christian Europe and its overly dominant claim to "the naming rights" of human knowledge, in the next chapter we turn to the current modern civilization for mankind – the European Western civilization.

In this chapter, I have discussed my seventh hypothesis of how to transcend our heritages of birth.

Hypothesis 1: The origin of all humans is in Africa.

Hypothesis 2: Even if the origin of all humans is in Africa, the Semites created the idea of one God as it is known to most of us and the Europeans created the modern world as we know it; the most important similarity shared by all humans is the collective unconscious.

Hypothesis 3: Even if all humans are similar, there are real differences and inequalities among peoples due to the differences in collective consciousness.

Hypothesis 4: Absence of evidence is not evidence of absence. Just because we don't have undisputed scientific evidence of civilizations before 10,000 BC does not mean that for certain periods between the creation of the earth

4.5 billion years ago and 10,000 BC, there were no advanced civilizations (humans or other creatures) that inhabited Africa and other parts of the planet.

Hypothesis 5: The six cradle civilizations, i.e. Ancient Egypt, the Olmecs of Central & North America, the Andean civilization in South America, the Mesopotamian civilization of the Middle East, the Indus Valley civilization of the Asian sub-continent, and the Ancient China civilization were multi-ethnic, multi-racial civilizations that hold significance for all humans.

Hypothesis 6: After the collapse of the African cradle civilization of Ancient Egypt, the Greco-Roman civilization became the intellectual foundation to what we know now as the European Western civilization.

Hypothesis 7: During the European Medieval ages, between the fall of the Roman Empire and the Italian Renaissance, the Islamic civilization played a critical role of safeguarding the ancient Greco-Roman classical knowledge which was resurrected in what we call the European Western civilization.

8

European Western Civilization

The present day modern civilization is the Western European civilization. It is the first civilization that has reached all the lands and all the peoples on the planet. The six cradle civilizations and the Classical civilizations (Greco-Roman and Islamic) each occupied only a small portion of the Earth. However, for the first time in human history, a civilization has risen to affect every culture and peoples of the world.

This civilization started with the Italian Renaissance of the fourteenth century, but one of the main seeds for its rise had been the ascendance of Christianity as the Roman State religion in the late fourth century. Before that time, Christianity was regarded as paganism by the Roman civilization, as the Emperor and most subjects of the Empire were adherents of Ancient Roman religions. However, when the Roman Emperor Constantine the Great made a decree legalizing the pagan Christian religion in 313 AD, and also following his calling of the First Council of Nicaea in 325, Christianity rapidly spread in the Roman Empire. It became the state religion in 380 AD by decree of Emperor Theodosius I. From that time onward, the meaning of the word "pagan" flipped to refer to non-Christian beliefs, while Christianity became the "true" religion.

The First Council of Nicaea is the body that created the Nicene Creed (the actual article of faith for Christianity). Until recently, you could not call yourself a Christian in the traditional sense unless you recited that creed or its variant, the Apostle's Creed. I remember in my school days in Uganda we used to recite the Apostle's Creed every morning during the morning services at my secondary school, King's College Budo. Christianity is summed up in this creed:

> **I BELIEVE** in God, the Father almighty,
> creator of Heaven and Earth.
>
> I believe in Jesus Christ, his only Son, our Lord.
> He was conceived by the power of the Holy Spirit
> and born of the Virgin Mary.
>
> He suffered under Pontius Pilate,
> was crucified, died, and was buried.
>
> He descended to the dead.
> On the third day he rose again.
> He ascended into Heaven,
> and is seated at the right hand of the Father.
> He will come again to judge the living and the dead.
>
> I believe in the Holy Spirit,
> the holy Catholic Church,
> the communion of saints,
> the forgiveness of sins,
> the resurrection of the body,
> and the life everlasting
> Amen.

When the Italian Renaissance started in Florence in the fourteenth century, Christianity was the accepted "universal" religion and the Pope of the Roman Catholic Church was the most powerful position in the whole of western Europe. Upon recovery of the classical antiquity from Constantinople and the old Roman world, the Renaissance was basically the revival of the old Greco-Roman civilization, but this time with worldwide implications.

The Renaissance was the age that started Western man's modern value of humanism – the idea that man is the measure of all things. From then onwards, history has recorded Western man achieve enormously in all human pursuits, including modern philosophy, creations in the arts, politics, architecture and the sciences.

The most famous of such men was Leonardo da Vinci, who exhibited superhuman genius in the way he left great works in mathematics, painting, astronomy, engineering, literature, botany, music, invention, cartography and many other fields. To a lot of historians, there has never been anyone to match da Vinci's genius; he is regarded as the universal genius, or simply "the Renaissance Man." There are people who even credit him for the invention of the helicopter, parachute and war tanks, since he drew pictures of them hundreds of years before they became a reality.

I remember at my university I was in the leadership for the engineering school's Leonardo Society before I knew why they chose such a random Italian name. When I did a little research and realized that Leonardo da Vinci was the ultimate jack of all trades (in all actuality, "master of all trades"), it made sense why my school had a study program characterized by all students (whether science or arts majors) taking at least one elective course from each of the subjects of engineering, humanities, mathematics, and the arts or social studies, and also completing one writing class before the end of their four years. The aim was to ensure that even if you graduate as an engineer, you know something about history, religion, art, philosophy and can write. I remember I learned my writing skills in the class Writing

101, where we used to make four rounds of edits for each piece of writing before Professor Blake would grade the fourth one. From that I learned how each of the three versions of your piece of writing aims for a different level of "completeness."

From the Renaissance onwards, the Western man gained a sort of turbo-engine in self-awareness and fortitude of personal will as he embarked to put himself squarely at the center of co-creation in this world. The first co-creation venture for the European man was during the age of discovery. Men from Europe sailed for months on vast oceans to discover and map foreign lands for their kings and queens. You have men like Vasco da Gama who sailed around Africa to India and back, Ferdinand Magellan who made the first circumnavigation of the world, Christopher Columbus who sailed westward without knowing what lay ahead only to end up in North America and the Caribbean Islands, and Captain James Cook who sailed most the whole world and mapped New Zealand, Australia, Antarctica and hundreds of islands in the Pacific for the British Crown.

Western man also embarked on the scientific revolution that brought us immense discoveries and creations in mathematics, the sciences, chemistry, biology, and astronomy, just to mention a few. Large on the list of achievements are Nicolas Copernicus and Galileo's objective evidence that the Earth is not the center of our immediate universe, but instead the sun is. Large also are Isaac Newton's discovery of the spectrum of light (the colors of the rainbow) and his superhuman discovery of the three laws of motion and gravity, and the unfathomably universal mathematics known as calculus.

Because of the achievements of the Renaissance, and the scientific revolution, European man also embarked on the Age of Enlightenment. Philosophy based on man's ability and greatness of thought were laid out by giants of human intellect like Voltaire, David Hume, Immanuel Kant, Jean-Jacques Rousseau and Adam Smith. We also can't forget earlier works by the likes of Spinoza, Descartes, Francis Bacon and John Locke. Fast-forward to the nineteenth and twentieth centuries, and we have the post-modern existentialist great thinkers like Kierkegaard, Nietzsche, Heidegger and Sartre, who all hail from the Western European civilization.

All the achievements in human thought and science played a great role in igniting the small island called Great Britain to spearhead the Industrial Revolution that brought us factories, steam-powered engines, trains, and gas lighting, to mention just a few.

We can't talk about Western civilization without mentioning the great and sacred creations of classical music. From the Middle Ages up to the modern era, music giants like Wagner, Mozart, Bach and Beethoven created masterpieces that still speak to the human spirit. The sublime feeling one gets upon listening to these European masterpieces should lead any civilized man to concur with Nietzsche that music is straight from God, and to live life without music is a mistake. It is from this personal belief that when I read about extremist groups that prohibit their members from listening to "western music," which I term as universal human music, it leads me to conclude that indeed such groups are evil.

On the collective side of things, the Western Europe civilization unleashed political philosophies and nation building which culminated in the creation of what we now call "nation-states." Besides Europeans making their own nation-states in continental Europe, they spread out to all continents of the world and named or actually created nation-states out of native people.

The concentrating agents used by the ascendance of Western European civilization were as follows: On the post-tribal grouping side of things, the holy alliance (or unholy as some may say) between the Roman Catholic Church and the Kingdoms of Europe gave a formidable collective consciousness to diverse groups of people to pray to the same God and use nationalism and their love of empire, country or king to build the frameworks of the civilization. On the writing system side of things, Western Europe used the Latin alphabet (A, B, C ... Z) to bring different languages under one easily translatable writing system. Apart from most of the world using the Latin alphabet in one form or another, the most important international language currently is English, which is used in many areas of the world, even in those that did not have a writing culture, e.g. my own mother language adopted the English Latin alphabet in order to make our language written.

Western European civilization was the first civilization to use humanism as its engine. Humanism, as the idea that man is the measure of everything, meant "man" in a singular way. Its radical assertion is that the independent thinking human mind is the one that creates the collective society. All other civilizations before it and the present day, non-modern societies believe that the collective is what defines the individual. On a general level, to understand the Western individual, you must read about the psychology of man – a good start are the ideas articulated by the father of psychology, the German Sigmund Freud. You can't say you understand the Western or European man without ever reading Freud's theories of the mind. Also, to understand the place of the individual in the Western nation-state, you must be familiar with the ideas of secular republicanism as exemplified by the history and the bedrock of the French nation.

However, specifically, crucial to understanding how modern Europe came to the value of individual liberty in thinking is to know the following two things: 1) the theories about the development of the modern mind, and 2) the Christian religion.

Origin of Consciousness and the Modern Mind

****This sub-chapter is dedicated to Lynn Gilbert of Austin, Texas ****

You cannot analyze any civilization without understanding how people thought or the collective consciousness of the people. It is extremely important that I devote a special sub-chapter to the development of modern man's consciousness, and what that portends regarding the functioning of his mind. Both in its collective sense and its individualist sense, modern man as a subject in the prevailing Western European civilization is unlike any other time in man's history. Unlike in any other civilization, for the first time we have a civilization that is built on individualism, where individuals can go and live in any part of the planet and even out in space. This is special.

Since the topic of consciousness is wide, for effectiveness I am going to approach it from a very narrow and precise angle, so that it makes sense to the overall thesis that this book concerns. The thesis gives recognition to the fact that despite all humans having the same collective unconscious, over the past thousands of years of human civilization, none of them has been built on an individual's free consciousness except for the Western civilization. Even if the civilization started with the Christian collective consciousness, for all intents and purposes, the current civilization is purely based on individualistic consciousness, which largely go beyond the Christian collective consciousness – case in point is the post-Christian Europe of today. A good testament to this is the fact that the Japanese, who are so removed from the Christian collective consciousness, are able to be a modern nation, which in fact is bigger and more modern than all the European countries. In my humble opinion, this Western civilization is our first attempt at building a truly human civilization (see the last chapter for further discussion).

Consciousness has been defined as "a state of awareness, being aware of external objects and also of something within oneself." Unlike "unconsciousness" which has stayed dormant as far as we can possibly tell, "consciousness" has an evolutionary history (or development over time) that is traceable and is still unfolding even at this juncture. While the collective and personal unconsciousness have stood quite still throughout time, with perhaps very negligible changes, the essence of consciousness has been characterized by tremendous changes and upheavals which have shaken the world and redefined our human civilizations over the ages. For example, even if for thousands of years people have had the same nature of dreams and largely the same archetypes about spirituality or respecting elders, in just a hundred years most societies have changed their collective consciousness regarding whether women can hold public office or vote in public matters, and that has drastically changed the way society looks at women – at least the modern society.

To discuss this very important topic as a buildup to my thesis, I am going to rely largely on the theory of consciousness by the American neurologist Julius Jaynes, as proposed in his masterpiece *The Origin of Consciousness in the Breakdown of the Bicameral Mind*, which is his only published book. It is considered by some people to be one of the most significant and groundbreaking books of the twentieth century, as it is so bravely original in its theory of consciousness and the development of the human mind. As someone who was born among people with a tribal mindset, this book filled a big void that I left in my first book; the nature of tribal mindsets versus modern man's mindset.

In my first book *The Fourth Heritage*, I talk about how the most important book I had read up until the time I wrote that book was Carl Sagan's *The Demon Haunted World: Science as a candle in the dark*. It is fair to say now that the most important book I have read in terms of giving me the theoretical framework to understand my tribal mind and that of any tribal relatives is Jaynes' book. Unfortunately, it is a very academic research book, and too complicated for the ordinary person who cannot concentrate long enough to read 500 pages of scholarly research. However, if you are like me and you still are conflicted about reconciling a tribal psychology and the beliefs that come from foreign religions and the European way of thinking, it would be a worthwhile investment of time to read this masterpiece.

I would not have known about this supremely relevant work by Jaynes had it not been for randomly running into a woman named Lynn Gilbert in Austin, Texas as I was on a cross-country trip driving across the US just before returning to Uganda in late 2011. Lynn Gilbert was an elderly woman, old enough to be my grandmother. She became interested in my book *The Fourth Heritage* when a friend of mine introduced me as the author of a book about the integration of African cultural beliefs with religion and colonial heritages. We exchanged books – she gave me a copy of a book on humanism, and I gave her a signed copy of *The Fourth Heritage*, which she later told me she had placed in her Austin library. As I write this, my third book, Lynn is still the record holder for reading my first book in the shortest time possible, finishing it in one night. The next day, after she had read the book, she emailed me a long feedback note, and central to that email was a reference for me to look up Julius Jaynes and his works on consciousness in regards to the subject of traditional practices where young people in my African village, and also people in some Brazilian cities, are made to undergo spiritual trances and get possessed by spirits.

In *The Fourth Heritage* I wrote about how I had noticed a link between such practices in three separate geographical locations: 1) the cultural practices in my village in Iganga, Uganda where we were made to go through rituals to put us under mental trances, 2) the same thing happening to people in the Brazilian afro-religious ceremonies I witnessed while visiting Rio De Janeiro in early 2003, and 3) the practice of hypnosis that we were entertained with while at university in Pennsylvania, US. I had written that I thought there was something similar in these three examples of behavior, but I stated that I didn't know what the link was. I was more than thrilled when I realized, upon reading Julius Jaynes' theory, that it answers the biggest gap I had in my first book. As such, I devoted a great many nights reading Jaynes' 500-page book and researching more about the topic of consciousness and its implication regarding traditional tribal collective psychologies. Jaynes' work is just a theory, so it is not a law of nature like gravity which would be beyond critique. However, the theory worked for me in regards to my outlook on life and, more importantly, it aided me tremendously in my effort to find a cure for a mentally sick relative who had severe schizophrenia. So reading this book was personal and had practical implications; it was not a mere exercise in mental gymnastics. What more is knowledge supposed to be for?

Even if there seems to be a universal consensus that non-living things are not conscious, there seems to be a lot of controversy surrounding consciousness in living things. While many ancient civilizations held, and present day east Asian beliefs (e.g. Buddhism and Hinduism) hold, the view that every living thing is conscious (that is, it has a soul, just like human beings), the Western world – which Africa now is part of by virtue of being colonized by Europeans and adopting their Christian outlook on life – believes that only humans are conscious as far as having a conscious soul. According to the traditional western belief, other creatures don't have spirits / souls and hence, some say they are not conscious. I cannot go through untangling all these beliefs, which is why I want to narrow my analysis to only the consciousness among human beings.

According to Julius Jaynes, consciousness is a learned skill; not so much an evolved attribute of our being, but rather one that was learned by humans quite recently. The actual human biological evolution took place over millions of years. Jaynes' assertion is very controversial among academics, but its investigation answers perfectly well the gap I had in my first book, and it also sets the final analysis I need before I can propose my core thesis of how to transcend our heritages of birth. Jaynes' theory postulates that consciousness as we know it is not more than 6,000 years old. Even if humans have been on Earth from about 2 million years ago (though in different phases of the "*Homo*" genus, i.e. different hominids), according to the theory, for most of that time humans were not self-conscious the way we know what self-consciousness is in the modern world today.

Self-consciousness is the consciousness of our own person over time, a sense of who we are, our hopes and fears as we daydream about ourselves in relation to others. Animals don't imagine themselves anywhere else, or think of their lives over time, or introspect in any sense that we can tell. This is the definition of consciousness that I have in mind in this chapter and it is the one that Jaynes said was born just a few thousand years ago.

At first, our human ancestors lived pretty much the way chimpanzees live today (with an ape-like mentality and low sense of self), but over a long time they evolved until reaching a sort of zombie-like existence where their minds were in a very primitive form. Jaynes calls this primitive state of mindset "Bicameral." While man evolved over millions of years until he reached the bicameral stage, the breakdown of the bicameral mind-frame to produce a mindset we now call modern consciousness happened quite abruptly and only about 3–6,000 years ago. There are other scholars who put the birth of modern consciousness up to 10,000 years ago, but I will go with Jaynes' research. Below is the brief discussion, not of the evolution of the mind until bicameralism, but rather, of the sudden origin of consciousness in the breakdown of the bicameral mind. This sets the stage for the development of the human mind from an archaic mind-frame to the current modern man's mind-frame.

In my discussion in this book, I have added the middle stage "pre-modern mind" – Jaynes did not include it in his discussion – for my personal reasons, to illustrate what I see as the transitional stages from bicameral to modern mind-frame. Below is a brief model of the three types of mindsets I will be discussing.

```
|  Bi-cameral  ⇨⇦ Pre-Modern ⇨⇦  Modern  |
                1              2
                     3
```

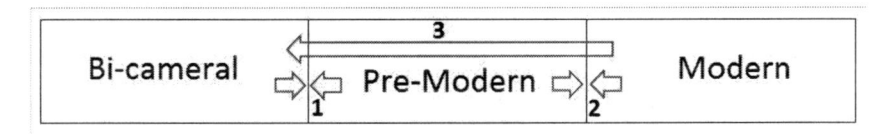

Figure 1: The Spectrum of Mindsets

Transition 1 is animism: when someone with a pre-modern mindset is animistic, they revert back to bicameralism. Transition 2 is individuality: the more a person with a pre-modern mindset develops their independent individuality, the more they bear the modern mindset. Transition 3 is consciousness: when a person with a modern mindset can be made to lose their consciousness, e.g. in hypnosis, they revert into bicameralism.

THE BICAMERAL MIND

In *The Origin of Consciousness in the Breakdown of the Bicameral Mind*, Julius Jaynes theorizes that consciousness is a learned skill, and the modern version of it emerged only between 3,000 and 6,000 years ago out of an archaic human mindset characterized by people living in a hallucinatory state of mind. According to Jaynes, before the breakdown of the bicameral mind, people lived in a perpetual hallucinatory mindset whereby they did not have the word or the meaning of "I" or "me," and instead lived and acted by hearing voices and seeing visions (attributed to gods) that emanated from the right hemisphere of the brain. In other words, the gods spoke to people's heads as if the gods lived in the brains, and the commands from the gods were to be respected without personal volition, the way a robot responds to programmed instructions.

According to this theory, people's brains were split into two parts (bicameral) with a command / follow or master / slave relationship between the two parts. The "master" part is where the gods dwelt, in the Wernicke's area of the right brain (the counterpart to modern man's Wernicke's area which is in the left brain for 95% of people today), while the "slave" part was a dormant part in the left brain that acted as per the dictates of the commands coming from the god part. It is well understood today by modern neurological study of the brain that the Wernicke's area, together with the Broca's area (both in the left brain for 95% of modern people, especially right-handed people), are the main part of the brain concerned with language. Their counterparts in the right brain are largely dormant in normal modern people. There have been experiments where people's comprehension, speaking or structuring of language sentences is directly affected by electrically manipulating parts of the Wernicke's area. For example, depending on what part you put the electrical pulse, people can become unable to tell time, or cannot put objects and subjects in sentences, or people can forget the first, second and third person in speech. So the heart and engine of the bicameral mind was the language part of the brain.

In a bicameral mind-frame, whenever man received commands by way of auditory hallucinatory commands (hearing voices), e.g. a command to sacrifice animals in order to bring forth abundant harvest, man did not have any choice, but rather acted robotically as the commands said. Presently, this is the brain relationship in people who are psychotic (the most severe mental sickness). When a mentally sick person whom society calls a mad person, e.g. a schizophrenic person, hears voices in his head or sees images in his head, he responds to them without choice. The response is automatic obedience. That is why it is so important for some of us who are "normal" to try and be compassionate and understand such people before we judge them. These people have no choice or personal volition. If the voices tell them remove your clothes or break the window, they automatically do it with no personal power at all to think or act otherwise.

Before the breakdown of the bicameral mind, people with this type of mindset did not have the analog "I" that we now use in our everyday language. Their consciousness was wholly tied to the visions and voices from the "gods" in their heads, and even a simple task like eating would be attributed to the will or wishes of the gods who wanted them to eat. Jaynes gives compelling evidence to show that some pre-historic writings, e.g. those of the Ancient Greek, Homer, and other epics of which the earliest books of the Bible are derivatives, were written by people who had this state of mind. And since the language of the gods is music or poetic discourse, all the great books of the pre-historic era are in fact long poems that were sung by people in public places. It is almost inconceivable by modern man to think how a book as big as Homer's Odyssey would be passed down over generations by singing sages – before it was written down – without you considering the fact that people during those days had a different mental makeup. They lived with the gods in the right part of the brain which gave them a type of consciousness wholly rooted in a super-active musical and poetic right hemisphere of the brain. Jaynes spends many pages giving modern neurological evidence of the functionality and attributes of that section of the brain.

When you consider Jaynes's assertion that the bicameral mind, with its controlling hallucinatory gods, existed during the final stage of the evolution of language, it is easy to understand the prevalence of many gods and whole civilizations of people believing in numerous types of gods. Have you ever debunked the mystery of "where did all the Greek gods go?" We know they lived on Mount Olympus, and were felt by every person, and had temples built in their honor which we can visit even today. Or in the case of Uganda, have you ever stopped to think "where did all the gods go that used to guide the daily lives of our forefathers?" People used to experience manifestations of different gods, and in the case of the Greeks, we have specific texts that go something like, "This God came from Mount Olympus and mated with a woman who used to live in this part of town and their daughter became Queen from this time to that time." It is not that the civilized literate Greeks who wrote such powerful accounts were crazy. The credible answer is that those people had a mind frame very different from what we modern people have.

Due to modern scholarship it is now a known fact that those Greek and Baganda gods did not physically exist back in those days until just disappearing into the heavens, but rather it was people's minds that "created" those gods. The gods were external symbolic realities representing purely internal psychological states such as anxiety, guilt, loss, etc. For example, when a plague or an epidemic broke out and people attributed it to Kawumpuli (god of plagues) and they sacrificed all kinds of animals until the plague went away, it was well within reason back then to attribute the eradication of the plague to Kawumpuli. It is not because Kawumpuli existed, or that he did anything. It is because back then people lived 100% for the gods and with the gods in their minds. In a way, they lived in a supernatural realm where they attributed all phenomena to gods, because they did not understand nature objectively. Now we know nature quite a bit better, such that when an epidemic breaks out, we can trace it to specific bacteria or viruses and we can call it AIDS or Ebola or cholera. There is no longer any need to give it supernatural attributes – at least for most modern people.

As people study science and understand nature in more and more fundamental ways, most of the beliefs we used to attribute to supernatural causes are now well known natural occurrences. In the Appendix I discuss in great detail many African people's belief in the supernatural, which I will show to be mostly an issue of natural phenomenon that nowadays one can study and indeed comprehend to be independent of the gods. While natural occurrences are neither right nor wrong, good nor evil, the minute people give supernatural attributes to them, automatically they allot them good or evil attributes. For example, when a natural thing like an earthquake occurs, according to nature it is neither good nor bad. However, if your brain is rooted in a supernatural realm, it is very easy for people to say how Musisi (god of earthquakes) is showing his anger whenever an earthquake happens. By extrapolation, people would go as far as believing that the god is annoyed, therefore to appease him they would sacrifice a goat or child (remember morality in such a mental state is not about you loving your child, but rather obeying the dictates of the wishes of the gods).

It is my hope that this intellectual journey and the personal discoveries I am taking you through can enable you to realize that we need to discard the overbearing superstitious beliefs we hold about many natural occurrences. The superstitious beliefs play a big role in holding people back and preventing them from getting a mindset that can delve into the mystery of nature (not super-nature) and understand the fundamental laws that govern the universe. We now know more than a dozen laws that govern pretty much all of the observed occurrences and events in the universe – be it here on Earth or on the moon or on a star a billion miles away. Without the transition from looking at everything with a belief in the supernatural to actually understanding the natural world (or what I like to call a paradigm shift in our mindset), many Africans as a group of people will not be in a position to develop our societies and shall keep looking at the modern Western world as the masters of their destinies. This is because the modern Western person devotes most of his life to investigating and understanding the natural universe and the laws governing it, as opposed to many African people who see supernatural significance in even the most mundane of occurrences. For instance, we need to transition from the state of consciousness where if it doesn't rain at a public event during the rainy season, people believe that God blessed the event. People can now study and understand the meteorological explanation of why it is that sometimes rain clouds don't form even if it's the rainy season.

When we look back to our forefathers, it is not enough to say that those people used to have false satanic beliefs in the wrong gods. There is a big unknown to this topic of people organizing their whole social communities and empires based on gods who were "real," only for us in the modern world to not attribute a single thing to those long-gone gods. The issue comes to be understood only when you grasp that it is not that the gods existed per se, but rather humankind had a mindset that easily "saw" and "heard" hallucinatory visions that the modern mind is no longer attuned to experience. However, presently there are tribes in which when someone important dies, like the head of the family, during or shortly after burial the dead person's hallucinatory voices can be spoken by a family member in exactly the same way that Jaynes talks about the talking dead kings during their burials. For almost 3,000 years, people in the Egyptian civilization used to call God "Osiris" or "Ra," but now it would be unthinkable to use that name for God. By the same token you should extrapolate the reality that just because for 1,500 years one group of people have been calling God "Allah" or "Jesus," doesn't mean that after another 1,500 years the people of the future won't have forgotten the word Allah or Jesus as names for God.

The bicameral type of mind came to an abrupt halt mainly due to two factors: 1) the advent of writing, and 2) the weakening of the divine authority in the brain. According to Jaynes, since hallucinations had auditory input as their main driver, the transition to writing caused the biggest catalyst to the growth of the subjective consciousness. Once people could read or see god's command written on a tablet, as opposed to hearing them as commanding voices that they had no ability to disobey, people naturally started realizing that by personal effort they could turn to or avoid the dictates from the gods as they could see them statically written down. This personal effort is one of the catalysts that brought forth the birth of people using the analog "I." From then on, a war started within society as people could still hear the commands from the gods, but at the same time were able to use free will to opt for an action that was contrary to the divine command.

Over time, this struggle was exacerbated by the failures of the gods in saving mankind from the cataclysmic events that were taking place, e.g. floods, earthquakes, fallen empires, rampant wars, etc. During this social transformation of the psyche, man was able to develop the left part of the brain at the expense of the right part to such a degree that today, most "normal people" don't hear any voices in their heads and don't have visions of spirits, ghosts or divine images. It is not a mere coincidence that the Wernicke's area and Broca's area, the two parts of the brain that are responsible for language, are in the left hemisphere for 95% of people, while their right hemisphere counterparts are no longer active parts of the brain. There are clinical experiments which show that mentally sick people like schizophrenics hear voices and see visions out of those areas of the right brain that are now dormant for most people.

Since spirituality and religiosity have a lot to do with people "hearing God's voice" or for some, actually "seeing visions of God," it is crucial that we all take some time to investigate what is truly God's voice versus the right hemisphere playing tricks on us. For those who have never witnessed within themselves or seen someone else who has a mindset that "hears voices or sees things," the 2001 movie *A Beautiful Mind* does a good job of illustrating what those phenomena are. But of course for some of us who lived in the African villages and have been around tribal rituals, we are very much aware of people who "see things" and "hear voices." Actually, if you are in a modern city somewhere in the world, just go to a hypnosis show (or just google it or search on youtube.com) and see how evidently natural it is for someone to see things and hear things that are not there.

Jaynes gives compelling evidence of the struggles between people who had crossed over to the new consciousness and those still in the bicameral mind. He gives historical examples of societies massacring bicameral-minded people like oracles, prophets, witches, etc., because after the breakdown and transmutation to the non-bicameral mind, it became the norm to label bicameral people as "abnormal" or worse, "evil." Even in present day society, the people with vestiges of the old bicameral mind are not looked at favorably; just look at schizophrenics who are often labeled as "mad people" and locked away from society. The only time modern society gives credence to vestiges of bicameralism is when it is in our favor, e.g. we accept that there are people gifted with this ability and we call them mediums, spiritual healers or prophets. But for the larger part, when someone says they hear voices, see visions, or talk to God, we as a society think they are abnormal and often prescribe drugs to stop the visions and voices.

THE PRE-MODERN MIND

This is the term I have created to aid with my analysis and the buildup to my thesis. Jaynes does not discuss this type of mind. In my thinking, the pre-modern mind is the type that is no longer bicameral, that is to say the left brain does not get commands from the right brain, but it is not modern yet because it has no grasp of objective rationality. The pre-modern type of mindset is similar to the period right after the breakdown of the bicameral mind and before the dawn of the modern mindset. Instead of acting robotically according to the voices and visions that dictated actions in bicameral people, the pre-modern mind does not hear the commands of the gods but tries to reach out to the lost commands through divination – the idea that things supernatural control life and you can appease them in your favor by performing specific acts.

The four types of divination as outlined by Jaynes are: omens, sortilege, augury, and spontaneous divination.

1) Belief in omens: this is the belief that if things happen in a certain sequence, then in the future that sequence will happen again. For example, when lightning strikes on a Tuesday morning, such a mind then thinks that on another Tuesday morning lightning will strike again. This is the most primitive type of divination as it is purely passive. People with a pre-modern mind who believe in omens are living a totally superstitious life.
2) Sortilege: this is the belief in chance in order to know how to proceed in life. Examples are rolling of the dice, the casting of lots, etc. This mind believes that there are chance occurrences that contain divine messages. For example, when there is a problem and at 6 pm on the sixth day of the week you roll a die and a six comes on top, then there is an important message from God or the spirits. It is not as passive as believing in omens, but it is still a pre-modern state of mind.
3) Augury: this is extrapolating information magically from specific things. Examples include sacrificing animals or children in order to get divine intervention in your worldly affairs. According to this mindset, by taking part in such sacrifices the gods / spirits will be appeased and in return those exuding this behavior will get favorable outcomes from the supernatural realm.
4) Spontaneous divination: this is the reading of God's intention spontaneously from anything. Examples include getting a

divine message from touching a sacred object and getting divine significance from hearing thunder or seeing a black bird fly by.

According to my life's experience, most of the people with a background like mine have a pre-modern mindset and many of them fit the belief pattern I have given above. This belief pattern is purely of a superstitious nature as opposed to understanding the ways and laws of the natural world. When I was young in the village, I remember many times going for traditional ceremonies where animals were sacrificed and people were induced into trances so that the tribal spirits could guide the community on important matters. It is from such personal experiences that upon reading Jaynes' book, I was able to quickly fill the gap that there is a transition stage between a total bicameral existence and the modern mindset.

The pre-modern mind cannot acquire objective knowledge on its own, and because it cannot understand the fundamental laws of nature it deems natural occurrences "supernatural" in an effort to attribute events to the gods or, as Jaynes calls it, in its effort to reach out to long lost bicameral gods. It needs to superstitiously believe in outside things, because it doesn't have the capacity to understand them according to the known laws of nature (what modern science is doing a good job of revealing to us). For example, for many tribal people, when someone is schizophrenic and starts "talking to himself" or "seeing things," they are quick to attribute it to ancestral spirits or ghosts from family enemies. They don't know that modern science has deconstructed what schizophrenia is and we can now pinpoint what bio-chemicals can be given to that individual in order to lessen the excitement of the right hemisphere of the brain in order to stop the auditory hallucinations.

The pre-modern mind is largely based on "oralising" (oral tradition). Where it ventures into the literate world, it passively reads and believes blindly because it does not have the analytical faculties to comprehend the real essence of what it reads. Both the bicameral and pre-modern minds can bring about a type of mind that is not "concentrated" but rather what I call "a porous mind." A porous mind is the type that can be read by other people like hypnotists, traditional healers, sensationalist preachers, etc.

THE MODERN MIND

This is the present consciousness exhibited by modern people. A person with a modern mind has self- consciousness or self-reflection that does not require invocating gods, spirits or superstitions, but rather has a mature left brain that is analytical, exacting and can conceptualize time – both infinitesimal and cosmological time. The modern mind arose out of the breakdown of the bicameral mind and transformed beyond the pre-modern aspects by analytical reading and writing. I hope you the reader are able to see, especially if you can go back to my first and second book, that the purpose of all my writings in these three books is to call to attention the fact that people born like me were destined to be underdeveloped and powerless in this world unless we embrace a literate culture to aid our minds into becoming modern. I am more than convinced that the real solution to our problems is not political or economic development per se, but in a more fundamental sense, the solution has to start with our people transitioning from an oral culture to a written one as this transition has huge implications on what type of consciousness people develop. Once people grow a modern consciousness, they can be analytical in everyday life and then everything will follow, i.e. social, economic and intellectual development, and general modernity.

Modern man has his consciousness in the most developed part of the brain, the one that analyses and can create new symbols and new meanings. To that effect, you find that even when modern man believes in a religion, e.g. the European Christian or Jew, their consciousness is no longer tied to the Bible or the Torah, or for that matter, to a church building or a synagogue, but is tied squarely within the upper left brain. Earlier I discussed the vestiges of bicameralism in the four superstitious practices of omens, sortilege, augury and spontaneous divination. The modern person does not exhibit these four vestiges. Presently, even if you eradicate Jesus' birthplace and the places where he lived from the face of the earth, the modern Christian, armed with a modern consciousness, would not become disoriented psychologically or become non-functional akin to natives when encountering the European colonialists (see the next sub-chapter for more details). No shrine is sacred enough for the modern religious person. He has outgrown his mindset of superstitious beliefs in sacred objects; no wonder the more people ascribe superstitious beliefs to objects, the more they revert to a pre-modern mindset.

Reading by the modern mind is a personal effort that is both rational and based on subjective consciousness (self-reflection). The modern mind can read and interpret the written word according to complex rules and logic. It can write complex ideas and sentences to communicate to other people, both today and in the future.

The consciousness coming from a culture with a writing tradition is more robust and stronger than one coming from an oral tradition. For example, the acuteness of mind that a European gets when he consciously understands the world based on "mental pictures" or "unconscious archetypes" from reading works like *The Iliad* or *The Odyssey*, which were written over 3,000 years ago, has more food for the mind than one coming from mental images based on the vague, non-exacting stories from oral traditions. The oral-based cultures also have a claim to humanity, but unfortunately, they are at a big disadvantage as they can't amass as much power as literary societies. And power as exhibited by the European man is what has shaped this modern world. Even when Europe was still an observing Christian society, it is the power that the Church wielded that indeed spread the European civilization to the four corners of the world.

Therefore, the power that the Western modern man obtained from his modern consciousness was amplified in society collectively by way of the concentrating agents I mentioned at the beginning of this chapter. The enormously developed concentrating agents have made modernity to mean people having a mindset that is not tied so closely to blood relations as it is to the general human family and to the overall universe. When you read that a man like Einstein (after being persecuted in Europe because he was a Jew) was able to turn down the request by the State of Israel for him to be its president because according to him, his life and his work were not just for Jews, you get to understand that he was a modern man with a modern mindset whose consciousness was directed toward the whole of humanity and the whole universe.

A Brief History of Christianity

Christianity is the world's biggest religion, with more than 2.4 billion people, and it was started in the first century as a Jewish cult centered on a man called Yeshua (Jesus from the Greek language). Before you can talk about and understand Christianity, you need to understand its source, Judaism – that is to say the traditions and beliefs of the Jewish people.

The Jewish people have been known by different names in history, such as the Hebrews and the Israelites. Their story starts sometime between 1500 and 1000 BC. That is more than 1000 years after the beginning of the ancient Egyptian and Mesopotamian civilizations, hence both Judaism and Christianity learned a lot from the beliefs of those two earlier civilizations. Some of the things they learned from their superior predecessors are highlighted in the following paragraphs.

There is historical evidence in the form of Egyptian written records that between 1500 and 1000 BC there was a group of people called Shasu or Habiru or Kabiru. They were nomadic people and some of them were enslaved just like many of the lower class peoples in those days, and much like in the days of modern slave trade for that matter. The Kabiru peoples, who were not the main ethnic grouping during the time of the Egyptian civilization, talk of their origin in the distant past, much in the same way the Baganda talk of "Long, long ago, Katonda created the world, and he created Kintu the first person and his wife Nambi ..." The story of the Kabiru people goes that in the beginning God, created the world. The earliest records of that time come from the Egyptians and show that those nomadic people called God YHWH. Each ethnic group calls their highest deity and creator by a different name, e.g. the nomadic peoples of western Uganda call God "Ruhanga" while there are other Ugandan tribes that call God "Ojok" or "Were." The ancient Egyptians called God "Ra" or "Isis / Osiris." When the Kabiru people started telling their story of origin around 1000 BC, they did so in exactly the way Mazrui's quote in the first chapter of this book states, in that: "All these ethnocentric traditions of the origin of mankind are variations of the image that the village is the world and the social group is the human race." The Kabiru or Jewish story is no different; it holds them as the special people at the center of the purpose of creation.

The Kabiru taught that the first man created, Adam, was their oldest ancestor, and so on (see my first book for details about the parallels between this ethnocentric origin story and the stories from Ugandan tribes). Central to their story of "being the human race and their village being the world," they said that in the beginning God created man pure, but man disobeyed God's commandment and fell from grace, therefore in order for God to reunite himself with the lost man he sent prophets, from the different tribes of the Kabiru, to reveal his message (e.g. Moses, Jeremiah, Elijah). This whole Jewish story is told in a big collection of books called the Bible, which the earliest records indicate was written no earlier than 1100 BC. Because of the date of its being written within close proximity to the time of the Egyptian and Mesopotamian cradle civilizations, the Bible copies a lot of its core themes from those civilizations, but nothing from the other four cradle civilizations (see my discussions in chapter five).

As centuries passed, the Jewish story developed the theme that there would be an anointed leader or king who would rule them, this leader was called "Messiah" of "Christ" from the Greek language. Unlike what we Christians now believe about the Messiah, the traditional Jewish belief is that he would be directly from the lineage of King David, and he wouldn't be a son of God or divine being, but rather a powerful political leader. I remember on Christmas Eve 2004 while in Washington D.C. I was watching Larry King host a Jewish rabbi and a Christian father, when the rabbi said something that I had never been taught as a young Christian boy. The rabbi said that in his long years in a Yeshiva (Jewish seminary school) he was never taught about a coming Messiah; he further said that most Jews don't consider the Messiah theme as a central tenet of their belief. Upon further research I found out that throughout history not all Jews have believed in this Messiah article of faith, and presently very few do.

So, the central Christian article of faith is based on a minority view about Jewish tenets.

The Jews who ended up starting Christianity believed that a man called "Yeshua" (or Jesus from the Greek language) was born and he fulfilled all the requirements of being the Messiah for the Jewish people. The Jewish leadership rejected this belief because according to them Yeshua was not from the line of King David, not a great political leader, did not rebuild the temple in Jerusalem, and did not show expertise in the teachings of the Jewish Bible. The above were some of the cardinal prerequisites that the Messiah had to meet. The followers of Jesus, who were very few at the time but super passionate about his story, changed the traditional story to say that actually the Messiah was also for non-Jews, or "Gentiles" as they were called, and even to go further, they claimed that in fact he was the Messiah for all humanity.

There were dozens of people who wrote accounts of the life of Jesus (the gospels), starting with the gospel of Mark around 67 AD, to later writings like the gospel according to Thomas, Matthew, Judas, Peter, Mary and John. Around 400 AD, the Christian leaders met in North Africa (during the last days of the Roman Empire) and after rejecting some of the accounts of Jesus (e.g. the gospel of Thomas and the gospel of Mary), they agreed on the official books of the new religion. This officially sanctioned collection of books came to be known as the Christian Canon and it is the Bible divided into two major parts: the Old Testament (39 or 46 books depending on whether you are Catholic or Protestant, but generally they are the books which the Jews still call their Bible), and the New Testament (the 27 books centered on Jesus and the new message to Jews and Gentiles).

So the official story of Jesus and Christianity is not from Jesus himself, since he died between 30 and 33 AD without leaving anything written. Unlike Islam, which was started by one man at a specific time and place, and unlike Judaism which is really just a belief system for an ethnic group (the way the Baganda believe in their traditions and customs, or the way Indian traditional beliefs are called Hinduism), Christianity has been created by people over a long span of time. First, as canonized by the Catholic Church in the fourth century – as described above – then after the reformation of the sixteenth century, different Protestant groups agreed on a different canon of the official story. For example, the English under King James wrote their own version of the Bible, which is different from the Catholic Bible; the Germans started a new church called the Lutheran Church; the people from Scotland started a different church called the Presbyterian Church. Finally, in modern times the religion has completely fragmented and people are still coming up with new sects of Christianity – one famous example being the all-American sect of "Mormonism" (The Church of Jesus Christ of Latter-Day Saints) that was founded by Joseph Smith in the early nineteenth century after claiming that God appeared to him and revealed a New Testament of Jesus Christ.

When I lived in Salt Lake City, Utah where the Mormon Church is headquartered, I read a book about Joseph Smith by Fawn Brodie called *No Man Knows my History*, which is considered an authoritative publication on early Mormonism and the life of Joseph Smith. From that book, along with my reading of *The Book of Mormon* (viewed by the religion as a complementary but separate scripture to the Bible), I was amazed at how ingenious and creative Joseph Smith was to create a new theology that is now one of the fastest growing religions in America and has become mainstream enough that in the 2012 presidential elections, Barack Obama's opponent was a Mormon, Mitt Romney.

Central to the Mormon theology is the belief that when Jesus rose from the dead he went to North America to preach to the Native Americans. Another interesting doctrine of the faith taught by Smith was that the actual Garden of Eden was in the state of Missouri, US. In creating his new religion, Joseph Smith borrowed a lot from Mohammad, the creator of Islam, to the extent that according to Brodie' book Smith said, "I will be to this generation a second Mohammad, whose motto in treating for peace was 'the Alcoran [Koran] or the Sword.' So shall it eventually be with us – Joseph Smith or the Sword." After being chased out of upstate New York and then Ohio, by the time he found refuge in Missouri he had become militant and fought back all the way up to his death at the hands of a mob.

Here are some similarities shared by Joseph Smith and Mohammad: they both claimed to have received the last revelation from God, they both wrote a new holy book that God told them to write, they both founded their own religions, they both had many wives (Mohammad having 13 officially, while Joseph Smith had at least 45 documented wives), they both inspired their followers to fight for their religion after their people had been massacred or killed by non-believers, and they both made their home region the new spiritual center of the world (Garden of Eden and new Zion was in North America according to Joseph Smith, while Mohammad made Mecca the center of his new religion).

The general story of Jesus and Christianity as I have known it is as follows:

According to the traditional story, the first four books of the New Testament are called the Gospels or the books about the good news [of Jesus]. They are supposed to tell the same story about Jesus. The first three are called Synoptic Gospels because historians believe the latter two (Matthew and Luke) referenced the first one Mark (written anonymously around 66 AD, about 30 years after the death of Jesus but attributed to a companion of Peter by early Christians of the second century AD). The last gospel, that of John, is quite different from the first three and it was written a lot later (around or after 100 AD). The Gospel of John stretches to make a case for Jesus as the Messiah or God from the beginning of time. The author of John starts his gospel with the famous phrase, "The Word Became Flesh," and declaration that, "In the beginning was the Word, and the Word was with God, and the Word was God. He was with God in the beginning. Through him all things were made; without him nothing was made that has been made."

The main contributor to the creation of Christianity was Paul, "The Apostle of the Gentiles." Even if he was not one of the 12 apostles of Jesus, he wrote 14 out of the 27 books of the New Testament and created many churches among the gentile peoples of Asia Minor and Europe.

Overall, the story goes that Jesus Christ was born to a virgin called Mary. Before he was born, an angel appeared to Mary and told her not to be afraid, for she would be pregnant not by her husband Joseph, but by the Holy Spirit. She would have a baby boy whom she was to call Emmanuel or Immanuel – which means "God with us." Not much is written about Jesus between the age of one and 30. However, at 30 he started his ministry of telling people to turn to the ways of the Lord. He encouraged people, especially his fellow Jews, not to spend all their efforts in reading the old laws, but rather he said that there were two laws which replace the long list of old laws: 1) love your God with all your heart, with all your soul, and with all your mind, and 2) love your neighbor as you love yourself.

He said these two laws replaced all of the laws revealed by God to the prophets in the Old Testament.

Even if Jesus kept saying "I am the son of man," his followers believed he was the "Son of God" who came to be the savior of mankind. When his group came into problems with the traditional leadership authority (the Roman leaders and his fellow Jewish leaders), he was put to death. He was killed in the normal way of killing bandits those days, by crucifixion on a cross. Christianity teaches that he was crucified and died on a Friday (Good Friday), and was then buried only to rise from the dead on Sunday (Easter Sunday). After he rose, he ministered for a short time to his followers until one day he flew straight into the clouds, into Heaven. He is now seated at the right hand of God. At the end of days, he will come back and judge the living and the dead. If you accept him as your personal savior, you will be taken to live with him in Heaven forever. However, if you don't, you won't be spared eternal damnation in a lake of fire called Hell.

One of the major creations or traditions invented about Jesus and Christianity is the celebration of the birth of Jesus. Because no one knew the date and month when Jesus was born, it was not easy to pinpoint a particular day to consider his birth date. However, after the Roman Empire was made Christian by decree of the Emperor in the fourth century, the Christian leaders found a convenient way to celebrate the birth of Jesus. Since millions were already celebrating the 25th of December as the ancient Roman religious "Day of the Sun" (December 25th is the date in the northern hemisphere on which the sun first appears full following the winter solstice on December 22nd), the Christian leaders just switched the celebrations to mean "the birth of the Son (of God)." It made sense because in Christianity, Jesus is the light of the world or the sun of the world, and since he rose from the dead after three days and the sun becomes full three days after the winter solstice on December 25th, it was a perfect correlation to believers.

To understand the significance of Christianity in the spread of the Western European civilization, you must understand the fact that, unlike other religions, Christianity was actually created by men like Paul, the early bishops, and others solely based on the inspiration they got from the life of Jesus. Since inspiration is all you need in this life to achieve great things, it is no wonder that the spread of the civilization, both in its benign ways (good missionary works) and its ugly ways (crusades and genocides against natives in Africa and the Americas), was done by European men who truly felt inspired by the "good news" of Jesus' life. It sounds ironic that some Europeans could come to a peaceful village in Africa or South America and force natives to become Christians, but if you understand that these men were inspired by what they thought was "the good news of Jesus," dare to understand.

At the root of Christianity is a deep inspirational spirit that speaks to the depths of human psychological archetypes. Five of these psychological archetypes are: innocence of childhood, virgin vulnerability, personal conscience, love, and human sacrifice.

Which human being learns about the story of baby Jesus, and does not fall in love with it? The baby is so innocent and loving that even if you are the Devil, around Christmas time you smile when you take children to Santa Claus to receive gifts. Growing up, what a joy it was for us to sing in Sunday school "Baby Jesus, baby Jesus, I love you, I love you, you are my savior, you are my savior, every day, every day."

The second archetype is about the mother of Jesus, a woman who got pregnant without having sex with her husband. If you don't feel human tenderness toward a virgin and her vulnerability, especially when considering that she would end up having to birth a child without ever even having sex, then there is something really off with your moral compass. This Christian belief about Jesus' mother goes further, touching on her own conception too. The conception of Mary herself is believed by the first Christians, the Catholics, to have been immaculate. Non-Catholics confuse the Immaculate Conception to mean the conception of Jesus by a virgin, but actually it refers to the conception of Mary herself in her mother Anne's womb. Immaculate Conception means that even if Mary was conceived by human biological means, God blessed her from the instance of conception such that she would live her whole life pure and holy until she bore a child, Jesus. If you don't get any inspiration from the power of the vulnerability of this holy woman, then indeed you need Jesus! It is important that I say the virgin birth has universal psychological power because its claim was not started by the Jesus story. In fact, there are critics who say that it was copied / plagiarized by the early Christians. Examples of other religious figures believed to have been born by virgins are the Egyptian Horus (around 3000 BC), the Greek Attis (1200 BC), the Indian Krishna (900 BC), and the Persian Mithra (1200 BC).

The third and very important mountain-moving creation in Christianity is the idea of the Trinity. Rather than holding that there is one God, as do the Jews or the Muslims, this archetype holds that God is in three persons: 1) God the father – the Almighty One, 2) Jesus Christ – the Son, and 3) the Holy Spirit. The three are all equal and the same, yet different. The Trinity was codified as a Christian doctrine around the fourth century. You need to contrast this concept with Judaism and Islam. In Judaism, God is one according to the most important prayer simplified as Shema: "O Israel, the Lord our God, the Lord is one." In Islam, according to the doctrine of Tawhid, God is one indivisible and absolute being.

By making God into a human being and at the same time a mysterious holy spirit, many Christians get tremendous inspiration from the human attributes of Jesus, which are exceptional even if you are not a Christian (peace, love thy neighbor, no matter how much evil you commit Jesus will always forgive you, etc.). Personally, in my Christian psychology I treasure Jesus' redemptive powers as the most important aspect of him. In fact, my favorite Jesus motif is the Statue in Rio de Janeiro, which is called Christ The Redeemer (which I visited in 2003). In my heart of hearts, in my doubts and weakness of mind, it is very comforting to know that I can be redeemed by the eternal redeemer. And from the Holy Spirit, Christians get insurmountable inspiration from the fact that no matter where you are and in what condition (even on your death bed), what you hear from your conscience can be interpreted as the Holy Spirit. Thus, human conscience is equated to the ultimate creator of the universe in one stroke.

The fourth theme of Christianity which is universally inspirational to all human beings is the idea of equating God with love. Love is a universal emotion that even the most despicable of sinners understands and feels. Throughout the New Testament, e.g. in John 4:8, the Bible specifically says that, "Whoever does not love does not know God, for God is Love." The theme of God as love, brought down to everyday life as Jesus is love, has such a strong emotional pull on people that it is impossible to imagine Western civilization without the passion expressed by Christians in the great musical creations, personal sacrifices and universal love for the poor and least fortunate among us – as inspired by Jesus' message.

"God is love" as an archetype is so drastically opposed to the slave / master relationship that the bicameral mindsets dwelt in. It is more about an unconditional love, kind of the way a mother loves her child or as a husband is supposed to love his wife in a good relationship. Like a child is able to feel loved and safe to the point that they dialogues with their mother without fear, so too do Christians dialogue with God in their daily lives, without fear. Unlike the Islamic "submission to the will of Allah," Christians are largely drawn toward "loving God and feeling loved by God, especially when you don't follow his will." It is this kind of mental disposition that has led some Christian women to feel loved by Jesus to such an extent that they don't need to get married to earthly men.

And last but not least, the fifth archetype is human sacrifice and it contends that Jesus offered to die for all of us sinners so that we never suffer again. Jesus is the redeemer of mankind. However sinful you are in this world, Jesus forgives you and you can go to Heaven just by quietly saying, "Jesus take this yoke of suffering from me, I accept you as my personal savior." Even though I have not gone to church in many years, just thinking about this doctrine is as awe-inspiring as anything that a human being has ever created. When I was visiting Rio de Janeiro and saw the big statue of Christ the Redeemer, even in my agnostic mind frame at the time I felt great spiritual inspiration from looking at that gigantic statue whose truly phenomenal message is that "No matter how much you sin, I, Jesus have redeemed you from Hell and Satan, and you don't have to suffer." I have read so much about religion and so much about non-Christian beliefs, but have yet to find something so spiritually freeing and, despite not being a scientific fact, capable of really making man know that he is not damned and will always have a second chance.

One criticism of Christianity is its lack of originality. It is indeed true when people say that there is hardly anything in Christianity that is original or that was not borrowed from Judaism, Egyptian or Mesopotamian religions. However, as a blessing in disguise, because the creators of Christianity borrowed so much from other belief systems, they ended up creating a system of belief that is so powerful and universal that no matter how much fault you find with it, you can always go back to the motif of the man Jesus himself and all you see is a poor man who was humble, never married or killed anyone and his prince of peace image is encapsulated in his command, "Love your enemies, and pray for those who persecute you." I believe any human being will appreciate such qualities, especially in a leader.

These are some of the beliefs and things that people have borrowed from other belief systems in order to create a robust Christian religion that indeed has been the soul of the Western civilization: 1) the idea of a god born by virgin birth was told about the Egyptian Horus (around 3000 BC), the Greek Attis (1200 BC), the Indian Krishna (900 BC), and the Persian Mithra (1200 BC); 2) the idea of Hades or Hell was held by the Greeks; 3) 25th of December was a Roman pagan worship of the sun god; 4) the cross was a very common symbol in pre-Christian religious beliefs, e.g. the Egyptians used it in various forms as the Ankh – a symbol for priesthood power, and usually gods and goddesses were drawn holding it, e.g. the goddess Sekhet; 5) the idea of the trinity was there in the Egyptian trinity of Osiris, Isis and Horus (the son); and 6) the flight to Egypt by Mary and Joseph to safeguard innocent baby Jesus from being killed is an exact replica of Isis' flight to the Nile delta to safeguard innocent baby Horus from being killed by a powerful enemy.

A very important episode in Western Christianity and its further development of the five universal themes mentioned above is what happened in the sixteenth century. By that time, Christianity as represented by the Catholic Church and the Pope had reached all known corners of the world and was so powerful that the abuse of power was evident to common people. Besides the fact that Latin was the only language to be used in church services – which essentially was a power play to keep non-Roman people who didn't speak Latin from rising to church leadership – the Pope was also extorting a lot of levies from the parishes all over Europe and the known world to fund the lavish lifestyle in Rome. In order to fulfill Jesus' message of being a personal savior to mankind, some church leaders led by Martin Luther of Germany officially protested by defying the powers of the Pope, a process that ended up being called the Protestant Reformation. I wrote details about this in my first book.

The Protestant Reformation ended up being a theological challenge to the Christianity preached by the Catholic Church. Central to this challenge were the following: 1) the Bible didn't have to be printed only in Latin, because that worked to prevent other indigenous peoples like the Germanic tribes from accessing Jesus' message. 2) The salvation that Jesus offers to people has nothing to do with all the traditions and the dos and don'ts that the Catholic Church preached (traditions like praying of the rosary, going through several sacraments, confessing your sins to the church every week, etc.). Led by Martin Luther, the northern European peoples protested and claimed that for a person to go to Heaven they did not have to do any work to earn it but rather needed only to pray, and by God's grace they could be saved. Hence the entry of the "saved by grace" as opposed to the "saved by works" concept in Christianity. 3) People did not need intervention by church leaders in order to access God. Each person in their private quarters could pray to and have audience with God. 4) God is a personal God. People have to have a personal private relationship with God, as opposed to following the type of public prescribed dictates that the traditional Catholic Church demanded. As I mentioned in the first book, it is this last article of reformation that greatly led to the Western man internalizing "individualism" as opposed to "collectivism," hence the civilization has been progressed by great individuals.

The Reformation led to decades of wars between Protestant Northern European communities and staunchly Catholic Europe around Rome and the South. When it was all said and done, several countries of the north officially broke off from the Catholic Church and started Protestant churches like the Lutheran churches in Germany and the Scandinavian countries, the Presbyterian Church in Scotland, and the Anglican Church in England and Wales. In a way, Protestantism became its own kind of religion as its new sects came up with new Bibles which rejected some of the books in the Catholic canon, and it also abolished many traditions like the confession, the praying of the rosary, the multiple sacraments (except for baptism and upon death).

Psychologically, the Protestant movement brought to the European person an individuality that was very different from the hierarchical collectivism of the Catholic Church. Since Western civilization is based on a high regard for the individual's liberty to free thought and personal conscience, after the Reformation, Protestant Europe took on the mantle of progressing the Western civilization. Soon after that, the scientific revolution took off in England with individual intellectual pursuits like those of Isaac Newton. The Industrial Revolution was also ushered in by the Protestant countries, specifically Anglican England. There is a clear correlation between industrialization and the countries of Europe that became Protestant, such as England, the Netherlands, Germany, Scandinavia, and the places in the world where Protestant Europeans settled, e.g. North America, Australia, New Zealand and South Africa. Over the years, the Catholic Church has also "reformed" to the extent that now whether you are in Catholic France or Protestant England, there is no real difference between the societies as far as the form of Christianity they exhibit – both are indeed reformed compared to the sixteenth century status quo. The conservative Catholic Church has opened up to the extent that it now officially accepts evolution as the best explanation of man's origin in Africa, a theory long championed by Protestant peoples like those of the Anglican Church, the religion of the theory's creator, Charles Darwin.

Generally, the Christian religion helped solidify the notion of individuality in Western man. From the start of this civilization in the Italian Renaissance, up to the scientific and industrial revolutions of Protestant Europe, individuals have been at the center of creating and discovering knowledge and the laws that govern the universe.

Western Civilization is Not Dead, but Hurting

Unlike all the other civilizations mentioned before, the Western European civilization has not yet fallen. The cradle civilizations collapsed thousands of years ago, and I discussed how the Islamic civilization had its peak in the Golden Age between 800 and 1100 AD. Currently, all the peoples of the world are organized in post-tribal groupings called "sovereign countries," whose creation is largely a Western European legacy because the basic tenets of nation-states originated with the Treaty of Westphalia, Germany in 1648. Even the various worldwide groupings of these sovereign countries are mostly Western initiatives, e.g. the UN, World Bank, IMF and World Trade Organization. Even international sporting organizations like the Olympics or soccer World Cups were created by Western peoples.

On the international communication side of things, most of the world languages are written in the Latin alphabet with English and other European languages as the major languages used especially for business transcending national borders. Even in the countries which don't predominantly use a European language for communication, e.g. China, which I visited in 2014, I was amazed that they use a keyboard inscribed with Latin letters.

On the social scene, a lot of the initiatives and trends coming out of the West quickly become international initiatives, e.g. the practice of liberal democracy, the capitalist economic system with its main centers in New York and London, the idea of human rights as proposed and written by the UN, and the current idea of rights for minorities (transgender, gay, and minority ethnicities).

Even if Christianity has waned in most of Europe (e.g. France is a staunchly secular nation), and it is facing a lot of pressure in the US where the major centers of innovation, commerce and education are liberal and post-Christian in the way they accept other religions, the Western-induced Christianity is now taking root more in the less developed countries, especially Africa, South America and even Far East Asia. With this shift of Christianity to non-European centers, you find that some Asians have come up with an image of Jesus that has Asian features, some black people have a black Jesus, and even the current head of the Catholic Church, Pope Francis, is from South America.

However, even if the civilization is not dead, it is facing a lot of pressure from within and from without.

From within, I would like to use the summary of Sir Kenneth Clark's masterpiece TV series *Civilization: A Personal View*. Sir Clark's work was a 1969 program that the BBC promulgated to commemorate the revolution of changing from black & white TV to color TV. It is a story of Western civilization from its inception to the modern age – In other words it was a fully-fledged, well-researched work that makes my mini discussion about the subject look amateur. In it, Clark walks through history by visiting all the major historical areas where Western civilization took root, and along the way he gives his personal take on things. One of the most important takeaways I got from watching the series was its beginning and its conclusion.

At the beginning, Clark talks about civilization in general after mentioning the fall of the great Roman Empire and with it its classical European civilization. He says every civilization, however complex and solid it seems, is actually fragile and can be destroyed easily from within by either of two enemies. One is fear. Fear of war, fear of invasion by an outsider. The other is boredom. Boredom is a feeling of hopelessness which can overtake people with a high degree of material prosperity. To counter these two enemies, he asserts that far more important than material prosperity is confidence. Confidence in the society in which one lives, belief in its philosophy and belief in its laws.

When you read about the fear in the US society – the present bastion of Western civilization – and you consider the boredom as exemplified on reality TV and celebrity life, and you add in the apathetic view toward politics or the outright decay of law enforcement as evidenced by the rampant police murders of innocent people all over the country, you would be an ostrich not to see that Western civilization is hurting.

In Europe, this fear is now expressed in an overly sensitive and effeminized political correctness of "respecting other cultures" as evidenced by the reaction of the police and the German men toward the massive gang rapes of women in Cologne on New Year's Eve 2015. No one can understand how the Mayor of Cologne would blame the hundreds of women attacked instead of coming down hard on the criminal migrants who committed the attacks, unless you deconstruct this situation within the theme that European society has reached a level where it can't even protect its own way of life. Actually, the Danish journalist Iben Thranholm went further to suggest that the environment that has brought about such an ugly situation for women is the death of masculinity among European men, because feminism has demonized the old masculine virtues of "protecting one's women, children and culture."

Reading about that sad story, I felt that I would rather be called a savage who can protect his women and girls, than be labeled a civilized modern man who cannot muster the courage to fight other men raping your women and girls. In fact, a 16-year-old German girl posted a YouTube video that went viral around January 2016 in which she begged German men to protect her and the women in their society. Looking at her totally demoralized young face, lamenting how she and her friends cannot go out walking to supermarkets or movie theaters because they could be raped, as an African, for the first time in my life I felt pity for the European society and way of thinking. It dawned on me that there is something large that is really missing in the way modern European society looks at life presently. Central to this mess is a pathological fear about offending other people, even bona fide criminals like those raping innocent girls and women.

At the conclusion of the series, Clark goes to America and to New York specifically. While facing the camera with the New York skyline of skyscrapers behind him, he concludes his epic program by saying three key things: 1) That he believes in the God-given genius of certain individuals, and that he values societies that make their existence possible. Think of the genius of Einstein; it was not allowed to stay in pre-World War Europe, but found a comfortable home in the US. 2) He alluded to what he said at the beginning, that lack of confidence is what kills a civilization. He said a civilization kills itself more by cynicism and disillusion than it does by bombs. He said the dreary fact remains that even in the darkest of days, it is institutions that make society work and if civilization is to survive, society must somehow be made to work so that people have confidence in their leaders. 3) He ends by reading that all-time famous WB Yates prophetic poem, *The Second Coming*.

> Turning and turning in the ever widening gyre
> The falcon cannot hear the falconer
> Things fall apart; the centre cannot hold;
> Mere anarchy is loosed upon the world,
> The blood-dimmed tide is loosed, and everywhere
> The ceremony of innocence is drowned
> The best lack all conviction, while the worst
> Are full of passionate intensity

He goes on the say, "Well that was certainly true between the World Wars and it damn nearly destroyed us. Is it true today? It is not quite because good people have convictions, rather too many of them." Then he ends the series by saying, "The trouble is that there is still no center. The moral and intellectual failure of Marxism has left us with no alternative to heroic materialism, and that is not enough." Dear reader, our worship of material consumerism is not going to cut it. Since the Christian center that held and propelled the civilization to unimaginable heights has died in the West, is there a way to salvage the virtues of Jesus the man, without the organized Christian church that society has rejected?

From without, the main challenge to Western civilization is radical Islam which, as evidenced by Islamic terrorist propaganda, is going on a barbaric rampage to destroy all remnants of pre-Islamic civilization in the Middle East, and its outright rejection of Western European values as unholy values means that it sees itself as a better civilization to humanity.

Despite these challenges, Europeans and their offspring need to be proud of what the civilization born in their backyard has achieved for them and, more importantly, for all of us. They should not feel guilty of some of the sins that have occurred during the civilization because every civilization has its cons. And they definitely should not be apologetic for all the grandeur that was conceived in the Italian Renaissance, advanced by the Church, and made universal by the inspiration of grace. For example, when I hear many Europeans being apologetic about the crusades to the point that they want to reject all the moral successes of Christianity, I remind them that starting with the first crusade begun in 1096, crusades were defensive enterprises by a resurgent Christendom aimed at reclaiming lands taken away by the conquering Muslims. It is the same reason that the Spaniards and Portuguese took back their peninsula in 1494 after almost 800 years of Muslim rule. It was a sort of "The Empire Strikes Back," but with a vengeance.

In this chapter, I have discussed my eighth hypothesis of how to transcend our heritages of birth.

Hypothesis 1: The origin of all humans is in Africa.

Hypothesis 2: Even if the origin of all humans is in Africa, the Semites created the idea of one God as it is known to most of us and the Europeans created the modern world as we know it; the most important similarity shared by all humans is the collective unconscious.

Hypothesis 3: Even if all humans are similar, there are real differences and inequalities among peoples due to the differences in collective consciousness.

Hypothesis 4: Absence of evidence is not evidence of absence. Just because we don't have undisputed scientific evidence of civilizations before 10,000 BC does not mean that for certain periods between the creation of the Earth 4.5 billion years ago and 10,000 BC, there were no advanced civilizations (humans or other creatures) that inhabited Africa and other parts of the planet.

Hypothesis 5: The six cradle civilizations, i.e. Ancient Egypt, the Olmecs of Central & North America, the Andean Civilization in South America, the Mesopotamian Civilization of the Middle East, the Indus Valley civilization of the Asian sub-continent, and the Ancient China civilization were multi-ethnic, multi-racial civilizations that hold significance for all humans.

Hypothesis 6: After the collapse of the African cradle civilization of Ancient Egypt, the Greco-Roman civilization became the intellectual foundation to what we know now as the European Western civilization.

Hypothesis 7: During the European Medieval ages, between the fall of the Roman Empire and the Italian Renaissance, the Islamic civilization played a critical role of safeguarding the ancient Greco-Roman classical knowledge which was resurrected in what we call the European Western civilization.

Hypothesis 8: **The European Western civilization is the current modern civilization and it is the first known civilization to unite the whole of humanity through individualism.**

9

THE THREE SINS OF ISLAMIC AND WESTERN DOMINANCE

The whole world currently is directly and indirectly influenced by the Islamic and Western civilizations. From the ascendance of the Islamic civilization in early seventh century and the Western civilization in the fifteenth century, both civilizations stretched their reach beyond Arabia and Europe. The nature of their outward reach, though benign to them, was in fact a gross act of sin that has been camouflaged over the years because of their insurmountable dominance.

We are only talking about both currently due to the fact that they are facing off with each other in some kind of clash of civilizations and all of us are victims. But since we all have been victims since their very beginnings, if we don't talk about the sins of these two civilizations, we will not heal as a human race. Even if we all have a case of Stockholm Syndrome – a psychological phenomenon in which hostages express empathy and have positive feelings toward their captors, sometimes to the point of defending and identifying with the captors – we should at least talk about it. If not for ourselves and our own healing, at least for the memory of all the millions of our ancestors who will never be remembered, who were slaughtered just because they were different or they believed differently.

The three gross sins of Islamic and Western civilizations have been: 1) slavery, 2) genocides and displacements of indigenous peoples, and 3) colonization.

These three sins first dawned on me when I went to New Mexico, US for my last two years of high school at the United World College.

Living in the American South West, I went to visit some of the Indian reservations and after learning a lot about the first peoples of the Americas, it dawned on me that indeed the few remnants of the Native American population are the super lucky few that have survived genocides against their ancestors. I visited Canyon De Chelly, the general Navajo nation, and even penetrated to reach the Hopi nation. After graduating from college I spent two years working with several Native American nations in northern New Mexico, primarily the Picuris Pueblo, and I cannot forget some of the conversations I used to have with the elders of their communities. It is not a small matter that right now in both America and Canada you can hardly find one per cent of indigenous people, yet the whole continent used to belong to them.

When I saw millions of black people in America and many more in Brazil when I visited there, for the first time it really dawned on me that the middle passage of African slaves from the West African coast to the Americas resulted in such massive scattering of my fellow black people all over the Western hemisphere, and even if I don't psychologically identify with the trauma and collective consciousness of slavery, because we never had slave trade in my country, I will forever be associated with such black peoples whether I want it or not. I had read about how Arabs had actually been the first slave traders on the East African coast, but I have not lived in Arab countries to connect the issue of black people in Arab countries with the East African coast slave trade.

My North American experience had a profound psychological effect on me, and I remember telling some of my close friends that I think the gross suffering of black people in the Americas has in part contributed to how soulful and spiritual they are in their music. Nonetheless, I felt that their history is quite different from the one that runs in my blood as far as all the oral traditions from my grandparents and what we study in my landlocked country.

As I outlined in the previous chapter, the Islamic civilization started with Mohammad in Mecca and the surrounding Arabian Peninsula in the early 600s, but spread to nearby North Africa by way of the Arabization of North Africa shortly after that. We know very little about the native peoples of North Africa before it became an Arab and Islamic region, but as a standard rule when immigrants meet natives, the Arab expansion into North Africa must have been characterized by genocides and ethnic cleansings. It reached up to the Sahara and West Africa by the ninth century.

The Arabs had conquered the rest of the Middle East starting with Jerusalem in 637 AD when they built the Al-Aqsa Mosque at the Temple Mount (the holiest site in Judaism), conquered Persia (Iran) by 651 and completed the conquest of present day Turkey in 1453. Islam conquered a big chunk of the Balkans and Caucasus countries, and for 800 years it ruled what we now know as Spain and Portugal. Eastward, the civilization reached present day India, Pakistan, and Far East Asian countries like Malaysia, Indonesia, Brunei, etc. On the East African coast, the civilization at one time controlled the whole coast from the Somali Peninsula all the way south to Mozambique. In fact, after centuries of ruling the East African coast, in the early eighteenth century the Oman Arabs moved their capital from Muscat to the Tanzanian island of Zanzibar. One of the lasting impacts of the Islamic Arabs over the East African coast was the birth of the culture and language called Swahili – which is a mixture of Arabic and Bantu languages (my mother language falls in this category).

The European participation in this sin of world domination emanated from the post-Renaissance European man who was emboldened with world knowledge and a will to conquer. Men from the various European Christian kingdoms ventured out to traverse oceans and unknown jungles to settle in new lands. In Australia and New Zealand they displaced the Maori and Aboriginal peoples, in the Americas they displaced the Incas, the Aztecs and numerous other peoples, and of course in southern Africa they displaced the native black peoples. They found it fitting within their Christian religion, and also incentivized by their trade, to take slaves from Africa and various Asian countries to the new world. In the new world, slaves worked like beasts of burden for hundreds of years until the modern era when they came to be recognized as equal citizens in their new countries.

What led to the last sin is that over the centuries, it so happened that the settlers out of Europe started looking at themselves as different from their kingdoms of origin. Hence, the birth of new countries all over the world. The third sin of dominance was committed by the mother European countries, upon being cut off from direct control of their people who had settled and began living independently as Australians, or New Zealanders, or Americans. These mother countries and kingdoms went on more direct missions to exploit and dominate other natives. This is where the colonization of much of Africa, the Indian sub-continent, and numerous islands in all the oceans of the world came from. The main culprits of this sin were principally Germany, France and the U.K., but the blame also goes to Belgium, the Netherlands, Spain and Portugal. I am a product of this third sin in that my people, the Basoga, were amalgamated from 1862 until 1900 with other tribes – the Baganda being the biggest – to create a country called Uganda (which name was a mispronunciation of Buganda kingdom). That is why I speak English, and despite all the negatives that history brought, I am very proud to be able to pick only the good from that dark chapter of human history. So, being able to write in this international language is one of the benefits I picked up from the colonial experience.

In this chapter, I have discussed my ninth hypothesis of how to transcend our heritages of birth.

Hypothesis 1: The origin of all humans is in Africa.

Hypothesis 2: Even if the origin of all humans is in Africa, the Semites created the idea of one God as it is known to most of us and the Europeans created the modern world as we know it; the most important similarity shared by all humans is the collective unconscious.

Hypothesis 3: Even if all humans are similar, there are real differences and inequalities among peoples due to the differences in collective consciousness.

Hypothesis 4: Absence of evidence is not evidence of absence. Just because we don't have undisputed scientific evidence of civilizations before 10,000 BC does not mean that for certain periods between the creation of the Earth 4.5 billion years ago and 10,000 BC, there were no advanced civilizations (humans or other creatures) that inhabited Africa and other parts of the planet.

Hypothesis 5: The six cradle civilizations, i.e. Ancient Egypt, the Olmecs of Central & North America, the Andean civilization in South America, the Mesopotamian civilization of the Middle East, the Indus Valley civilization of the Asian sub-continent, and the Ancient China civilization were multi-ethnic, multi-racial civilizations that hold significance for all humans.

Hypothesis 6: After the collapse of the African cradle civilization of Ancient Egypt, the Greco-Roman civilization became the intellectual foundation to what we know now as the European Western civilization.

Hypothesis 7: During the European Medieval ages, between the fall of the Roman Empire and the Italian Renaissance, the Islamic civilization played a critical role of safeguarding the ancient Greco-Roman classical knowledge which was resurrected in what we call the European Western civilization.

Hypothesis 8: The European Western civilization is the current modern civilization and it is the first known civilization to unite the whole of humanity through individualism.

Hypothesis 9: The dominance of the Islamic and European Western civilizations led to their people committing three sins with worldwide implications: 1) slave trade, 2) genocide against native peoples, and 3) colonization.

10

AFRICA IN THE MODERN WORLD

Since the advent of the modern civilization in the Italian Renaissance, Africa and Africans have been thrust into this modern world, sometimes positively and other times negatively. I have dedicated the entire appendix to this topic of Africa in the modern world; however, I would like to give a brief summary here. The appendix is for the reader who is interested in knowing my in-depth analysis of Africa and Africans in the modern world; both the good and the bad. For it is my genuine conviction that what happens in Africa in the near future will determine a lot of things for the future of the human race.

How low Africa is determines how high we can go as a human race. It determines how much peace we can have in this world. Failed states in Africa can be the exporters of the next wave of terrorists. To an extent, how safe the world is, in terms of disease, may well be determined by the next epidemic coming out of a jungle in Africa. I am not saying this to demonize Africa; the fact is that in the recent past, diseases have come about due to certain peoples eating monkeys or other wild animals in the jungles of Africa, which has led to transmutation of disease causing viruses in the world. The French eat frogs and snails, the Chinese eat dogs and monkeys, so I am not singling out Africa as if it is the only place that has people who engage in eating "non-traditional" cuisine. By the way, it is not all Africans, in my country monkey meat is not edible. And when you watch the 2010 documentary movie *Russian Lessons*, in which Georgian women talk of being forced to eat their husband's eyes after being raped in front of their husbands, I know that primitive behavior largely levied against Africa is in fact a human condition that any "civilized" human can resort to, given desperate circumstances. I watched the movie at the 2010 Sundance Film Festival, at which I also met the director Andrei Nekrasov. By the way, when we talk about "desperate circumstances", we shouldn't forget the little historical detail of how the Europeans besieged in the city of Stalingrad in World War II ate each other just to survive.

Since the days of the cradle civilizations, and possibly even during the many unknown civilizations before that, people from the African continent have had a mark on the rest of the world. However, the modern civilization which started with the Renaissance and Western European dominance has not been kind to Africa. The main reason for this is that when the modern outsiders came into contact with current Africans, they found us in pre-modern mindsets. Gone were the days when we built advanced stone edifices in Egypt or southern Africa or traversed to other parts of the world in pre-historical times. The six examples of our mindsets, which disadvantaged us a lot and up to now have played a big role in keeping us behind, are: 1) a porous type of mind, 2) religion in Africa is largely within the bicameral paradigm, 3) most Africans have a herd mentality, 4) most of us Africans lack the notion of spatialization of time, 5) for most Africans, everything is supernatural, and 6) most Africans lack agency. Disadvantaged with such pre-modern mindsets, it was easy for the Arabs and the Europeans to come to our land, force or manipulate us into believing their religions, and generally make our minds think about the world according to their ideas of the world. While doing this, they exploited our resources, enslaved and colonized us.

By knowing the above state of our minds, the outsiders knew our weakest point. The Arabs and Europeans left behind religious systems that pretty much keep us in pre-modern mindsets. They left behind a spiritual system that keeps us enslaved to their creations. They control our spiritual minds forever by the devices and narratives they implanted in our minds. These devices and narratives speak to the pre-modern mindsets largely by emotional and identity triggers. We have a situation where we are still enslaved by the way we emotionally identify with the images and paradigms the Arabs and Europeans planted in our minds. And universally triumphant is the African mind that can individualize the interpretation of the religious and social paradigms left behind by the Arabs and Europeans.

The first major negative effect of our encounter with the dominant civilizations of the Arabs and Europeans is that it dismembered our psyches. Whether historically since then, or currently in many instances of our interacting with the outside world, we exhibit the following four psychological ills: 1) a mentality of victimhood, 2) an inferiority complex, 3) an eagerness to consume foreign things, and 4) the African's eternal dilemma.

The African's eternal dilemma is the gravest of the four psychological effects. While I discuss the other three in the appendix, below is the detailed discussion of the dilemma. The dilemma is, "The more educated and advanced we get in this modern world, the more we are cut off from our African traditional roots."

The African's eternal dilemma

While the first three ills are evidently apparent among the uneducated, we the educated elites face an even worse problem, a psychological dilemma which many exhibit even if they don't suffer from the inferiority complex problem. I am saying it is worse because feeling inferior due to lack of education does not necessarily mean psychological conflict will ensue, even if it is a psychological malaise. However, when the educated person faces this dilemma, it is a psychological conflict that makes us even worse off than uneducated people who live blissfully in their reverence of white / European people.

The dilemma is this: For the African, the more educated and advanced we become in this modern world, the more we are cut off from our spiritual, emotional, intellectual and traditional African roots. This separation causes what I have called an eternal dilemma, because while we are full of Western education and ideals, they are usually incompatible with African traditional ways which require we respect and revere certain cultural customs. We are forced to pay lip service to the "merits" of such customs, yet at the same time our Western education and research shows them to be primitive, backward or immoral. With more Western education, we get removed from our roots, but no tree can stand tall and reach far into the sky if the roots are cut off. The dilemma creates a cognitive dissonance that can create the greatest of psychological conflicts in all of us educated Africans.

I argued in my first book that most developed modern Asians don't have this problem due to the dominance arrangement on their Naki[1] diagram. So for the Western people and the modern Asians, the more they are educated, the deeper their psychological roots grow in relation with their traditional ways, and the result is that they face no dilemma as we do.

A good example is that for many Western educated Christian Africans, they embrace and practice monogamy as a core tradition of Christianity. Because the traditional culture allows and even encourages polygamy, you find that many of us who come back from studying in Europe or America look at the polygamy practice as a backward one. In our time abroad, we have been taught that women have equal rights with men and that if a man has more than one wife, the women in that relationship are not being treated equally. Once back home, however, it is almost impossible for us to even start questioning polygamous arrangements, especially if they involve our parents or close clan relatives.

The result is that we end up holding some ideals in our heads, but when it comes to public debate we shy away from intellectual honesty. Once we compromise on this authenticity, we slowly slide down the slippery slope of ethical compromises. Ultimately we end up with an African society where even the educated people can never act as strong moral agents, who have sacrificed their lives in the pursuit of moral principles.

The more educated we get the more we increase our rationality but for most of us, the consciousness stays pre-modern. As we know, mentality is not a product of rationality alone, but rather largely it is "a state of being," or consciousness. That is why you can find many people without any education but who have a modern mind frame or modern consciousness. This is very easy to witness among societies with a writing culture; some people can grow up and drop out of school in primary / grade level but due to their society's collective consciousness, those people end up contributing to the modern world because they can engender a modern mind frame. A quick example of this is the school dropouts who have started world class I.T. companies that are currently the driving force of modern advancement. For us, because of the eternal dilemma, even some people with PhDs fail to attain a modern mind frame because they can't escape the African collective consciousness which is pre-modern.

This explains why some very educated people who return from America and Europe to live back home in Africa easily succumb to living like the uneducated masses (stealing public funds, wasting money on unwanted material goods, generally doing everything but uplifting the public). They fail to use their foreign modern knowledge to create value in our society to improve the quality of life of the uneducated masses and also guide them on how to understand this modern world and contribute to it. I know how we, the educated elites, have failed our societies because I returned from spending 13 years in the West, and realized that the situation in our societies is very worrying. It is absolutely immoral for some of us who are educated and privileged to have so much money and power in society, get very rich off stealing government money or running big businesses to the tune that we think in terms of millions of dollars, yet the poor neighbor down the street is illiterate, does not know that Earth is round, and the minute she sees a white person she is ready to prostitute herself with the dream that she will be taken as a trophy wife to Europe. Actually, some of our young people in society are so desperate and hopeless that they are taken as willing slaves to Middle Eastern countries where they work without pay, have their passports confiscated and are held as sexual slaves against their will. To me all these are outcomes of us, the educated elites, not caring about the general good of the public, by refusing to sacrifice ourselves to create real value in our people's lives.

Some of the worst culprits of this behavior are many of our African leaders. They succumb to the eternal dilemma so badly that most of the time they are in office, they collude with Western peoples to keep power, never really working to lift their people out of the quagmire that the African person finds himself in, in this modern age. I once read an account of an African president, who is well-educated, castigating his fellow countrymen he was supposed to be leading. The newspapers quoted him saying something along the lines of, "These local Africans don't know how to make money. That is why

I fight very hard to bring in foreign investors. The Indians and whites have a natural skill of making money, that is why the government is doing its best to bring them here." A president is supposed to inspire the people he leads, but if you have problems understanding the African mind that produces such a mental specimen, then you have no idea about the psychological malaise that befalls even the most educated of us. In a modern society, a president who categorically castigates his own people would not last one day in office, or if he did, he would go on a massive PR campaign to do damage control. But in our African societies, the people who should pull us up, the people who should show us the way to modernity, many times are the real stumbling block to our advancement. It is due to my personal realization of this fact back in 2003 that I lost all doubt in how I can be original in my thinking and advocate a totally new social dispensation for our society.

I believe it is some sort of psychological malaise as a symptom of our eternal dilemma that causes people difficulty in concentrating their minds on a particular task for an extended period of time, be it in a work project, or reading, or dedicating themselves to something for a long time. The repercussion of this internal psychological reality manifests itself in societal inefficiency or outright retardation. Have you ever wondered why it is that in Uganda, and Africa in general, we have failed to innovate our own writing culture, and despite using European languages we have failed to produce national dictionaries or create world class theories in math and science? Or why it is that we have problems constructing world class infrastructure (hint: it is not for lack of money as billions of dollars are embezzled, and not by Europeans or Americans), or why we have failed to cultivate a culture of maintaining buildings / infrastructure that were world class in colonial times? For example, it deeply saddens my heart to see images of buildings and whole cities that were world class in colonial times, but currently are totally run down. It makes you wonder why this is, and I can tell you it is not from population pressure. I have been to the tallest building in Africa, the Carlton Building in Johannesburg, and its current state is despicable compared to how it was in colonial times – mind you, it used to have more traffic back then.

It is not enough to say that it is due to bad leaders or colonialism. There is something really lacking in the society's collective consciousness and individual mind frames in these modern times. I believe in order to acquire a mental staying power that can allow our people to dedicate long spans of time to a task, or appreciate the value of maintaining infrastructure, we need to have a lifelong dedication to something akin to the Heri of Kesa (see chapter 11). Otherwise I can't see a way we can motivate people to have staying power to go after mental pursuits and, in the process, strengthen their mental aptitude so that they dedicate themselves to tasks with a long-term view such that even if it doesn't benefit them in the present moment, it benefits their grandchildren's children.

This is very personal to me. It is no small matter that I have to wonder why it is that even if we Africans are the oldest race in the world, not one of us has been able to concentrate his mind on the divine realm the way the desert people of the Middle East did to create sophisticated ways of relating to God. We call these sophisticated ways "religions." Even some recent American guy like Joseph Smith was able to concentrate his mind for long enough in 1820 that he created a brand new religion, which denigrates black people by the way, but has still been exported to Africa where hundreds of thousands of black people consume it.

Because of the eternal dilemma, however much you find yourself proud of your traditional culture and norms, and happy about the fact that our countries obtained independence from the colonialist, you encounter cognitive dissonance when you consider that the general structure of our nations, our education systems, the books we use, and the subjects we study are still from Europe. After more than 50 years of independence we still have not been able to undo the colonial borders that we complain about, or come up with indigenous subjects of study independent of European studies, or even agreed to develop indigenous languages to access modern knowledge; we still study in English or French about English or French systems and their world views. Even the spiritual disposition of a typical African is still enslaved to who colonized his country. This conflict between feeling free and independent, yet relying on the former colonial master for everything that matters, leads to a serious psychological and intellectual dilemma that only an African can understand. I was able to break free from this psychological and spiritual enslavement in 2003 and my prayer is that with these three books I have written, I will be able to open some intellectual and spiritual minds of my fellow Africans. If I can do that for even a handful of souls, I will die a very content person.

Below is my diagrammatical illustration of the African's mindset due to the dilemma.

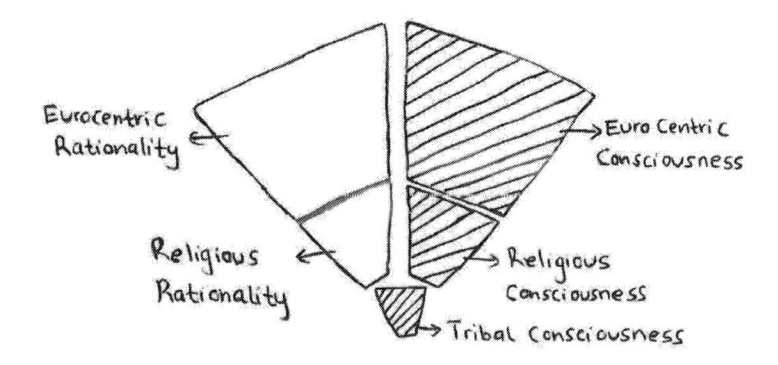

Figure 2: The Kamp Diagram Due to The Dilemma

The first layer, the tribal layer, is whole and intact, but only for someone with a strictly tribal mindset (without exposure to foreign religions or European colonial education). There is no psychological conflict between his tribal consciousness and the way he uses it to understand the "real nature" of the world.

The second layer, the religious layer, is intrinsically dualistic and conflicted, if not completely contradictory, for someone who is exposed to foreign religions. His religious sense of being or consciousness and the way he uses religion to rationalize understanding the "real nature" of the world butts up against the fact that the core of his existence is a tribal heritage.

The third layer, the Eurocentric layer, is likewise intrinsically dualistic and conflicted for someone who is further exposed to Eurocentric colonial education. There exists a cognitive dissonance between his Eurocentric world consciousness and the way he uses it (rationalizes it) to understand the "real nature" of the world, given his consumption of foreign religious teachings that are conflicted with the tribal core of his existence.

I offer a solution to this dilemma by way of what I have personally used to triumph over it, the Heri of Kesa (see the next chapter). Also, I specifically propose a cure for the other three psychological ills in the appendix of the book.

In this chapter, I have discussed my tenth hypothesis of how to transcend our heritages of birth.

Hypothesis 1: The origin of all humans is in Africa.

Hypothesis 2: Even if the origin of all humans is in Africa, the Semites created the idea of one God as it is known to most of us and the Europeans created the modern world as we know it; the most important similarity shared by all humans is the collective unconscious.

Hypothesis 3: Even if all humans are similar, there are real differences and inequalities among peoples due to the differences in collective consciousness.

Hypothesis 4: Absence of evidence is not evidence of absence. Just because we don't have undisputed scientific evidence of civilizations before 10,000 BC does not mean that for certain periods between the creation of the Earth 4.5 billion years ago and 10,000 BC, there were no advanced civilizations (humans or other creatures) that inhabited Africa and other parts of the planet.

Hypothesis 5: The six cradle civilizations, i.e. Ancient Egypt, the Olmecs of Central & North America, the Andean civilization in South America, the Mesopotamian civilization of the Middle East, the Indus Valley civilization of the Asian sub-continent, and the Ancient

China civilization were multi-ethnic, multi-racial civilizations that hold significance for all humans.

Hypothesis 6: After the collapse of the African cradle civilization of Ancient Egypt, the Greco-Roman civilization became the intellectual foundation to what we know now as the European Western civilization.

Hypothesis 7: During the European Medieval ages, between the fall of the Roman Empire and the Italian Renaissance, the Islamic civilization played a critical role of safeguarding the ancient Greco-Roman classical knowledge which was resurrected in what we call the European Western civilization.

Hypothesis 8: The European Western civilization is the current modern civilization and it is the first known civilization to unite the whole of humanity through individualism.

Hypothesis 9: The dominance of the Islamic and European Western civilizations led to their people committing three sins with worldwide implications: 1) slave trade, 2) genocide against native peoples, and 3) colonization.

Hypothesis 10: In this modern era, Africa has suffered greatly due to the three sins of the Islamic and European Western civilizations, but in order for the whole of humanity to find peace and wellbeing, Africa – inspired by its unique universal spirit that is not Islamic and not European – must rise up again to take its rightful position in human civilization. How high the human species goes in finding peace and wellbeing depends on how high Africa can lift itself up.

PART 3
TOWARD A HUMAN CIVILIZATION

I hope you have been able to see from what I have discussed so far that: 1) all humans are similar as far as the human soul is concerned, this is evidenced in our collective unconscious, and 2) there have been many civilizations since the cradle of man in Africa and the current one we are living in is the Western civilization – each civilization has guided its people within a distinct social–psychological envelope of collective consciousness. All the other civilizations rose and fell, however the Western civilization has not yet fallen. That being said, it is currently going through a lot of stress and strain.

What is the way forward?

We have to find a way to build on this current civilization so that it truly becomes a human civilization. This is possible, because Western civilization is the first civilization that started with humanism at its center - the belief that an individual can make the collective, in other words, the mind of one individual has the potential to create the whole.

The author in front of the Pyramid of the
Sun, Teotihuacan, Mexico (2007).

With some of the people who showed up at the first book
event for my first book, Austin, Texas (Fall 2009).

Skiing trips in the mountains of Utah in the winter of 2010 allowed me a lot of time to think, and the symbol of the Heri of Kesa was born on one of those days while riding on the gondola.

Snowboarding in Park City, Utah (Winter 2010).

The author at Arches National Park, South Utah. During the summers of 2010 and 2011, I spent many weekends driving to Southern Utah to experience the magnificently breathtaking landscape. These trips also gave me lots of time to think about the Heri of Kesa.

With my first two published books. Once I was confident about the finality of the symbol for the thesis of the third book, I put it in the second edition of the first book which was published on March 7th, 2011.

11

THESIS: THE HERI OF KESA

****This chapter is dedicated to my ancestors Yowasi Kampala and Bamwise Kampala, two illiterate men whose lives I know little of, yet whose reference point is my eternal struggle to put into writing ****

All the previous ten chapters have been preparing you, the reader, to reach this main chapter which contains my core thesis and primary reason for why I wrote this book. Earlier I discussed how the modern mindset, or modern man's consciousness, arose firstly due to the emergence of a writing culture. Writing cultures use literary devices to propagate the communication of ideas and also to concentrate people's minds. For example, words like "god is great" versus "God is great" hardly have any difference when spoken, but when written words, they can be the difference between war and peace or the difference between someone feeling offended or appeased about his idea of God. When written down, words become devices that enable a group of people to think and concentrate their minds on a specific subject. In the repetitive exercises of using these devices to concentrate their minds, people from a writing culture end up developing their minds in ways that are more powerful than people without a writing culture. Over thousands of years, history has shown that the people from writing cultures have been able to amass power, starting with the power of the mind, which transforms into power of society, economic power, military power, and so on. And that is why my people, who never had a writing culture, were colonized by Europeans, and not the other way round.

This is the only explanation that can give reason to why a small number of European men were able to come to Africa and colonize millions of people, or why about 200 Spanish men were able to conquer the mighty Inca Empire, which at one time might have had as many as 12 million inhabitants. It is the only explanation that can give reason to why a small island called Britain (with only a few million inhabitants) was able to colonize and take dominion over millions of Africans and half of the world, such that even today that small island with its few people still affects the way we think, the way we organize our societies, and of course, the way we speak to other peoples of the world. It is also the reason why the Jews, who are 0.2% of the world population, have such profound importance in world affairs … they wrote down their tradition and later peoples like us (Christians and Muslims, who are more than 50% of world population) still can't create ideas about God that are divorced from their age-old written ideas.

My written device, "the Heri of Kesa," is meant to be a tool that people without a modern mindset can use to obtain one through embracing a writing culture, interrogating the written word, and ultimately to concentrate their minds. For those who already have a modern western mindset, the Heri of Kesa is meant to broaden their humanity.

There is a profound paradox felt within many non-Western minds. I have heard people preach how Western civilization is largely bad. One would think that the world would be a better place if we all went by the Chinese, or Indian, or Islamic, or Japanese, or other "traditionally non-European" ways. But no, there is no proof of that. The whole world still congregates in Western capitals, children of the richest people in the world end up studying in Europe or America, and every nation has signed up to the Western economic and political structure of capitalism or the other, also European-created, system, communism. Even the most powerful non-Western country now, China, uses a system created by two Europeans, Karl Marx and Vladimir Lenin.

My introspection has led me to realize that the bad which many people see in Western civilization blinds them from seeing the overwhelming good that the civilization has brought to the world. Or they forget that Western civilization is individual-based, so whether you are of African or Asian descent, you can migrate to a Western country and live a successful life, your son or daughter could even grow up to be the President of the US. I have heard many African leaders publically proclaim their strong faith in Christianity while admonishing that traditional tribal beliefs are Satanic, and then in the same breath they blame colonialism or Europeans for all of Africa's problems. See how inconsistent this is? Such leaders would not profess a very Euro-centric religious heritage if the Europeans primarily brought bad things to our countries.

It is a very inconvenient truth that we often avoid admitting to the fact that many of us still have pre-modern mindsets that drive us to manifest a victimhood mentality in relation to more powerful Western minds. Instead of teaching our children to cultivate modern mindsets that can make them compete anywhere in the world, we cower inwards and find reasons to point out only the bad within the Western heritage. Such thinking at best is disingenuous, and at worst hypocritical. The bottom line is that the Western civilization has a positive balance sheet, and if there are gaps within it, we should fix them or improve on the system. It is a gross hypocrisy for us not to realize that in history there are Africans who committed similar sins as those we charge Western man with (see my discussion of the Bantu migrations in my first book). When you consider the horrific ethnic cleansing promulgated by the Arabs in North Africa during their civilization's expansion in the seventh century, you realize that the guilt we pile on Western civilization is shortsighted at best, and false at worst.

So this is my take on the subject. Instead of asserting that Western civilization is bad for the world, I want to look at it in a way that is useful for my diagnosis of the real problem and proposal of a solution. Many people (Europeans included) used to have a bicameral or pre-modern mindset which Western civilizations has attempted to modernize, but in the process committed the three sins I have discussed in chapter 9. My proposal, which is very specific, and one that I have not read any other human being make, is that now in 2016 we Earthlings need to create a new way of looking at the world. A new way that enables us to become a species whose whole purpose is to act as a light to illuminate the pre-modern mindsets that countless peoples still have. Since these mindsets were intact even before Western man spread to all corners of the world, my proposal of the Heri of Kesa is *sub-specie eternitatis*[2] and independent of the political debates people have about the merits of Western civilization. I have spent many years incubating this final chapter in my Fourth Heritage series, and I have no doubt it is a ray of light on the paradoxes of our thinking about how the West has written world history and made us all into its own image, but then there exists the politically correct sentiment to make the West feel guilty for the rest of time. In a way, I am going to borrow from that most enlightened of Western men, Jesus, and say, "Why can't we all forgive our enemies?" Forgiveness will make both the former victor and the former victim find a way to see the humanity in each other – both the positive and negative aspects. The key is for us all to find a formula of transforming people from pre-modern to modern consciousness.

The Heri of Kesa is a detailed description of my personal solution to the topic of "what we in Africa need in order to develop." I discussed this in the first book, but due to the interest of non-Ugandans in my writing, I have opened the discussion to broaden the reach of my analysis. So, my proposal here will reach and encompass topics to do with bringing optimism to the wider world.

The hindrances to development are problems that we in Africa would still have even if the colonialists hadn't come; insomuch as we maintained the pre-modern mindsets. By the same token, the misery and suffering going on in the world would have happened even if the Western civilization had not reached all corners of the Earth. There is no historical evidence that if the Chinese, Indian, or Islamic civilizations were the ones to have reached all corners of the world, the world would be a better place. It is totally disingenuous and utterly false for many of us to try and convince ourselves that we are underdeveloped or "backwards" as some say, because of colonialism (which lasted only 68 years in Uganda). We cannot hide from the fact that our peoples were around for thousands of years before Europeans arrived. If we Africans had been in a position to repel the outside influences, we would still be standing tall the way the Japanese are. We are underdeveloped / backward mainly because of what transpired in those thousands of years leading up to colonialism. It is not because of the minute 68-year span that Britain was the colonial power in Uganda, or in the little time that the Europeans were carving up the Middle East and the rest of the world under their spheres of influence.

For us Ugandans or Africans, even if the Europeans had not committed the three sins discussed earlier, we would still need a heri in order to develop (as per my analysis in the first book). In many instances, colonialism or Western influence is used as an excuse by our leaders, because they fail to design real solutions to our deep predicament. Look, there are other societies that were colonized or brought under the influence of the West, but have been able to develop; cases in point are South Korea, Japan and Singapore. In fact, since the tangible effects of Western civilization tend to be a net positive, I am sure there is a way to use the history of our encounter with Western civilization for our own good, as opposed to looking at it only as detrimental to our development.

We have to realize that our political problems aren't necessarily going to be solved by politicians, our economic problems aren't necessarily going to be solved by economists, and our health problems won't necessarily be solved by doctors. Rather, they will be solved by someone who, at the right time, designs an idea or policy or something that will galvanize the whole mass of our being into realizing our potential as thinking humans. A good example is how a super-rich person with enough resources can deploy them to solve problems in the health sector even if they are not a doctor.

At first, I started writing this book by proposing what our Ugandan or African heri could be. However, I quickly ran into difficulties and challenges that I could not overcome. To be more manageable and effective, I changed the subject, so instead of writing a proposal for the collective heri, I am writing to explain and define my personal heri. This way anyone, either in Uganda or any other country, can objectively debate and critique it openly in relation to me, as opposed to it seeming as though I am imposing my way of being and thinking on the populace. I would love to see people debate the four heris I proposed in the first book, then by contrasting them with the Heri of Kesa, we shall reach a consensus.

The concept of the Heri of Kesa has two primary objectives: 1) to engender a modern mindset or develop a concentrated mind, and 2) to enable people to unleash their creativity.

Without further ado, I welcome you to my personal proposal of "How we should be, and what can propel our creativity." I believe if we redefine who we are, "The Fourth Heritage," hopefully we restructure our society, "The Fourth Republic," and then embrace a robust heri, the sky is the limit.

Definition

The Heri of Kesa is **the authentic, individualized interpretation of one's experience of phenomena such that one grows a consciousness and rational mind frame that actualizes the understanding of the fundamental laws of the universe and one's duty to contribute to creation here on Earth**. This happens before one reaches the age society calls "adulthood," or before marriage. This is because when one becomes an adult, one usually stops searching for the universal truth, choosing instead to protect a societal truth.

There are two prerequisites (and one optional condition) for attaining the Heri of Kesa.

1) <u>The Fourth Heritage:</u> You need first and foremost to redefine who you are as an individual in regards to reconciling what is good within each of the three heritages we inherit at birth. In my first book I showed and gave you a framework on how to achieve this. This is a personal endeavor. Similar to the origin of consciousness in the breakdown of the bicameral mind, you have to go on a personal journey to define who you are independent of your heritages of birth. Personally, as I described in detail in the first book, I was able to start on

this personal journey by changing my tribal name as per the below lineage diagram – note that unlike the Western world, where surnames are family names or names of the father, in my culture surnames are random names picked from a set of clan names. And each clan within the tribe has a group of distinct names to choose from – that is how within a tribe you are able to avoid incest because people from the same clan cannot marry. A name in tribal heritages is more than just a word, it connotes your whole being, your connection to your ancestors and basically your destiny regarding the tribal universe. By choosing a new name, it made it possible for me to formulate all the details of the Fourth Heritage because I have lived my whole life with internal conflicts and questions regarding every detail of my being, or what they call "the self." And from that conflict has resulted my impetus for personal inner healing and the creation of the fourth heritage and heri of kesa.

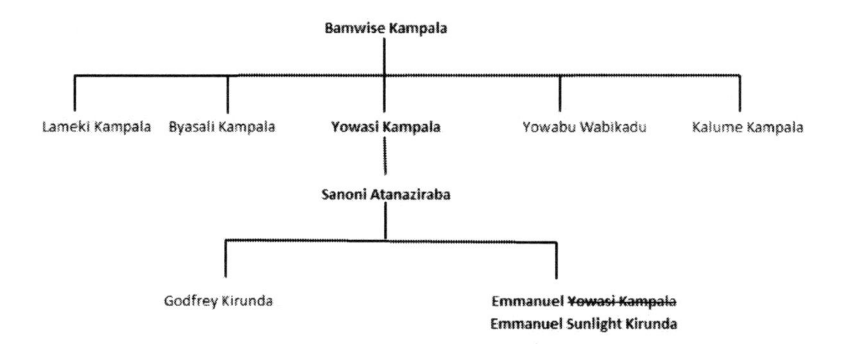

```
                        Bamwise Kampala
                               |
   ┌──────────┬──────────┬─────┴─────┬──────────┬──────────┐
Lameki     Byasali     Yowasi      Yowabu      Kalume
Kampala    Kampala     Kampala    Wabikadu    Kampala
                          |
                   Sanoni Atanaziraba
                          |
              ┌───────────┴───────────┐
         Godfrey Kirunda        Emmanuel ~~Yowasi Kampala~~
                                Emmanuel Sunlight Kirunda
```

Figure 3: My Family Lineage

Similar to how "the self" is not a mere sum of body parts, the Fourth Heritage is not a mere sum of the tribal, the religious and the

European heritages. It is more than the sum; it is unique and stands alone as a dominant identifying paradigm.

Generally, the journey to attaining a Fourth Heritage means re-creating yourself and your world. As I alluded to, it can be as simple as children giving themselves nicknames different from their birth names, or as complex as people coming up with groundbreaking new concepts. In the religious arena, it could be as strenuous as unlearning all that you have been taught traditionally in order to embrace ideas from another religion or from purely human secular reasoning. In fact, it could also be choosing to belong to our traditional Islamic or Christian traditions, but willing to doubt their conservative dogmas so that you stay grounded in a human universalism that transcends the religions we adopt as an accident of birth.

As I said, you still remain identified with your parents' tribal and religious heritages, and of course every modern society is influenced by the Western civilization, but all three of these MUST be individualized by you. While you are on this journey of attaining an individualized rational and conscious mindset, the second prerequisite is crucial.

2) <u>Learn to read critically:</u> For me as a Ugandan this meant learning to read critically in English. The nature of the language matters here. Learning to read and write in a written language like English will lead you to harvest the two knowledge bases that are crucial to your understanding of the fundamental ways of the universe / nature; 1) mathematics, which is the pinnacle of human reasoning – the language of the universal God and 2) the natural sciences (physics, chemistry and biology) which are the cumulative models that man uses to understand nature and life. Science is special

today because, more than anything else, it alone indeed has the monopoly on the production of factual knowledge.

If some national projects were to make any of our local African languages achieve the same written stature as English, then at that time those languages could play the role that English played in my lifelong germination of the Fourth Heritage and the Heri of Kesa. This second prerequisite is a categorical rejection of oralization or oral tradition. It is a must that we transform to a written-down tradition (see the part in chapter 8 where I write about the birth of consciousness in the written word).

> Live in a conducive environment: This is not a prerequisite, but it is a condition that would ease your attainment of the Heri of Kesa. Since this heri is all about consciousness and the accumulation of a more refined rationality, it is possible to attain it in any physical environment, be it a dictatorship, a village or a city. But for ease of this journey, the social environment needs to be accepting of individualized existence and personal change. For us Ugandans, I made an attempt to model such a social environment in the second book, *The Fourth Republic*. In a nutshell, if Uganda had an environment close to the one I drew up in that book, our children would quickly redefine their integrative identity within the triple heritages and also easily attain modern consciousness and rationality, which are the core ingredients of a modern mind frame. Personally, I went through a lot of struggles due to growing up in a family with illiterate parents and spending the first five years of school failing to pronounce simple English words like "three" or "knowledge." However, while I grew up with such a conducive environment only in my

head, from an early age I knew that even if I was faced with poverty, or racism, or any other obstacle that could come my way, as long as I redefined myself in regards to what I ended up terming "The Fourth Heritage" and "The Heri of Kesa," the universe / God would conspire to make me succeed in life.

The Heri of Kesa is based on something truly fundamental to all of us as human beings, such that you can use it to understand and relate to any person from any culture. More importantly, you can use it as a framework to be creative, productive and prosperous in your endeavors.

After conceiving of the Heri of Kesa by the above prerequisites, it has to be propagated by these four pillars:

Propagation Pillar 1: Acknowledging the fact that modern humans can learn a great deal of knowledge from the long lost ancient civilizations and the six cradle civilizations.

Propagation Pillar 2: Unknowable God. If you use your rationality, the best you can know is an ethnocentric God. If you use your consciousness you may acknowledge the existence of God, but also realize that you can never know God.

Propagation Pillar 3: Post-tribal identity. Each individual has to have independent thinking, such that they do not accept something just because the group accepts it, or reject something just because the group rejects it. This means that an individual must take on a post-tribal identity.

Propagation Pillar 4: Don't be a slave to the Islamic and Western civilizations. Even if the modern world is dominated by Islamic and Western thinking, we are not born to live life as slaves to these two systems of thinking.

Below is the diagrammatical representation of the Heri of Kesa. In a way these two diagrams represent the gist of the entire book. Each diagram has two legs: 1) the rational leg represented by the lines, which can overcome the three limits (see subsections below), and 2) the consciousness leg represented by the shading which represents one's internal experiences and specifically the evolution from the bicameral mind to the modern mind.

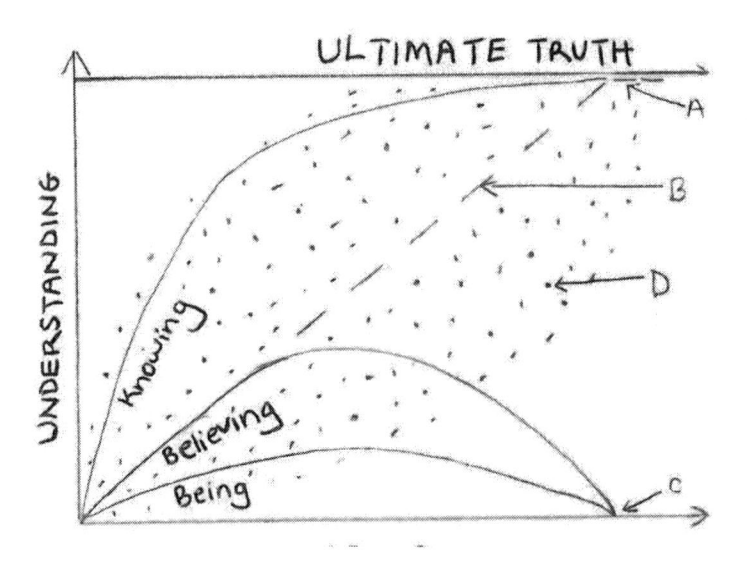

Figure 4: The General Heri of Kesa

A: This is the asymptote[3] of the relationship between objective knowledge and the ultimate truth. No matter how refined and great objective knowledge gets, it can never reach the ultimate truth.

B: The dashed line signifies that even the best way of believing (which is subjective knowledge) theoretically just leads you toward the potential of attaining the maximum level of understanding that is possible for us as human beings, but it ends at the asymptote.

C: It has two angles. First, it shows how bad beliefs or superstitious beliefs (believing what you don't understand) can lead one to zero understanding. Second, it shows that if you just stay in your initial position of being, without making any rational effort to believe something (whether that be through seeking subjective or objective knowledge), you are guaranteed to have zero understanding.

D: This is the propagation of consciousness. Based on your state of being and how you refine your mindset, you can reach the highest understanding that is possible for humans beginning at any time and via any given avenue.

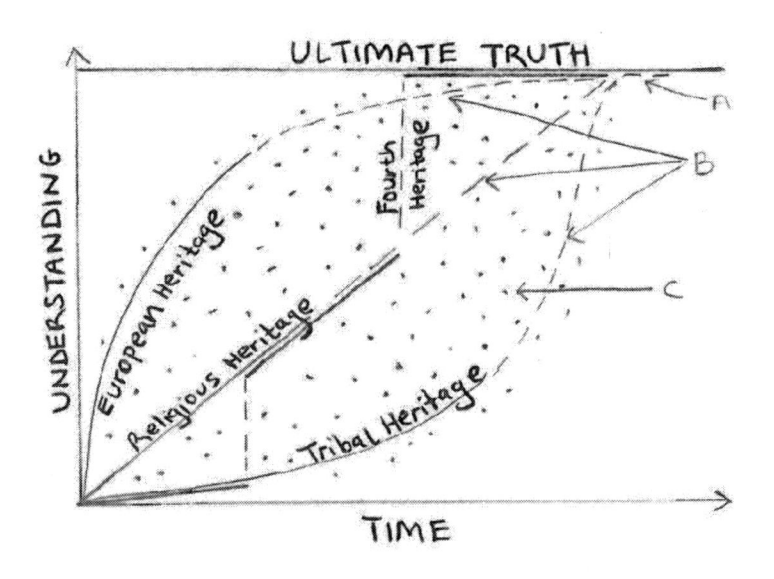

Figure 5: The Specific Heri of Kesa

A: This is the asymptote of the Fourth Heritage objective knowledge curve and the ultimate truth. Rationality through the Fourth Heritage guarantees you to reach the maximum understanding possible to man.

B: The three lines that end up as dashed lines signify the pure potentiality that tribal knowledge, religious belief, and elements from the Western heritage could all theoretically lead you to reach the maximum level of understanding that is possible for you as a human being.

C: This is the propagation of consciousness. Consciousness alone could lead you to reach the maximum understanding that is possible for humans.

The wise people nowadays derive their insight about nature or life by using the scientific method[4], then spread their knowledge based on verifiable propositions. They spread their knowledge by way of light (objectively and skeptically) and like a candle in the dark, over time that light of objective knowledge gets rid of ignorance in the human mind. However, the way the not-so-wise people spread their ideas is analogous to the spread of heat (coercion or raw power). While light shines away the darkness, heat burns things. No wonder tribal and religious methods, by virtue of them using coercive methods to instill knowledge in people, have led to a lot of bloodshed throughout man's history. By contrast, the science of men like Isaac Newton and Einstein has shone brightly and illuminated the human minds of Christians, Jews, Muslims and the rest of the human family. I want the Heri of Kesa to be like a candle of light in the darkness of our pre-modern mindsets.

Explanation

In the definition section above, I started the conversation of how the Heri of Kesa is about the quality of rationality and the state of mind (consciousness) that we should espouse. You need to be a free person in order to fully embrace the Heri of Kesa. Free from the societal limits you were born into, and free to create new assumptions about nature. If all you are is "being" (being "a woman" or "a man," being in "this or that tribe," or belonging to "such and such a race") there is no source of understanding in such an inertia state. "Being" is true and it is a fact for you, but it has nothing to do with facts or truths beyond you. Unless by "being you" you mean also being an embodiment of the universal consciousness or God, which is a totally different proposition. If you don't go beyond "being" and start believing in something (e.g. mythology, religion or ideology) you end up with only the most rudimentary understanding of the world and your place in it. This is why our tribal ancestors were easily overpowered by the outsiders; they were existing in only a rudimentary way.

On the other hand, though, if all you do is "believe," there is equal possibility of you knowing and understanding a lot, or ending up having the wrong subjective knowledge which can lead you to zero knowledge of the world. For example, we read in history that at some point people believed that the earth was flat and that it was the center of the universe. Other people who doubted these dogmas were even killed. Now when we look back at that history, we realize that the believers in "Earth as the center of the universe" relied only on subjective knowledge – they believed something because it validated their religion, not because it was true in and of itself. "Belief" is all about personal truths, but not about facts or the ultimate truth. The main folly with "believing" is that most of the believers are not taught that the aim of the belief is not so much about physical facts but rather about the "non-physical" realm that may be called the spiritual world. For example, if the believers of old were able to understand that the statement "we are at the center of the universe" is a spiritual construct with only spiritual significance, and then been mature enough to disassociate that said belief from their acquisition of factual evidence of the shapes and positions of the planet Earth and the sun, then there would not be any misunderstanding about "religion being wrong about the earth as the center of the universe." So, "believing" is solely about the non-physical world and truths we can feel or behold as "spiritual beings". The actual facts about the physical world are outside the realm of believing and squarely in the realm of objective knowledge.

If you set out to understand what you are in terms of "being," and you grasp that "belief" is all about the "non-physical" realm, but more importantly you put most of your life's effort in searching for knowledge from all cultures and civilizations of the world – both living and dead – then you will be on the way to knowing the maximum truth that a human mind can possibly know. "Ultimate truth" is out of the question; it cannot be reached. Knowing the ultimate truth is equal to knowing the mind of God. And whoever says they know God's mind is at best a liar, and at worst an evil person – cult leaders come to mind. However, as humans, the best way to trend toward "the ultimate truth," even if it is given that you can't reach it, is if you dedicate all your life to searching out knowledge, beyond just "being" and "believing." This knowledge can either be through rational means, or consciousness, or both, but since consciousness is more chaotic and supremely subjective, I will concentrate most of my analysis on the rational method of searching for knowledge because it can easily be shared and embraced by wider humanity; case in point is the way modern science is embraced by all people, even those who don't believe in it. If I were to use the consciousness method, I would have to attribute my knowledge to a societal authority like God in order for my message to permeate to anyone beyond me.

When we look at our triple heritages of being / believing / knowing, in order to understand the truth from the three, a truth that will be beneficial for our living, we have to struggle very hard to search out knowledge that will make the limit of each of the triple heritages very clear. This is because the limit on the utility of each triple heritage is the beginning of the creative force that we must harness to create models and ideas that are useful to our societies (more about this in the follow up sub-sections about such limits). Only through the understanding of these limits can cognitive dissonance[5] be prevented.

The medium for the Heri of Kesa is literacy, which has been primarily the English language for me. If we, in Uganda, were using another language for mathematics and the natural sciences, I am sure I would have employed the use of that other language. From the time I began cultivating the Heri of Kesa that day in fourth grade, when I took upon myself the name Kesa and spent countless days writing it out tirelessly in different calligraphy fonts, English has been the language that played the critical literacy role, not my native language of Lusoga. And as such, the transformation of people's consciousness from the pre-modern mindset (based on primitive parts of the brain) and its outside centers of reference (shrines, sacred objects, etc.) into a frontal lobe-centered[6] consciousness which characterizes the modern mind frame has to be based on learning how to read and write critically (for more information, see the role of writing in the breakdown of the bicameral mind).

Consciousness beyond the bicameral vestiges in the cerebrum part of the brain (of which the frontal lobe is part) can lead you to look at the whole world as a playground. In fact, you are also able to look at the whole of history with its long gone civilizations. In everyday life, you can feel free to go on solo trips to any part of this planet, you are able to scale any mountain or dive deep to remote areas of the oceans, or indeed take off in a rocket to discover outer space. All these you can do only if you have a modern mind frame, whose consciousness is not tied to some object back in your village, like a shrine or a sacred tree. Have you ever analyzed why many of our tribal people become less functional when placed out of their environments, or placed with foreigners? I have witnessed grown men, who command respect and stature in the village or in our small towns, act awkwardly when you bring them to talk to young kids from Europe or when they are placed in front of an interviewer on the BBC. All this is because many of our people are still wallowing in a pre-modern type of mind frame, even when they get PhDs from Oxford.

The exercise of writing helps people's spatiality of time tremendously. Traditionally, tribal people didn't have a concept of time until the outsiders brought the idea of modern time defined by minutes, seconds, centuries and millennia. The pre-modern mind cannot spatialize time (to exact events in the space-time continuum). By ensuring that you understand time from the infinitesimal to the cosmological levels, your pre-modern mind modernizes so that you can place events in their exact time and position of occurrence. You cannot do this using the oral system from our grandparents which based time on how tall a human shadow was on the ground, or mentally recording events and memories only by way of the changing of seasons, animals migrating, etc. Do you realize how impossible it would have been for me to have a modern mind frame if all I spoke was my native language? For example, when I speak to my extended family in Lusoga, no one can tell me simple things like when my grandfather or his father moved to our village, got married to his wives, or generally where and when our clan was formed. The elders simply resort to using mythological language about simple things that transpired during our forefathers' time which happened just 100 years ago. So when you observe that the graves for my ancestors in the village are all marked "Date of death: 1st January," with a random year, it is because they did not keep calendar dates of when people were born or died. Psychologically, this translates into a people who cannot place events in their rightful place in time.

If we are traditionally unable to know about and understand details regarding events a mere 100 years ago, then do you better comprehend how we grow up to have a pre-modern consciousness compared to a kid born in England or Germany whose conscious mind can discuss details about specific events down to the day and month of their occurrence 500 or 1,000 years ago? As I mentioned, while all human beings are the same as far as the collective unconscious is concerned, there are groups of people who have been left behind in civilization. Not being able to contextualize events in precise time is a sign of pre-modernity. Without me learning English and being able to understand time, space and history with exact reference points, my consciousness would have remained shallow and led to me have an inferiority complex.

Since we pre-modern peoples don't have thousands of years of history and literature to reference in order to develop our consciousness, the way the modern peoples of Europe, America and Asia naturally do, you have to realize that we need to catch up with modernity in a different way. By us embracing devices like "heri," "fourth heritage," "fourth republic," and "Naki," we can develop a system of reference that can substitute the thousands of years that modern people possess in their cultures. These literate devices will help someone with a triple heritage develop the same robust consciousness that came to modern peoples through study of history and literature.

When you roll back all history or all civilizations, they all come back to Africa. So why don't we use that as the ultimate reference point? That fact as a reference point would be stronger than any religious or political ideology, which are recent creations. For example, out of our existence as a species over a period of about 200,000 years, the biggest religion we follow in Uganda is Christianity, which is less than 2,000 years old, amounting to less than 1% of the total time humans have been on this planet. And as for political ideologies, none of them are more than 500 years old, so it is easy for us to choose to overlook any political ideology, especially as they all emanate from colonialism which is one of the three sins of the Western civilization. Capitalism, socialism, communism and everything in between were all created in Europe by Europeans, and if we need to create a really human civilization that goes beyond the hurting Western civilization, what better way than us reimagining all systems that are failing to rescue humanity from the emptiness of material consumerism?

On my mental wandering journey as a teenager lost in imagination, I used to have a vision. Seeing as how the history of humanity rolls back into Africa as our cradle, I always wondered: why can't we have a museum dedicated to humanity that is built in Africa? It could be something so profound and magnificent that wherever, whenever any human being thinks deeply about humanity and all its creations over the millennia, they feel an urge to take a pilgrimage to Africa to visit that museum.

A Fundamental Concept in Mathematics

Mathematics is the pinnacle of human reasoning. Of all the knowledge that man knows, or as some people would rather say that

God has allowed man to know, mathematics is the king of kings of knowledge. In fact, many scientists and anyone who ever delves deep into the nature of things or of the universe conclude that mathematics is the language of God. I mean, everything in life, in the universe has a mathematic angle to it. For example, there is a mathematical angle to why the day is 24 hours and not 25 or 20, there is a mathematical angle to why when you jump up you must fall to the ground (while on Earth, but if you jump in outer space, since there is no down, you stay in the direction in which you jumped), there is a mathematical equation to how a circle is round and a square has four equal sides, there is a mathematical implication to why oil floats on water and not water on oil, there is a mathematical angle to why a baby human spends nine months in the womb of a woman while a baby elephant will spend 22 months in its mother. And my favorite: there is a mathematical explanation as to why when the sun rises up in the morning or sets down in the evening, it is red, yet at noon the sky is blue.

It is from mathematics that all the natural sciences (physics, chemistry and biology) derive their meanings and implications. As we casually acknowledge, all other forms of knowledge, e.g. political study, religions and history, become more credible if they have a scientific / mathematical reference supporting their claim. For example, when physics shows us proof that the earth is not the center of the universe as religion used to teach for thousands of years, modern day religious people spin it and say that "the fact that the universe is much bigger is a testament of God's grandeur" – of course dodging the fact that religion used to teach something wrong. Mathematics is the pinnacle of man's reasoning or understanding of the universe, and it is not an option that some people should study math because they are "smart" while others should study non-math subjects because they are not "smart." If you don't know some of the fundamental concepts in mathematics, you are a human being who is immensely disadvantaged in regards to how you can ever understand the ways of the universe or the language of God.

On our first days of primary school, we are introduced to the rudimentary type of mathematics called "arithmetic." Arithmetic is the mathematics of counting and adding, e.g. $1 + 1 = 2$. After learning basic arithmetic, in around the second year of primary school we are introduced to the second type of mathematics called "geometry." Geometry is the mathematics to do with shapes and their angles, e.g. circles, squares and rectangles. As we progress in primary education, the third type of mathematics we are introduced to is called "algebra." Algebra is the mathematics to do with operations like minus (-) and addition (+) and their application to equations, e.g. if $3x + 4 = 10$, what is x? The fourth type of mathematics they teach us is called "trigonometry." Trigonometry is the math of lengths and angles of geometrical shapes called triangles; e.g. a right-angled triangle has only one angle equal to 90 degrees, and its longest side is called the hypotenuse.

Usually it is when you go to secondary school that you are introduced to the fifth type of mathematics called "calculus." Calculus is a very wide and deep type of mathematics. If I had my way, I would make it a human right for every person to study some form of mathematics up to understanding basic calculus. Why?

Modern calculus is the type of mathematics that was independently discovered or created by the English mathematician and physicist Isaac Newton and the German mathematician and philosopher Gottfried Leibniz. There were other mathematicians before them in other parts of the world who flirted with the same kind of mathematics, but modern calculus is as invented by these two men in the seventeenth century. They independently landed on the same fundamental equations of nature using different symbols, and living in different countries. What a pity if you go through life without reaching to study and understand elementary calculus!

Without boring the reader with specifics, calculus is the mathematics concerned with change in things or processes. For example, if you want to find the speed of the earth moving around the sun, or if you want to know how your money is compounded at a certain rate in a bank, or if you want to design a shock-absorber so that when your car hits a pot-hole the car can, for a short time, jerk you up, but then quickly stabilizes so you are not shoved up and down uncontrollably, you have to use equations that fall within the field of calculus. Another vivid example is that algebra alone will take you forever to calculate the volume of an irregular shape. However, if you use calculus, you can instantaneously calculate the volume of such an irregular shape. Calculus in its more advanced forms is what has enabled modern man to create immensely powerful systems like super-computers, or advanced technology that allows us to have rockets defy Earth's gravitational force and have manmade objects orbit other planets or hover over Earth the way the International Space Station does. This is all possible because through very advanced forms of calculus equations, one can calculate how a moving object will change direction and what change in speed can cause specific changes within the internal properties of that object.

The "limit of a function" is a fundamental concept that you have to understand before you can delve into learning calculus. In fact, it is a fundamental concept that is the bedrock of a lot of other mathematical analysis.

A "function" is a mathematical sentence. The "limit of a function" is a mathematical statement that says: if you have a function $f(p)$, there is a predictable, calculated output that the function gives when the variable 'p' approaches a specific value. For example, the function f (t) – where t is the action of increasing water temperature – gives you the output of "steam." This means when you keep increasing the temperature of the water, the outcome is that the water will keep warming up until the temperature is 100 degrees centigrade at which point water becomes steam. So if you have mathematical eyes, when you see that function f (t), you instantaneously know that the limit of that function is "steam."

This "limit of a function" concept is fundamental to a lot of mathematics, and as math is the pinnacle of human reasoning, I want to say that if you benchmark your reasoning in line with this concept, by definition you can reach a way of reasoning about a thing that constitutes the pinnacle of reasoning regarding that thing.

From knowing the implication of this fundamental concept of mathematics (that for a given function, there is a predictable, calculated output that the function gives when its variables approach a specific value), I want to borrow that reasoning to analyze how any human being can transcend the limits of one's heritages of birth, if those heritages are defined as the triple heritage of being / believing / knowing. I want you the reader to see my points in the most fundamental yet "natural" way of seeing things. They are "fundamental," in that the implications have an effect on everything in our societies and touch all people whether in Africa or outside. They are "natural" in that it is self-evident – their reasoning is not based on any ideology (which by definition is a social creation, usually by Europeans, e.g. the ideology of Marxism or capitalism). So I want my line of reasoning to be simple and self-evident to any rational person. This is in line with Einstein's thinking that "things should be made as simple as possible, but not simpler."

As someone born with the triple heritages (the first can be tribe or national identify, the second is religious – usually Christianity or Islam, and the third is the Western European heritage or colonialism), whether you live life in Africa or other parts of the world, there is a particular predictable mental state you gravitate towards as a result of the inheritance of the triple heritages. And this mental state has specific fundamental qualities to it. These fundamental qualities that characterize our mental states are the limit of the tribal heritage, the limit of the religious heritage and the limit of the Western European heritage. For those people with just two heritages (no one has just one heritage), the third limit might not apply to you.

You cannot give value or understand the value of a system until you reach its limit or you are out of its reach. A good example is that the notion of "Third World countries" is quite meaningless until you are in a First World country, or you see Third World conditions from the First World point of view. Similarly, you cannot see the value or the limit of the tribal heritage until you have taken to heart the religious heritage, and likewise you cannot see the limit of the religious heritage until you have gone beyond it. As you read the following sub-sections on the limits, remember there are two definitions of the limits: 1) that which cannot be surpassed when in the system, and 2) that which is the ultimate outcome arrived at by the system. I will not single out what definition I am referring to at the various instances of discussion.

The Limit of the Tribal Heritage

Since the tribal heritage is not based on a writing tradition, by extrapolation, you cannot develop a modern mind's consciousness when you live within the tribal confine (see the sub-chapter where I discuss consciousness and the development of the mind).

The limit of the tribal heritage is transition point 1 and transition point 2 as shown on the diagram "the Spectrum of Mindset" in chapter 8. When someone with a tribal mindset is animistic, they revert back to bicameralism, however the more that person individualizes their life, i.e. develops their individuality independent of the tribal teachings, the more they bear the modern mindset. The reversion to bicameralism can take the form of tribal people indulging in animism and ancestral worship. Ancestral worship basically comprises activities where members of the tribal group induce trances or changes in people's consciousness that allow the induced people to take on manifestations of the spirits of dead relatives or animals. The second transition point usually involves people physically leaving their tribal areas (traditionally, the reach of the tribal collective consciousness exponentially diminishes the farther people get away from their tribal land of origin) and they espouse religious or Western ways of thinking that they acquire via reading. I remember when I was a young boy my relatives in the village used to warn us that if we crossed the Nile to be on the land of another tribe, the ancestral spirits would not reach us and protect our lives. This is a classic example of how the tribal area builds a bubble of collective consciousness that engulfs the members.

The limit for the tribal heritage is that one cannot understand the fundamental laws of the universe. "Tribal" means the traditional indigenous peoples of the world e.g. my tribe of the Basoga, but there are also other groups of people who look at their race or religion in a "tribal way," so they are also governed by this limit.

As I have said above, firstly, this limit comes about because by definition one's not having a written tradition leads one to possess a pre-modern type of consciousness. The proof of this can only be found out if you were born in a tribal setting without a literate culture and brought up with tribal customs. The minute you graduate from this level and you learn how to read and write and keep cultivating more subjective consciousness, you will be able to see this limit as clear as daylight. I personally manifested this limit when I left my tribal traditional upbringing in Iganga town and went to the big city Kampala. This limit should be self-evident if you are a black African born in a traditional environment without the culture of reading books, or if you belong to any of the tribal groupings in whatever country you may be from. I believe it is within the confines of this limit that you find the breeding ground for the four psychological ills, mentioned in Chapter 10, which infect people with a pre-modern mindset (inferiority complex, victimhood mentality, eagerness to consume foreign things and the eternal dilemma). It is also the breeding ground for many to exhibit primitivism in this modern era, what Professor Ali Mazrui called idealized primitivism or "the tendency to revel in the triumph of simplicity and the virtues of non-technicality."

As a people born with a tribal heritage, we need to innovate ways that enable us to go beyond this limit. Tribal heritage should not be looked at as a static reality created by our illiterate forebears to guide our lives forever. Rather, we need to look at tribal heritages as dynamic social settings which continue to be defined by us in the present. And since, unlike our forebears, we can read and write, it means we have opportunities to actually create social settings that can enable all our peoples to bear modern mindsets. One quick strategy to propel our society towards such a future is that we should stop asking people what tribe they are but rather ask what tribe their parents come from, since a child from parents of different tribes does not necessarily take on all the traits and characteristics of the father's tribe. Over a generation or two, our population will end up being just "citizens of the nation" and not belonging to this or that tribe. And as I mention in the appendix, the nation-state is the civilizing entity for us Africans, not the tribes. Nonetheless, as outlined in the second book, tribes and their heritages need to be preserved for historical and reference purposes.

Note about a dominant tribal heritage

In my first book I explained the Naki Diagram of Heritage Dominance and showed how the tribal heritage is always dominated by the religious, and in turn the religious is dominated by the Western. When I visited Cuba last year, I came face to face with Santeria, an African religious tradition which was carried there by African slaves, more specifically the Yoruba traditional religion. It is the one example I have found in which the African tribal heritage is dominant over the European Christian heritage. In Santeria, the mediums between the people and God Almighty are called saints, but a more correct interpretation would be "gods," or "Orishas" in Yoruba.

All the Orishas are black people with Yoruba names like Ogun, Oshun, Oba, Yameya, Babalu Aye and Chango (there are 30 major saints). In the museum of the Orishas in central Havana, you marvel at the 30 giant statues of tribal African men and women staring at you. The religion is very similar to the Brazilian Candomble religion – which I was fortunate to witness in the summer of 2003 when I visited Brazil – because Candomble is also basically Yoruba tribal traditions and rituals. It is no small matter that after hundreds of years of slavery, the Yoruba traditions were so powerful and robust that even when people practice Christianity, they use Yoruba names for all Christian saints. Many books say about 70% of Cubans (blacks, mixed race, and white people) practice Santeria, however when I talked to some people at the Santeria museum and also my acquaintances, they told me it must be about 90%. In summary, Santeria – or Candomble – is the only example I have come across where the Naki Diagram does not apply, for the Yoruba tribal heritage as practiced in Cuba and Brazil is definitely dominant over the European Christian heritage.

In order to understand why the Yoruba African religious tradition has survived hundreds of years and continues to be practiced in its authenticity in Cuba, Brazil, and many other countries of the new world, you need to know that the Yoruba pantheon of gods was even older and more grand than that of the Greeks. When you read about the Greek Zeus, Athena, Poseidon, and all the other gods and goddesses from Greece of BC, the same is true of the Yoruba Olorum, Oshun, Chango, Obatala and Yameya. It is quite remarkable that whereas the Modern Greek person has abandoned the Greek gods and the psychology that used to come with them, the Yoruba gods have survived something as traumatic as slavery and the middle passage.

Nonetheless, given the objective of my thesis in the first book, even this reversal Naki diagram as evidenced by the Cuban and Brazilian practices does not invalidate my hypothesis that "we need a heri to develop and solve the invisible problems." For it is only the acquisition of a heri that enables a people to develop. The Yoruba culture is so old and complex that they have a calendar more complicated than the Christian calendar and older by 8,000 years, demarcated with 13 months in a year and four days in a week. However, despite this level of complexity, according to my hypothesis, that is still not good enough to lead them to development. I don't sense an original heri among the practitioners of Santeria or Candomble, hence we don't speak of them as developed societies or people with modern mindsets in the same way I explained about the Japanese, the American and the German heris.

So in a nutshell, even if a people can have their tribal heritage dominant, still they are governed by the tribal limit, and without them developing a heri, those people still lack the "it" needed for economic and intellectual development.

The Limit of the Religious Heritage

While I have tried to show in the preceding section that someone with a tribal mindset cannot at the same time bear a modern mindset, it is not the case for the religious heritage. Since religions are based on written words, theoretically they may lead to the conception of a modern mind frame and modern subjective consciousness. This is something good that can come out of religions. But something bad can also come from religions; they can also lead some people to exhibit a tribal mentality. This is when religious people look at their religion in a closed-minded kind of way. If this happens, then the religion is producing a pre-modern mindset, and the first limit applies. A very good example is the conservative religious people who don't find it within themselves to respect the beliefs of other people ... they look at their religion as a special closed entity, with no room to learn from other cultures, and also look at themselves as the only righteous people going to Heaven.

Due to religions having a literary foundation, the limit of the religious heritage is not made up of specific transition points within the spectrum of mindsets per se. **The limit of the religious heritage is the difference between facts about the universe versus truths as preached by a specific religion.**

The limit manifests itself in the form of cognitive dissonance that a person can develop when they believe in a specific religious dogma whose beliefs are in contradiction to objective facts about nature or life. A quick example is how the main religions preach that when you die you will go to a place called Heaven and live forever in happiness. If this was a fact, many religious people would conspire to die so that they could go to heaven. In fact, the fundamentalist Muslims who blow themselves up in suicide attacks have exactly this religious belief, just like the rest of us who will never blow ourselves up. So even if the terrorists believe in their truth and they die for it, we have our own truth which we can't die for and in fact we judge their truth as false. So the argument about dying to go to a happy place called Heaven, just like many religious claims, is not about facts. It is solely about how you believe what your religion teaches you. If your religion teaches that when you die you will go to Heaven and have pizza every day for the rest of time, hey, you could find it within yourself to commit suicide so that you go and enjoy the endless pizza.

This issue of religions being about subjective truths as opposed to objective facts translates into religions being about "one's faith" but not so much about knowledge. Despite what religions preach about their faiths, they all started as acts of self-knowledge by their creators, not objective knowledge of the universe out there. Unfortunately, many believers of the respective religions don't appreciate that their faith is more about the self-knowledge of the creators of the religion, as opposed to being about the objective knowledge of the universe. This is the main reason why people debate the difference between religion and science. Science is the knowledge of the universe and how it works, so science is objective and any other human being can observe and carry out experiments to understand and own that knowledge. Even if there is a trace of scientific finding emanating from people's deep consciousness, those people present the findings in impartial mathematical sentences which any one can access without alluding to the creators. For example, when Isaac Newton discovered the equation of the universal law of gravity $F = ma$ (for which, on Earth, "a" is the acceleration felt by an object, which is 9.8 meters per second squared), whether you know him or not, whether you love him or hate him, it is possible for you to understand the proof of this equation through your own experiments. And this scientific knowledge is truly universal because it is true and can be verified in an experiment in Uganda, or Japan, or Iraq, and more powerfully, it can be verified on Earth, on the moon or on any other planet or star in the universe.

When you take religion as a source of objective knowledge, that's when you find many religious people end up having a God who does and knows many things, but over time gaps appear in their God's knowledge. Philosophers call such a religious God a "God of the Gaps". Here are three examples: 1) for hundreds of years religious people believed that slavery was allowed by God, but now people of those same religions say that God does not allow slavery; 2) for most of religious history, women have been looked at as unfit to be religious leaders, but now the modern religious person accepts that women are equal and can be leaders in divine works, and 3) for centuries people used to say that the punishment for adultery was death due to God's commandment, but now the average modern religious person cannot even think about killing an adulterous person. And when the terrorists put that belief in practice by stoning to death adulterers, we "non-extreme" people say that they are distorting the truth.

There are many other examples that show that over time, society or people have been able to fill gaps within the religious realm. It should be evident to a rational person that religions are not about objective knowledge, but rather about faith. And this faith has to be "blind faith." If it is not "blind faith," then you are on the way to an objective kind of knowledge which will lead you to science and the findings of modernity. What I mean is that when God says "you should kill the adulterer," you need to believe it universally without giving excuses. If you question the command, then it opens you up to scientific inquiry, and you should be brave enough to go all the way with scientific explanations.

At the root of religion as a source of knowledge is that it is knowledge of the self, just like art, psychology, and literature. However, science is knowledge of the environment outside one's self. Hence, when you are talking about things that are beyond one's self, you must use science. If you want to use religion to explain things outside one's self, it only works under coercion or forced belief.

Besides religions filling the gaps of "their God's knowledge" over time, the other way that they try to argue in defense of religion being about knowledge is that religion uses allegory and metaphor, so you should not take it literally. But that is not true. It is only allegory and metaphor for people who can read and write, and especially people who can read and write in sophisticated ways. There is no way religion is just a metaphor and allegory, for when my illiterate relatives or the poorly-educated fools in our societies hear that "God created the world in six days," they think specifically about Monday to Saturday. The idea that six days could mean the 14 billion years of the universe is a privilege of us, the educated class. No small wonder that when these illiterate and poorly-educated people hear "slay the infidels," they literally go to war on behalf of their God.

On the flip side, if indeed religious texts are to be taken solely as allegory and metaphor, then people are at liberty to also conclude that when religion says you will go to Heaven, it is not a physical place but rather "a feeling of bliss one can feel here on Earth." If you start reasoning using metaphor versus literal meanings, you get into a small corner which can only be occupied by people like us, who are privileged to know the difference between metaphor and literal, and maybe we are less than 1% of the world population. Indeed, there are very few people in this world who understand what allegory or metaphor means. To the overwhelming majority of religious believers, God's commands need to be taken literally. So when a terrorist kills "infidels," he can find justification in his holy scriptures. When you tell him, "That applied in the seventh century, but not in the twenty-first century," who of you is now the one following the true message from God?

This kind of debate leads us to wonder why we don't admit that religious texts were written when humans had a very limited scope of natural knowledge. The more natural knowledge we have, the more the religious texts become irrelevant or we need to update them. Maybe we need God to reveal his words anew using more correct language and concepts. For example, God saying that, "Man should spread to the four corners of the world," is less correct and should be updated to, "Man should spread to the whole surface area of this sphere called Earth." Such a command would not arouse any debate about objective fact versus subjective truths, nor a debate whether 4,000 years ago God did or didn't know that the Earth was a sphere. Upgrading of religion could also be extended to the acknowledgment of historical biases like the one that has Jesus always depicted as a white, blue-eyed, blonde-haired man (sounds more from Sweden than the Middle East). We all know that there is a very slim chance that a Middle-Eastern person in the desert of 2,000 years ago would be as blonde and blue-eyed as the historical pictures we see of Jesus. With an updated sense of religion, no one would really feel offended if officially we started drawing Jesus as a non-white person.

As I said above, if religious people start using science as evidence for their beliefs, then they need to be brave enough to go all the way. For example, if you have been believing that the first people created by God were the Biblical couple Adam and Eve in the Middle East, then when DNA evidence shows you clearly that the first humans lived about 200,000 years ago (not 6,000) in Africa, you should be brave enough to doubt the objective knowledge not only of "Adam and Eve" but of the entire enterprise of "revealed knowledge from God."

Nothing in the revealed books of the past is as complex and awesome as some of the discoveries we are making in the modern age. For example, the discovery of DNA – the signature of our biology, which is so complex and so complete as far as telling the story of how living things really are – can easily lead people to ask themselves, "If God is omniscient, how come he did not reveal DNA in his revealed books of the past?" It is the simple questions like the above that lead many people who are mature in rationality to deny the existence of God as revealed in the past books. This is because they can easily conclude that all the things written in ancient books about God are simple hypotheses about life and the universe, not the truly awesome complex discoveries that we now know about life and the universe. In fact, when you read about the suspension of the laws of nature in the scriptures, AKA miracles, like when entities called "angels" appear always "as white people," or that some human being can fly into Heaven in violation of gravity, or that someone can walk on water in violation of natural laws about density, these assertions are not any different from oral assertions by tribal people that the first man came from the mountain, a sacred river came about from tears of a princess, that rulers descended from Heaven with their cows, or that the Japanese descended from the sun. If you can suspend logic and believe the written accounts, you should be brave enough to suspend logic and believe the tribal teachings too.

Some religious people's defense is that God works in mysterious ways, or that God's revealed books are actually allegorical with much deeper understanding to be inferred. If that is the case, then you have to accept that all the people that do evil in God's name are justified because to them they had the right to interpret the allegorical words as they saw fit.

My religious heritage, just like the vast majority of Ugandans (about 85%), is Christianity. There are tenets about Christianity that can lead to cognitive dissonance and moral dilemmas if one does not separate objective facts from the "truths as perceived only by Christianity." For example, when Christianity teaches that only Christians will go to Heaven, I used to suffer psychological nightmares thinking about how all my good Muslim friends would not go to Heaven. This became worse when I became friends with other people who were not religious at all. However, as I grew and saw so many evil things done by some Christians, I started getting confused about how come those bad Christians would end up in Heaven. In my mind I would rather not be in Heaven with such bad Christians, but instead be with my non-Christian friends who were dear to me. To make it even more confusing, when I would look at the peacefulness, good behaviors or the tolerance towards other people that my non-Christian friends exhibited, again I would go through psychological agony over their eternal plight because they would not end up sitting in Heaven with me.

It is only when I was old enough and had read many other sources of knowledge (besides the Christian Bible) that I realized that there are other "truths" that non-Christians believe in. For example, the Muslim truth is that only true Muslims will go to heaven / paradise. The Hindu truth is that when one dies, one does not go to heaven but rather re-incarnates as some other creature, until after several reincarnations, that person would fuse into the ultimate universal consciousness. Whereas each religion preaches their truth that only their followers will go to heaven, the objective fact is that all peoples – whether religious or not – will die, but no human knows what exactly happens after death. Through my readings I was able to understand that there is a big difference between facts of nature / life and truths as preached by a specific religion. One hindrance that keeps many people from realizing this is that religious heritage is taken by many people to be more about personal identity with the group than a way of thinking about the facts of nature. As such, religions lead to in-group loyalty and out-group hostility that prevent human beings from becoming truly universal and spiritual. When this happens, followers start preaching that their religion is beyond criticism. Even when some of their fellow followers act in uncivilized and savage ways, followers are blinded by in-group loyalty not to see that the actual source of the savagery is people's belief that their "religious truth" is a "universal fact."

When facts of nature are presented that are in contradiction with religious belief, many believers just decide to ignore the facts in order to keep their personal identity with the religious group. However, it is only when you understand the difference between religious truths and objective facts that you can then use the facts to comprehend the limit of the religious heritage. And only when you comprehend the limit will you be in a position to understand the fundamental laws of the universe.

It is unfortunate that when you reach this limit, i.e. being able to understand the difference between objective facts of the universe and the truth of your religious heritage, you have to swear an oath of silence. Only you and your God know the difference. It is similar to what the Chinese Taoists believe when they say, "The tao that can be told is not the eternal tao." This is sad, because as a civilization it translates into people being afraid to speak up about the evils in religion. As I said at the end of the chapter about Western civilization, "fear" is one of the two factors that lead to the collapse of a civilization. In history we read about people who were brave enough to go against the prevailing culture and collective consciousness (examples are Zoroaster, Gautama Buddha, Jesus and Mohammad). In the process those people progressed human civilization into the future and their teachings are what started some of the most important religions of the world.

Nowadays we follow religions that reference those brave people of the past. Those brave souls were able to bring forth moral teachings into the world as a result of their heightened consciousness. Their teachings, which we call religions, started as sparks of consciousness, or what we call spiritual experiences with the divine. Unfortunately, many of us religious followers never have any spiritual experiences of the divine as we blindly follow historical teachings. We attach to religions for personal identity and social power, yet true spirituality that dwells on God has nothing to do with power and personal identity, but all to do with universal consciousness. We only use our rationality to follow traditions of religions, usually in ways that are devoid of spiritual significance because it is only spiritual consciousness that can lead us to the eternal source or God, which those founders were able to experience. Even if those founders experienced God at a certain time in history, because God is beyond time, it is only when you have spiritual experiences for yourself that you realize how, instead of looking backwards to historical events the way religions teach, you should just use your consciousness so God can manifest in the present.

When you reach the limit of the religious heritage, you start exhibiting transcendence and universal compassion towards all peoples, especially those who don't believe in your religion. The people who can't reach this limit are 100% enslaved by their "religious truths," and they never subscribe to the silent oath. Instead they go out in the public square (or on social media) to advocate for their religious truths. Worse, some of them go to the extent of forcing other peoples to accept their religious truth, or kill other people for not accepting their religious truths.

If you understand the limit but do not take the silent oath, then you reach out to the public through satire and parody. A good example of this is South Park's[7] take on religion, especially the episode about online religion, and "the Church of the Flying Spaghetti Monster," which parodies traditional religions by believing in its own God called the Flying Spaghetti Monster (FSM). Using the imagery of a god who is a cross between spaghetti and meat balls, the FSM engages in similar commands and behavior as the traditional gods that religions preach. When you analyze the humor in all this, it points to something very deep, which is that the creators of these two modern stories are indeed cognizant of the limit of religious heritage. In reminiscing about this limit, you need to appreciate that just because someone is serious about their belief in God, it does not mean they are righteous. Concurrently, just because someone is funny and goofy about God (FSM is a good example), it does not mean they can't teach deep religious lessons. I have seen many serious religious people take part in embezzlement of people's money, sexual abuse, even killing. On the other hand, I have witnessed many light-hearted funny people (who might not be religious) do a lot of noble things in this world.

In my discussion about the Islamic civilization, I mentioned how between 800 and 1100 AD the Islamic world was the center of human knowledge. It is important to note that even if the Jews and Christians have had the greatest contribution to human knowledge post thirteenth century; it is not specifically because their holy books are better. No. To my understanding it is largely because within the teaching of their religions, individuals are able to go beyond the limit of their holy texts. We know it is a fact that many Jewish and Christian societies were also categorically against progress in sciences (a good example is the story of Galileo), however within the teaching of Jewish Christian texts, individuals have had the courage to go against the grain and push the frontier of human knowledge.

Many have risked death or banishment from their community. A very good example of this is the young 24-year-old Jewish Dutchman Spinoza (see the sub-section "A brief discussion about God" for details on him) who had the courage to write a strong critique of his society, and specifically his Jewish religion, to the point that he was excommunicated by his community leaders. However, all humanity has benefited from Spinoza's audacity to point out something so fundamental that, even 300 years later, in his reflection about a cosmological spirituality, Einstein is quoted to have said he believed in Spinoza's idea of God, as opposed to the one forced on individuals by a powerful cultural machinery. It is no small matter that many intelligent people claim you cannot say you have read philosophy or understood Western knowledge unless you are versed in some of the insights that this twenty-something lad, Spinoza, wrote in the 1600s.

Since the burning of the House of Wisdom in Baghdad in the thirteenth century, it is because individuals within the Jewish / Christian tradition have been able to go beyond the limits of their religions that we have a situation where 10% of all Nobel winners have been non-religious (atheists, agnostics and freethinkers) despite these people having lived within the Western Jewish / Christian world.

The issue of transcending religious heritage in the arena of knowledge is very vital because as I mentioned in Chapter 7, with just 0.2% of the world population, the Jews have contributed so much to our human knowledge to the point that 20% of all Nobel laureates since inception and 22% in mathematics and the sciences have been of Jewish descent. I am mentioning this statistic because the foremost British biologist, Richard Dawkins, was quoted in 2013 saying he was bewildered that it is no small coincidence that Jews with such a tiny fraction of world population have won an overwhelmingly big chunk of Nobel prizes, especially within the natural sciences. A very clear illustration of the Jewish domination is that modern physics and a lot of the discoveries to do with nuclear knowledge were mastered and advanced by Jewish minds like Einstein, Bohr, etc., and modern psychology or the mapping of the human mind squarely sits on Jewish minds like Freud (the father of modern psychology). Any serious modern research about this objective fact does not conclude that this is because Jews are God's chosen people, or that they are superior to other humans. Rather it is because individuals within those heritages are able to transcend the limits of their heritages of birth. That is why someone like Einstein was able to turn down being the President of Israel in 1952, because to him his identity was more with the whole human race, not just his Jewish tribe of birth.

It is paramount that as a human race, we encourage our societies to transcend religious limits. We need to transcend limits on everything from women's place in society to the investigative inquiry of the natural world. As a young immature Christian, I used to argue with people about the wrong depictions of the Bible and of Jesus himself in modern times. But when I matured in knowledge, I reached a point where I am now able to watch movies that negatively depict Jesus (e.g. *The Last Temptation of Christ*) or read books bashing the religion, and for some reason I know that the people who make such material do so from their vantage point. They have the right to do that. And whatever they do has nothing to do with my beliefs or the validity of Jesus. I am now mature enough to know that there are two Jesuses: a historical Jesus and The Christ. While as the historical Jesus is fair game for critique (e.g. did he have a wife or not, was he white or black or brown, did he fake miracles or not), all those have nothing to do with The Christ. The Christ is all about spiritual knowledge and transcendence, which is 100% within the realm of personal subjective experiences. If you feel offended by the negative portrayal of Jesus, then you have not understood the difference between Jesus the historical man and Jesus the spiritual Messiah, and you surely do not understand the deep meaning of "the living Christ" or "the Christ consciousness."

You cannot talk about The Christ to non-spiritual people, because they have no faculty in their mind to comprehend. But for me I know that it is the distinction between the two facets of Jesus that make him no longer a Jewish male, but rather a universal malleable symbol. People have even given him feminine traits, and many diverse societies have claimed him as their own. For example, there is an Asian Jesus I saw in a Korean text who had Asian facial features, I have seen a black Jesus among black people, and of course the blue-eyed blonde Jesus among Europeans. All the different images of Jesus are localized (for the Europeans, for the Asians, for black people, etc.) because The Christ is different from the historical Jesus. This acute difference is an example of knowing the difference between "objective facts" and "religious truths" and when you do, by definition you have gone beyond the limiting aspects of the religious heritage.

When we can reach the limit of the religious heritage, we can't forget the biggest benefit that the monotheistic traditions of the Western civilization have brought to the world in general and Uganda in particular. The benefit is that of enhancing our development of consciousness by exacting our minds. While our forefathers' beliefs in many gods (polytheism) or in a general god without specific attributes (the predominant tribal belief) created a type of consciousness, that consciousness is not as strong as the one emanating from the belief in one God. It is the difference in minds that I discussed in Chapter 8, i.e. an exacting concentrated consciousness akin to the one that came about at the breakdown of the bicameral mind when people started reading (which the monotheistic traditions bring to us, unlike the tribal traditions) versus a general porous mind which can't even transcend the limit of the tribal heritages.

It is only if we adopt a modern mind frame that we can understand modern science and the implied true knowledge within the Western religions in such a way that we adopt only the good, without the bad. Trust me, there are a multitude of bad things within these Western religions that can play a big role in enfeebling people's minds or leading people to commit all kinds of evil. But potentially, there is a lot of good which you can only get out when you are able to rightfully critique religions.

On your journey to understanding the limit of the religious heritage, it is important to know the difference between religions and cults. Cults are religious organizations whose devotion is more toward an individual and inducement toward dying than a spiritual transcendence or divine reality. For example, we read in history that when Christianity started, it was a cult. People were following it mainly because of specific beliefs about Jesus the person. However, over the years Christianity became a religion whereby, as exemplified in modern times, it is not so much about reverence of the person Jesus but more about "the good news." The good news is the set of good teachings that Jesus espoused, which can inspire you to live a noble Christian life without emotionally attaching yourself to the fine details of Jesus the man. For example, when you consider Jesus' only violent act to be that of chasing traders away from the temple of God, a true believer can't find reason there to be a warmonger, but instead they follow Jesus' teaching of "love thy enemy." So if we understand the religious heritage beyond the cult of the founder, we as a human race will find it easier to transcend our religions of birth so that we only hold onto the good messages from the religions, and not have merely emotional attachments to the person who started the religion.

Islam and Christianity are the most prone to turning into cults, because they are the two religions that claim God Almighty revealed himself through a human being. Judaism doesn't claim that, and all the other non-Abrahamic religions don't claim that. When this cult transition happens, religious followers focus largely on their emotions toward the person of Jesus or Mohammad, rather than spirituality toward The Eternal Source. I have met women who talk about Jesus in terms of loving him like a woman loves a man – it is no longer about enlightenment and spiritual transcendence. I have met Muslims who talk about Mohammad the way cult followers emotionally defend their leader. When looked at this way, religions actually prevent their followers from enlightening their consciousness, or rather they work to prevent the human spirit from reaching out to the God Source. It is only an enlightened consciousness that can go beyond the human mediums of religious knowledge to focus solely on the universal Eternal Source, or what many call God.

In order to go beyond the limit of religions, you need to appreciate the equality of the sexes in accessing spiritual knowledge and leadership. It is not enough that out of the triple heritages, it's only the religious heritage that has exclusion of women from certain positions or from behaving in a certain way. In tribal settings, women are enormous spiritual leaders in all kinds of ways. In the Western heritage, women are leaders in society (prime ministers, presidents and equal in numbers at universities). Even in research and science, women are increasingly well represented. I was amazed at the number of women at MIT; women were visible in all facets of that technical institute regarded as the best technical school of higher learning in the world. In the religious heritage, it becomes headline news when women can become bishops and pastors or rabbis in Judaism. It should not be such a rarity.

Note on a mental imagination

The following is the abstract thinking that led me to conceive the concept of the limit of the religious heritage. If you don't appreciate the above lines of reasoning, try engaging in the below thinking exercise.

The main religion in the world, which I happened to be born into by random circumstances, is Christianity. I say random because had I been born among the family of our neighbors in Iganga town to the left or to the right of our house, I would have been born in a Muslim family. So I am a Christian, 100% because I was raised that way. There are Christians who convert into the religion, but that is not my story.

My religion of birth preaches that God inspired Moses to write the first books of the Bible, but historians show that there are four sources for the books attributed to Moses: the Yahwist, the Elohist, the Deuteronomist, and the Priestly strain. This means that despite what tradition says, there might not have been an actual figure called

Moses. The traditional belief is borrowed from the Jewish teachings. Nonetheless, for argument's sake, let me believe that God inspired a man called Moses to write down the first books of the Bible. All accounts point to an authorship date between 1400 BC and 600 BC.

When you look at it both from a Biblical point of view, about Creation or the scientific point of view about the origin of man, both ways lead you to realize that for many thousands of years God did not have any word or command written down. No one knows the length of the silent time between Adam (the first man) and Moses (the first person to write God's word) or the silent time between the first human in Africa to the time of Moses, but according to current biology, the first humans arose in Africa between 200,000 years to 500,000 years ago. So the silent period could be as long as 500,000 years. During those silent years, Adam and his offspring or the first African and his offspring lived without a written account from God. Even when Jesus came, the most important person for Christians, he lived on this Earth for about 33 years, but did not write down anything. It is about 30 years after his death that someone (who people called Mark) first wrote down Jesus' story. So, during Jesus' time, God speaking through Jesus did not see it fit to write down Jesus' message. That silent period in Jesus' case was more than 63 years – the length of time between Jesus' birth and the first writing about his life.

Why didn't Adam or his offspring write down anything? Why didn't Jesus write down anything? To me it is revealing that 1) God's message, as Jesus had it, did not have to be written down, and 2) all the people who lived before Moses did not have to rely on written word. Pass forward to 2016, what makes any of us sure that God's message can't come down today by non-written method? Or in other words, since you realize that man had to write down God's message thousands of years after God created the first man or decades after Jesus died, isn't it only self-evident that the men who finally wrote down God's message might have made some errors of omission or commission? Maybe due to human error, the people who wrote about Jesus missed something or wrote something incorrectly? If you don't possess this train of doubting thoughts, then you find yourself reading the holy book literally and we all know where literal reading of the word of God has led mankind (see Chapter 6 in my first book *The Fourth Heritage* for a detailed discussion of God and morality).

The more plausible and liberating explanation, given the above critique into God's word, is that maybe God can communicate his message to you and me even today, without it being written down!

To really gravitate toward comprehending the limit of the religious heritage, you have to open your mind's eye to the fact that when people do write down God's message, because of human fallibility, there is need for you to rely on the prerequisites of the Heri of Kesa to analyze whether what anyone says is God's written word. You cannot just believe that something is God's word just because it is written.

In summary, we have to conclude that God worked with people for thousands of years before writing was ever invented, and so he can still reveal himself and his ways to you or to anyone in this present day and time in an unwritten way. And as such, it becomes your duty to search for the facts about life / nature and separate them from your subjective truth as preached by your own religion of birth, which could possibly be erroneous.

The Limit of the Western Heritage

The Western Heritage in regard to my heritage of birth is the British colonial experience. Just like other colonized people, the Europeans had an enormous effect on me and my destiny in that they created the entity called the nation-state of Uganda, they set the physical boundaries of the country, installed English as the language of national communication, set up the nature of government and the type of law in the country, created the education system we use, etc. In a way, it is the Western colonial experience that ultimately has led me to interact with the wide world, for good or for bad, to the point that I am writing to you in the English language.

It causes great cognitive dissonance every time people like me open our minds to deny the ubiquitous extent of the Western heritage in all facets of our lives. The people who deny that reality also always end up blaming the colonialists for the reason we are underdeveloped. But as I have said before, there are many other people who were colonized but have been able to grow modern mindsets and are actually also developed peoples just like their former colonizers. Examples are the USA, Singapore, etc. Specifically, when you go through our education system learning more about European history, science and literature than anything about any of our tribes or other African countries, you really find yourself under a great intellectual hypocrisy every time you open your mouth to blame colonialism for our problems.

By and large, the inconvenient truth is that we non-Western peoples have failed to create any system that is truly indigenous and independent from the Western influence; not in religion, not in the models of the nation-state, not in language, and not in education, to mention just a few. Because of this reality, by definition when you are born in our African countries, or any other Third World place, the historical burden makes it so that you live not so much with agency, but rather as a product that the Western world created. Trying to achieve agency in our thinking or the social set up of our economies and societies becomes a herculean task that most of us don't even try to contemplate. And this means settling into a defeatist existence where your mind is programmed to feel inferior to white people / Europeans and you have an insatiable urge to blame them for every shortcoming within our societies. For those who don't capitulate quickly, they think deeply about it, but it is a source of great psychological repulsion and shame. Many turn this psychological conundrum into anger toward "the white man" or the outside world. And unfortunately even many of our leaders and writers also exhibit this anger.

This psychological struggle can consume some people for life, and they live emotionally supercharged lives characterized by anger towards the colonial masters, but unfortunately this anger is at the expense of them living peacefully with sober minds that can create things and ideas which could truly help our peoples to understand the wider world. Putting aside the negative repercussions of the colonial experience, we sometimes forget that the colonialists also gave us great tools by which we can understand the rest of the world, e.g. the tool of the international languages, alphabets, religions, etc. We should keep our indigenous languages, because they are invaluable repositories of our human souls. However, it is the international languages like English and French that have a tremendous amount of power and source of learning in the world.

Whomever speaks a language like English has tremendous advantage when conducting any business in this world or learning state-of-the-art knowledge through computers. It is the language used at the best universities in the world, and most of the scientific research writings every single year – writings that have the repository of what man is discovering and creating in the present time – are largely in English. So if you speak only a tribal language, you can't be privy to cutting edge findings in molecular biology or the latest discovery about DNA.

The Western Latin alphabet is the cornerstone of computer programming, and since computers run every facet of the modern world, what a disadvantage we would be at if we did not understand and use the Latin alphabet. Maybe we could have developed alternatives, but the fact that currently we are not developing alternatives to the Latin alphabet means that it has great intrinsic value.

Nonetheless, the more we are entrenched in the English language and other facets of the Western civilization, the more we cut ourselves off from speaking our mother tongues and the more we lose many of our traditional cultures and norms. Therefore, I came to the conclusion that the limit of the Western heritage in our current modern world is that even if we have the possibility of understanding the rest of the world better and also learning what the human brain can learn regarding the fundamental laws of the universe, all this comes at the expense of us being uprooted from our indigenous heritages.

In other words, **the limit of the Western heritage is the beginning of a psychological eternal dilemma** (see Chapter 10 for the African example). Note that here I use the second definition for the word "limit."

Summary about the limits

I am not against tribal, religious or Western ideologies and ways of being. They are needed and they have potential for being used for good. However, the tribal and religious heritages must be constrained by a secular state. They can be sources of influence in society, but not actual power – that is the privilege of the secular state. Without this, these two have the potential to turn into barbarism and primitivism. The state must require its citizens to split their existence into private and public parts; this means citizens are obliged to justify their political views (which are in the public domain) exclusively in non-religious terms, while at the same time they are given freedom in their private lives to live per their conscience by exercising their independent religious convictions.

The onus on us is to ensure that the secular state provides universal education and freedom so that each individual will grow to understand the limits. When the limits are understood, the individual will be able to shun all negativity within each heritage and hold on to that which has the potential to be a source of positive morality and positive sense of community.

Convergence of Consciousness & Rationality

In the definition part of this chapter, I mentioned that the second leg of the Heri of Kesa encompasses how consciousness is the other half of the mental state that can allow a person to understand the fundamental laws of the universe. The first leg is the rational one. It is important to note that the fundamental laws of the universe are written down in a language that is rational. Even if they can be arrived at by consciousness, the language they are written in is mathematics – which falls squarely on the rational leg of the Heri of Kesa. Keep in mind that the laws I am referring to are those that all humans and all objects, whether on Earth or in any part of the universe, are governed by (basically anything that is in the universe as we have come to know it).

So the fundamental laws will not be about society or religion or politics or anything that each culture comes up with. It is a known fact that, by definition, whatever each culture comes up with, as long as it is ethnocentric (i.e. narration that presumes that the particular cultural group telling the story is special), it cannot be universally fundamental. For this reason, nothing in society or religion or politics is fundamental as far as the natural universe is concerned. For example, if you think democracy is fundamental, there are examples of undemocratic practices that can be shown to bring about good outcomes for a society. If democracy was fundamental, then undemocratic societies would not have any desirable outcomes, but history is full of undemocratic societies that have lots of good going on. For example, imperial Britain did a lot of good for the human civilization, yet it used to have a divine monarchy. If you single out only the bad within the undemocratic societies, you should also pick out the bad within the democratic societies and realize that democracy does not phase out bad outcomes, just as undemocratic societies are not void of good outcomes. Hence, democracy as a social value is not fundamental.

The fundamental laws I am talking about are those that are expressed by the pinnacle of human rationality, i.e. mathematics. Without losing the reader, I will not use any mathematical language but will talk about examples of them using the English language. Apologies to those who have studied beyond elementary mathematics and physics; you might find the following examples too trivial.

One such example is the law of gravity. Whether you like it or not, whether you know it or not, it is a law that if you jump up you must come down. Another example, also discovered by Isaac Newton, is the law of action and reaction: when you act with a force on something, there is an equal and opposite reaction to your action. All laws of nature have specific mathematic sentences (equations) that any person can read or calculate to know how the law governs nature. There are dozens of fundamental laws of nature, and my thesis is that for any human being, especially us who are products of the triple heritages, the only way we can get to understand them is by going beyond our tribal-religious heritages. If you think even for a minute that these laws can be found in religious reasoning, then you are using a definition of religion that is different.

For me there is a fundamental law that intrigued me ever since I was young. I remember I used to look up in the sky in my town Iganga at the planes passing, and it intrigued my mind how they could fly without flapping their wings. Around 10 or 11 years old, I remember fidgeting with some big books at our neighbor's home and one of the older sons there (who had studied some advanced physics) tried to explain to me that the planes are able to fly due to some natural law called "Banusi" principle (I later learnt it is actually written Bernoulli's principle). Roaming the dirty roads of Iganga and playing in the nearby forests with my friends as we hunted small birds with our slingshots, or stole telephone copper wires to create our toy cars, we kept coming up with all kinds of stupid explanations about how planes can fly. I remember at one point we used to think they were created by God.

When I was at university and we studied Bernoulli's equations in fluid mechanics, the mental feeling I experienced was akin to an epiphany, a spiritual experience. Just like that, I connected that those mathematical equations were what we were hypothesizing about in the forest of Iganga town with my boyhood friends. I vividly remember getting back to my room and crying tears of joy. For the first time, within my hands, within my abilities, I could understand the mathematics of a fundamental universal law that back in my teenage years seemed like "planes flying without wings" was a miracle of God. That event reminded me of the ancient Greek, Archimedes, who ran out from his bathtub naked into the street shouting, "Eureka! Eureka!" or, "I understand it! I understand it!" when he had his "aha" moment. When you understand the natural principle (derived from Isaac Newton's natural laws of motion and the natural law of conservation of energy) that describes how the pressure difference between the lower and the upper parts of a plane's wing causes a specific lift force that carries the plane in the air, it is such a triumph of the human mind in dissecting the way the universe works.

There are so many laws of nature that I have been fortunate enough to understand because I have studied mathematics and the natural sciences. Up to now my reminiscence about those laws brings a kind of euphoric awe, similar to what I used to get when I was deeply entrenched in my tribal and religious paradigms. While kids from Europe and America can study these laws of nature and never have any ecstatic feelings or experiences, for a kid like me born in an African village to two illiterate parents, it meant and still means something more than a rational exercise. It touched my consciousness. And it is from such deep emotional experiences, which are both in the remits of consciousness and rationality, that I have been able to create the idea of the convergence of rationality and consciousness.

I hope the reader now appreciates what I alluded to at the beginning of my discussion about mathematics, i.e. that if I had a way I would will for it to be a human right for everyone to study some kind of mathematics up to calculus. Everyone, including girls. It is not fair that many school girls in most traditional societies are rendered to reading only language and humanities subjects, while the boys are the ones who study mathematics and natural sciences. I feel great inspiration understanding the mathematics that explains complexities of nature, and I am sure if we had a country where the average person understood such basic tenets of nature, that country would be devoid of gullible citizens who are deceived by the low-level religious conmen who masquerade as men of God.

The fact is that the fundamental laws are written down and are communicated rationally. However, there are so many examples where it is illustrated that the knowledge of those laws came to the people who wrote them down by an "aha" moment, which by definition is a flash of consciousness. For example, when they say that Isaac Newton came up with his law of gravity when he saw a falling apple or when they say Archimedes came up with his principle when he was in a bathtub, all these and many other examples allude to the fact that understanding can come to people in a flash, not just through long drawn-out research (a rational activity). This flash is instantaneous and it falls in the sphere of consciousness. So someone can first become aware of a phenomenon in nature by way of consciousness, and then afterward they use language, which is a rational tool, to communicate to the rest of humankind what the knowledge is. The way religions start is a very clear example of this; their founders, after having a flash of consciousness – which they described as a divine encounter with God – go and lay out descriptive guidelines of behavior for their followers.

However, whatever knowledge someone comes about by way of a flash of consciousness has to have a mathematical angle to it in order for it to be deemed a fundamental knowledge of nature. If it stops at just being written in social cultural languages like Luganda, or English or Arabic, by definition whatever that person is saying is not fundamental, but rather it is biased in favor of the language and peoples they are among. The person writing that knowledge might not know that his writings are not fundamental and he might erroneously argue that they are, but the real fact is that nothing is fundamental unless it has a mathematical representation and it is beyond the language and people of one's birth. It has to be able to be understood fully by other people who don't speak the creator's social language. And by mathematical representation I mean either equations or geometrical shapes that have mathematical descriptions, e.g. a circle has a mathematical equation that describes it.

For propagation purposes, one needs to have a minimum level of rationality in order to grasp the proper laws of the universe, even if you have a heightened level of consciousness. Some examples to illustrate this are as follows: 1) if rationally you don't know that the Earth is round – maybe you still believe that it is flat because that is what your God commanded you to believe – no matter how enlightened your consciousness gets, you will not understand the fundamental law of nature regarding the force of gravity which governs the shapes and arrangements of heavenly bodies like planet Earth and every star in the universe; 2) if you cannot rationally differentiate the word "Earth" from "universe," or "mass" from "weight" or "force" from "energy," however developed your consciousness is, you can't grasp the natural law of conservation of mass – knowledge of how energy can never be created or destroyed, but it merely changes from one form to another forever; 3) theoretical physics is largely based on consciousness, e.g. Einstein's theories were first deduced by his abstract thinking, which is a rational activity, but if you consider the interplay between thoughts and the unconscious mind, it is fair to say that the source of the thoughts themselves was not the rational mind. However, it is only when he rationally put mathematical equations down to everything that other people accepted his theories via objective experiments; 4) music by and large is created by people's consciousness, but then if they can put math to it, e.g. the classical symphonies by the European greats, then it becomes a rational composition which other humans can consume by reading sheet music; and 5) people who start religions do it as a result of a personal experience of consciousness, but if they are not able to write it down and make sense so that others can use rationality to understand what their message from the divine is, then they can be left to be called "loonies" or "crazy" or "cult leaders". However, if they put a rational model of theology together, then it can be positively accepted by other people and that is how religions take shape in society.

Below is a simple model that shows how people understand life or nature around them and also within themselves. Rationality and consciousness are the twin tools that people swim in in an effort to understand life, nature or the universe.

Rationality ⇒	God
Education, Social systems, religions	⇕
Consciousness ⇒⇐	Consciousness
Cultural traditions, Spirituality, Being	

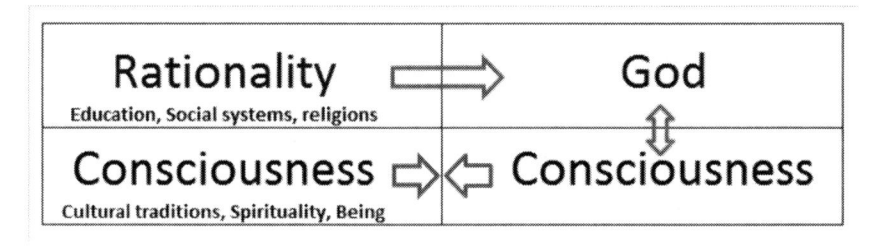

Figure 6: Convergence Model of Understanding Life

Consciousness leg: Even before someone can think, e.g. when still in the womb, they become conscious. When someone is finally born, their consciousness propagates their being through innate faculties in the brain. And outwardly, through cultural traditions, that person becomes an entity of the human family. The reach of consciousness ranges from the singular personal consciousness of the individual up to the union between that individual and the entire universe or the union of each individual consciousness with the universal consciousness, or God, or the ultimate source.

Rationality leg: From childhood, as the brain develops, the cognitive faculties in the cerebrum are developed and through social systems like education and religion one's rationality is further progressed. But as Immanuel Kant posited, and William James also affirmed, the limit of rationality is the beginning of God.

Hence, both the consciousness leg and the rationality leg converge in the entity called "God" and whether you define it as a supreme being, or an ultimate reality, or "the force in the universe" is just a small detail for us advanced primates. One can also call it the Ultimate Source or the Source Spirit. The limit of rationality determines the boundary of secular humanism, beyond which humanity has to obey the dictates of the universal consciousness, or God.

The issue of consciousness versus rationality has divided the world since time immemorial. For example, during the European enlightenment, philosophy was divided into two schools: that of the rationalists and that of the empiricists. You can say that empiricists really were advocating for consciousness as the main driving force of the human condition, because all experiences, by definition, emanate within one's consciousness, not abstract rationality. And all the major philosophers of that era could be divided into those two camps. On the rationalist side you have Descartes, Spinoza, Leibniz, etc., while in the empiricist camp you have the likes of Hume, Locke, John Stuart Mill, Bertrand Russell, etc. Kant played a major role in explaining a convergence of both schools. This dichotomy has also been created in modern democratic societies where at maturity the political parties settle into two large categorizations, either a conservative camp (more rationalists, and based on cold facts about society even if they are unpleasant facts) and a liberal camp (more concerned with the collective consciousness of the nation or humanity, more biased toward brotherhood even at the expense of the objective truth sometimes).

Heck, maybe this dichotomy is indeed a natural way of things, because even the brain is also divided into two: the left hemisphere (more analytical and logical, or you can say rational) and the right hemisphere (more creative and intuitive, or you can say it is more in tune with consciousness). So it is no controversy when you see the differences in the sexes, where women are more right-brained, hence more in tune with human consciousness, while men are more left-brained, hence more rational (how can I say this without seeming sexist? ... what I mean to say is that men tend to have more opportunities to develop the rational part of their brain). It seems it's natural that some of us see the world through rational eyes, while others are inclined to see it with eyes of consciousness. It all depends on which hemisphere of your brain you cultivate and develop. There are some who are able to see the world in a balanced way, but it takes a lot of effort to reach that state of mind.

So given this natural dichotomy, we are left with hoping that God can rescue us from ourselves by converging our opposing natures.

A Brief Discussion About God:

God is unknowable, or at best unknown. Throughout history people have approached God in one of two ways: 1) acknowledging God and stopping at that – this is the Creator or what my tribe calls Kibbumba or Katonda, or 2) using their social-cultural lenses to create images and attributes of God – this is the created God. So there is the Creator God, and then there is a created God.

My people, the Basoga, just like millions of other indigenous peoples who did not write down their ideas of God, fall into the first camp. When I was young and my grandmothers talked of Kibbumba or Katonda, they would never spend even a second talking about the specific attributes of God. The Creator God is truly unknowable and can only be described as a cosmological reality that is the source of everything, or the Spirit Source. When you find two people arguing or debating about God, they are not talking about the Source God who is unknowable, but rather they are talking about the anthropomorphically created God to whom they apply ethnocentric human images and attributes. This is largely because when two people argue about God, by definition they are using rationality, yet God is beyond rationality and 100% within the realm of consciousness. You cannot use your subjective conviction to persuade someone about the real Source God; each person has to have a personal subjective experience of God. Without that experience, it is futile if not useless to even start discussing the subject matter.

A very important aspect of God is that the Source God is eternal and also everlasting. Very often people usually interchange the meanings of these two words, and even dictionaries (which are created by language experts) also interchange the meaning of the two words. However, if the dictionaries were created by spiritual experts e.g. Joseph Campbell, they would give different meanings of the two words. Something can be eternal without being everlasting, and the opposite is also true; something can be everlasting without being eternal. Eternal means beyond space and time, while everlasting means unending passage of time, or forever.

Eternal is instantaneous, it connotes infinitesimal and intense and it is a multi-dimensional flow. Everlasting is within the four dimensions, and it progresses from one, two, to infinity. While eternity connotes value, a window into knowing, into changing and into multi-dimensional reality, everlasting connotes no value because it is passivity, it is meaningless because even infinity is a meaningless passivity. Remember in Chapter 1 I discussed in great detail how the thing called "time" is actually nothing. Time has no properties or qualities you can talk of, the way you talk about the qualities of space, or matter, or mass. Time is just a measuring tool for events. So when someone says this thing is everlasting, it means they are saying that there is an event that lasts from one, two to infinity durations. But there is no event like that. So when they say God is everlasting, which is true – as I have just explained, it is the only thing that qualifies for everlasting; note that God is not an event but rather a form of being. So the only thing that is everlasting, God, is actually only everlasting when you change the definition of everlasting to mean "ever-being," since in actuality there is no event whose passage we are to measure forever.

Whereas you can have an "aha" moment and grasp a concept (an example of an eternal reality), doing something forever is meaningless. For example, think of the best thing you can ever do: it has great value when you do it, but keep doing it over a longer period of time, and then it starts losing the value. This is because by natural law, any progression either increases, decreases or stays the same – and there is no event that can stay the same for infinite progression. Even when people talk about "living forever," they are actually talking about "being forever" which could be possible because "being" is not "an event," and therefore, when you just be, maybe you can be forever – but don't talk about doing any event during that "existing forever."

Consequently, when you talk of things like Heaven or Hell or any other thing which people put in the spiritual realm, they have to be talked about in terms of eternity, not unending time. And since humans live within this four dimensional space-time, we have authority to talk about only those things within the four dimensions. When it comes to the Creator God who is the only entity to be both eternal and everlasting, beyond the four dimensions, the best we can do is fool ourselves by reflecting human qualities onto what can't be reflected upon. A good example is because of our living within the time dimension, when we ascribe specific qualities of God based on this time or that time, e.g. in this year God did this, this is an exercise in anthropomorphic mental acrobatics. If God really did something in the past, because of the eternity quality, God can do that same thing in the present and in the future, and what that means is that you have to ascribe the same value to the past as the present as the future. It is wrong that society usually puts more value on the past. There is no event or person in the past that is more important than you here in the present. So, connect with The Eternal Source now and here, and you will be the best that you were created to be.

To further develop the above discussion, knowing the difference between objective facts and religious truths (see the limit of the religious heritage) is similar to knowing the difference between the unknowable God and the created God. Knowing this difference is the key that qualifies you to debate the issue of God. The debate between the unknowable or unknown God and the created God is the debate that Spinoza engaged in the 1600s that led to his excommunication from the Jewish community. When Einstein says he believes in Spinoza's God, he means that Spinoza acknowledged the existence of the Source God who is also acknowledged by all indigenous peoples that were dominated by the Islamic and Western civilizations. Einstein, even if as a scientist was maybe the greatest human mind of the twentieth century, actually acknowledged Spinoza's world view when he said, "I believe in Spinoza's God, who reveals himself in the harmony of all that exists, not in a God who concerns himself with the fate and the doings of mankind."

Spinoza says there are two types of God. The first is one who is universal and every human being, by virtue of living, is a testament to his existence because "what is, and whatever can be" is in God. That is the God my grandparents or my tribe believed in and I inherited that belief. Since the greatest rational philosopher Spinoza believed in that God, following his meticulous rational lines of thought, how far can my African rational mind take me? It is a no-brainer that my imperfect rational mind has also led me to acknowledge that God as the Eternal Source God. But Spinoza also goes on to describe a second God, the one created by each ethnic group, like his Jewish people. He says that God is a manmade God. For daring to raise his personal view about the two Gods, that unfortunate 24-year-old lad had stumbled upon an eternal truth that any thinking person is bound to struggle with, but that led him to face the wrath of his community. And if you hold any doubt about the power and depth of Spinoza's insight, ask yourself why, when he was excommunicated by his Jewish community, they cursed him with words that could have been mistaken as being directed at the Devil himself. The leaders of his community excommunicated him by declaring:

> By the decree of the angels, and by the command of the holy men, we excommunicate, expel, curse and damn Spinoza, with the consent of God, Blessed be He, and with the consent of all the Holy Congregation ... and with all the curses which are written in the Book of the Law. Cursed be he by day and cursed be he by night; cursed be he when he lies down, and cursed be he when he rises up; cursed be he when he goes out, and cursed be he when he comes in. We order that no one should communicate with him orally or in writing, or show him any favor, or stay with him under the same roof, or read anything composed or written by him.

With such a verbal thrashing from his elders and community, the poor lad was left to spend the rest of his life not able to be gainfully employed, he was expelled from Amsterdam by the municipal leadership, he never married, and died a lonely death but with his human spirit unbroken. What a giant of the human intellectual landscape! All of us, who are under the tyranny of any type of created God, have to thank heavens that such a soul ever graced this planet. And when you realize that nowadays, more than 300 years after his death, the Western intellectual world pays homage to him, one wonders, why does society always cut out its own members who dare to think differently, or contrary to the prevailing authority?

Traditionally, the societies that developed a writing culture have written about God or created an idea about God as an ultimate being in the universe who takes on human characteristics. The only people who write about God and give it attributes akin to the unknowable God are those with pantheistic views, e.g. some scientists. Einstein was quoted saying that, "God is the totality of all the laws of nature." In a way, if humanity takes scientists like Einstein as the true modern story tellers, then we have a chance of having the whole human race shun the manmade Gods, and instead acknowledge the real Eternal Source God. But as long as we know God from each society's ethnocentric writing, the Indians will keep having a God who is Indian, the Jews a God who is Jewish, and the Arabs a God who is very much a desert Arab God.

So when we have to discuss God according to the Heri of Kesa, the structure of that discussion is given in the below diagram.

```
                    ┌─ Believe in God ──→ theist, deist,
                    │                      polytheist, agnostic
         ┌ Rationality
         │          │
         │          └─ Don't Believe ──→ atheist, agnostic
  God ───┤
         │          ┌─ Acknowledge God ──→ pantheist,
         │          │                       Unknowable God
         └ Consciousness
                    │
                    └─ Don't acknowledge ──→ Unknown God
```

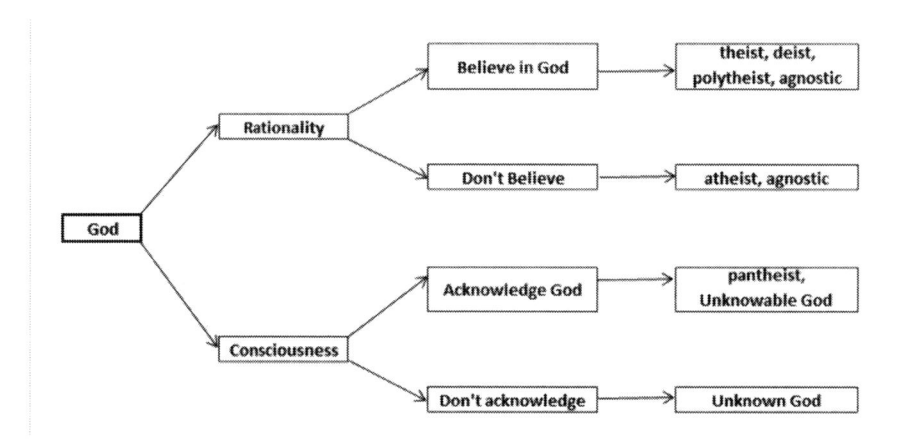

Figure 7: The Heri Discussion of God

The traditional way has been based on written accounts. This leads straight into a rationality-based discussion about God. Through rationality, people jump straight to the question, "Do you believe in God, yes or no?" If yes, you are a believer or a religious person. If no, you are a non-believer or non-religious person. If yes, and you believe God is a supernatural entity, you are a theist. If yes, but you believe God is purely a natural entity without supernatural attributes, you are a deist. If no, you are a non-believer or atheist. If you can't answer yes or no, or you answer yes or no but you accept that you don't know, you are an agnostic. Note that in this traditional way of discussing God, there is a thin line between the theist and atheist, e.g. the only difference between a Christian theist and an atheist is that even if they both don't believe in the thousands of non-Christian supernatural gods, it is just that the atheist goes one step further by not believing in Jesus, too.

Moving from the traditional to discussing God according to the Heri of Kesa, it can either be from an oral or written perspective. Either way, the discussion is 100% based on consciousness, which is to say that it is beyond reason. The relevant first question becomes, "Do you acknowledge the existence of God?" If "yes," you can be a spiritual or a non-spiritual person. Spiritual people are those who are pantheists, who believe that the whole universe and everything in it is divine, God is in everything. For the spiritual person, even if they have conscious experiences of God, it is a proviso that God is still an unknowable entity. For the non-spiritual people, they don't have the mental faculties to consciously experience God, so for them God is simply unknown. All indigenous peoples say "yes" and are spiritual. I have encountered people who are non-spiritual, i.e. they don't acknowledge God, but they are perfectly good members of our human family, and according to me, they still fall under the eternal dictates of the Source God, although they are not conscious of it.

If you are from a religious background and want to use Heri of Kesa to understand the Source God, you need to borrow the Danish religious philosopher Soren Kierkegaard's conclusion: "You have to take a leap of faith." You have to suspend reason. You have to decide to forfeit or lose your mind so that you can find "God." If you don't abandon reason, you end up being like one of those religious apologists who engage in mental gymnastics to rationalize that something white is actually black.

The most famous ethnocentric God we know of is that of the desert peoples in the Ancient Egyptian and Mesopotamia civilizations, "the Khabiru" or Hebrew people. They called God YHWH or Elohim (Elohim is actually a plural word, which means the initial writers actually meant "the gods," but in modern times its meaning has changed to a singular, hence we know it as the name for "one god"). They gave specific attributes to God, e.g. God is a male, God is jealousy, God likes some people but not others, and God requires that people pray to him.

There are other desert people of the Arabian Peninsula who since the seventh century have also given somewhat different attributes to God based on their social cultural lens. To give you an example of how the different ethnocentric stories of this type of God are, the Hebrew people wrote around 1400–600BC that God tested their forefather Abraham's faith by asking him to kill his beloved younger son Isaac, whom he had conceived with his wife Sarah, who was in advanced old age, because God did not favor the elder son Ishmael. They also wrote that Isaac was the ancestor of the 12 tribes of Israel. However, in 630 AD the Arabs write about the same story (2,000 years later), but with totally different details. The Arabic story says that God tested Abraham's faith by asking him to kill his only son Ishmael, who is the ancestor of all the major Arabs including Mohammad, and that Sarah did not bear any children.

You cannot appreciate the contradiction in such stories about God and his commands, unless you appreciate the fact that those are ethnocentric stories, even if written down and ascribed to God the almighty. When you see today's animosity between Arabs and Jews, maybe it has something to do with Arabs believing in a story that essentially retrospectively changes the traditional history of the Jews, who for more than 1,000 years had a specific story about their origin and lineages.

It is almost impossible to agree on even the simplest of story lines about this type of god so long as the stories are being written by different ethnic groups. So when the Indians and Buddhists call God Brahma and write an elaborate story line that does not mention Abraham or any of his sons, it gets to be obvious that each ethnic group over the years can create an anthropomorphic God with their society as the center of the divine story.

To sum up this whole topic of ethnocentric gods, Carl Sagan said in his book, *The Pale Blue Dot*, that over time science has disproved the human self-conceited notion that our planet is the physical center of the universe, that we are the most important creatures in the universe, and that God has human attributes. Our notion of an anthropomorphic God is a mere illusion, and thinking that the creator of billions and billions of galaxies and planets over a period of more than 13.7 billion years would look just like the *Homo sapiens* species that has existed for only 200,000 years is a deep-seated psychology of human vanity. It is more logical and statistically more plausible that the creator could look more like the dinosaurs who existed on Earth for more than 200 million years than humans who may not exist long enough to register even one million years. Sagan quotes the Ancient Greek philosopher Zenophilus, who said that man making God in man's ethnic image is a sign of arrogance: "The Ethiopians make their God black and snag-nosed, the Thracians paint their God white and with red hair, and if horses would write and paint, their image of God would look like a horse." So, we need not to be arrogant. We need to be humble and either acknowledge or not, but let's not commit blunder by dictating that we know the detailed qualities of God.

While spirituality and religiosity are interchangeable, or the same when talking about the unknowable God of indigenous peoples, there is a big difference between spirituality and religiosity when it comes to the God written about by the different ethnic groups.

Spirituality is an innate reality and excitement of people's consciousness in relation to personal experiences of awe, serenity and ecstasy toward the Source God. Because most people are wired by nature and society to ascribe spiritual status to many things, including our own psychological experiences, we erroneously interpret some altered states of our own consciousness as a universal occurrence that has to apply to everyone and everything. In a way, we interpret it as evidence of God singling us out as special people. For example, many people who have had "aha" moments, or a flash of consciousness, instead of interpreting it as an isolated incident, have been reported to interpret it using their social environment as a direct message from God as created by the social milieu. The difference is that if it is interpreted as an experience of consciousness reaching out to the Source God, it means it has relevance only to you individually; however, if it is interpreted as a direct command from God, this leads the affected people into believing that God is concerned with a specific social cultural environment more than the whole of humanity or the whole universe. The latter is what leads some people to say things like, "Our God commanded us to behave like so and so, and their God is not the right God."

Religion is a socio-cultural creation based on the insights about God brought about by the spiritual experience of the religion's founder. It is from this fact that someone like the great American biologist and religious philosopher William James concluded that most religious people never have spiritual experiences. Because spiritual experiences are ephemeral and they cause one's consciousness and view on life to change, many lifelong followers of religions actually never experience the spiritual transcendence that the originators of the religion claim to have actually experienced. Hence, many religions end up being social organizations focused more on cultural relationships.

By the same token, many spiritual people have transcendent experiences, but without being part of a cultural organization called a religion. Such people are fully in tune with their spirituality and indeed have more profound experiences of the divine than people who blindly follow religions. And when you see some of the negative things that have happened due to religions (examples are people killing other people who don't believe in their religion, or the Catholic scandal in the US and Ireland in which priests used to rape young boys), it is fundamental for you to understand that indeed there are religious people who are devoid of God. A better way of putting it is that there are some religious people who are really evil. Just as there are good religious and spiritual peoples, there are also very good people who are neither religious nor spiritual. The human spirit comes on a very wide spectrum.

Religions are people's cultural model about "life here on Earth," they are not descriptions of the nature or the universe. For example, the Jewish people's model, which most of the world has copied, is "God created the world and people at a certain time in the past and sent prophets to convey his word to the world, and chose the Jewish people to be the special people in the world." St. Paul rejected that model and started a new one which we call Christianity, which says that, "Yes God is a male figure, created the world and people, and after the Jewish people refused to heed the words of the prophets he had sent, God decided to send his only begotten son Jesus to be the savior of all mankind (not just the Jews)." Hindus have a different model which states that, "There is no specific beginning of creation, but rather cycles of existence, there are many gods, both female and male, that are manifestation of the ultimate God and you, as a person, live life here on Earth for a certain time, but when you die you are reborn as another creature and this reincarnation goes on until at last you abide by the doctrine of Moksa whereby you can attain the ultimate existence by becoming one with the supreme spirit Brahman, or the whole universe." My tribe's religious model is that, "Kibbumba created nature and people, there is no Heaven or Hell, when you die you become a spirit that hovers over the family /

community and can influence your family's daily affairs of life for a certain time before your energies dissipates into the wide universe. There is no eschatological doctrine, no end of days or judgment day."

Spirituality, on the other hand, is not about a human-made model of social life. Spirituality is 100% within the sphere of consciousness. It is the reality of consciously perceiving phenomena in nature in ways that may not be rational. Depending on the culture you are in, that perception is socially harvested with a specific cultural bias. This explains why there are stories of Catholics who have had spiritual experiences of visions of the Virgin Mary, and at the same time, Hindus have spiritual experiences not of the Virgin Mary, but of the gods and goddesses believed within their societies.

Myths are traditional stories within a culture that are a blend of real events or people and "spiritual entities" that could be beings or objects. In a way, myths are a blend of objective facts and man's imaginations. If myths are written down, they can morph into religions over time. And when they become religions the word "myth" takes a negative connotation, and the religious don't like their religions being referred to as myths. When this metamorphosis happens, myths are left as stories that don't have the backing of a social structure the way religions do. For example, during the Greek and Roman times, their practices were universally referred to as religious and the state gave people due space to practice them. However, now when we refer to them we usually denote them as myths – the reason being that they don't hold as much social power as the Abrahamic religions of the modern world. Nonetheless, we can't forget that myths are greatly steeped in spirituality or consciousness of the universal human spirit and they play an enormous role in holding a people together and making their culture cohesive.

The principle benefit of going beyond myths or knowing facts objectively is to enable you to understand nature and the real universe.

The principle benefit of identity is to enable one to be human in the most primitive and basic way of existing. The identity instinct could be stronger than myth and knowing.

Nonetheless, in order to advance and build a better human civilization, knowing has to be dominant over myth and identity. It is a fact that people get stuck in a specific identity paradigm, whether tribal or religious, and cannot comprehend that the real universe is working according to laws and dictates that are beyond how you believe from a tribal or religious perspective.

Frantz Fanon states in *Black Skin White Masks* that: "In terms of consciousness, black consciousness is immanent in its own eyes. I am not a potentiality of something; I am wholly what I am. I do not have to look for the universal, [I am the universal]." Immanence refers to those philosophical and metaphysical theories of divine presence in which the divine encompasses or is manifested in the material world. In the same spirit as Fanon, I believe that the consciousness that will come out of the Heri of Kesa is one that has immanence as one of its defining properties. If this heri is to be accepted by Africans or other humans, then by the above definition, it can't be described as "for black people," or non-universal. This consciousness has to apply equally to the young black child born in Uganda as it does to a Chinese or European person who comes to settle in the country. This is because one of the inspirations for creating this heri has been the universal truth that human beings have their cradle in Africa, and East Africa in particular.

The current Eurocentric world has produced a collective consciousness, which in both political ideology and religious theology is based on non-immanence or exclusivity. If you have a Marxist consciousness, the capitalist is excluded; if you have a Christian consciousness, the Muslim is excluded. What I am advocating for is that if you have the Heri of Kesa as a source of consciousness, the Marxist, the capitalist, the liberal, the conservative, the Jew, the Christian, the Japanese and the Indian are all part of this human crucible. That is the only consciousness that can truly be universal, and it can only grow out of Africa, and particularly East Africa. If we can't teach children in whatever part of the world they may live that the human story started in Africa, that the only true universal consciousness has to be born among people originating there, then I can predict with absolute certainty that we humans can't land on a universal consciousness or mind frame here on Earth.

It is no small detail that majority of black Africans, specifically those in East, Central and southern Africa, are ethnically called "Bantu," a word which in my tribal language and in all the other hundreds of Bantu languages means "people." To me this speaks to the primordial nature of our consciousness and spirituality as Bantu, such that we are the only people who have remained with a human consciousness that designates ourselves and all other humans simply as "Bantu." The Anglo or Latin peoples of the world have different words for themselves and other words for other people, but for us, the ethnic grouping of all our small tribes is called Bantu and from our languages we also call "other people" the same word, Bantu. Maybe it means that there is a primordial level in ours and other people's consciousness that is 100% the same. Maybe it is a sign that at some level the Eternal Source wants us to know that all Earthlings or *Homo sapiens* are simply Bantu.

The Tyranny of Experience:

Knowing the above general information about God, religion, spirituality and myths, we end up finding that people generally fall into two camps. Some people lean toward rationality, they have a mental disposition in favor of rational cold facts, while others lean toward consciousness, and their mental disposition is in favor of subjective social truths. Whatever your mental disposition, we all need to be on guard against the Tyranny of Experience.

The tyranny of experience simply means that just because you have an experience, in your head or physically in the world, it does not mean that it is universal or that other people should or can have the same experience.

Even if I believe that the limit of rationality is the beginning of God (I reached this rational conclusion borrowing heavily from the reasoning of Immanuel Kant and William James) or rather the limit of rationality is the territory where consciousness rules supreme, however refined your consciousness is, it has to obey the laws of nature (which are written down rationally). You may not know them, and actually our current human rationality may not extend to them yet, but the laws of nature need to be written down rationally for universal consumption, or else a universal human civilization cannot even be born, let alone endure.

I believe by embracing the Heri of Kesa, i.e. having a universal consciousness beyond our heritages of birth and singular but in sync with all humanity, and a rationality that understands the natural laws of life, one will be able to transcend the tyranny of experience.

It is paramount for the modern man to internalize that just because you experience real events within the tribal or religious heritages does not mean that those experiences are objectively universal facts that apply to all humanity. Take an example: there are tribes in Uganda whose female members have to kneel down when greeting males. To men in those tribes, such cultural norms by women make them endearing and attractive for marriage. However, you would be grossly mistaken and people would laugh at you with endless ridicule if you look at those tribes and think that all peoples (the other tribes) in Uganda, or indeed in the wide world, look at kneeling women as a sign of endearment and sexual attraction. Just within Uganda there are many other tribes in which when a woman kneels, they would take it as a sign of mistreatment or actual offense. So now if you are a young girl born in one tribal reality and you have to be married into another reality, you better know the difference. You better know quickly that women's kneeling is not a universal norm.

Another good example is how our African forefathers were easily colonized and subjugated by Europeans and the Arabs. Even if our forefathers over thousands of years had developed deeply in the sphere of consciousness (they understood and believed in the Eternal Source or the Creator of the universe, they had open hearts that loved all humanity sincerely, they welcomed visitors and strangers in their houses with open arms, they were deeply spiritual in that they knew the difference between the sacred and the profane, etc.) that did not save them when faced with foreigners who might not have had universal consciousness but were high on rationality. The development in rationality by the Europeans and Arabs led them to create alphabets to concentrate their languages and use those languages to write down stories which they said were revealed from the Creator, which put our forefathers at a big disadvantage. Our forefathers, with their less developed pre-modern minds, could not tell and rationally argue their case that the foreigners were presenting ideas of "created gods," and history has judged them harshly because they forfeited their agency and sense of self, which up to now I am struggling to overcome. My life's mission is that my grandkids are left with a written accord that they can use as an intellectual ladder to fight against ethnocentric creations from outsiders. The fact that our forefathers had "real personal" experiences within the conscious realm did not mean that those experiences were universal, and indeed they paid dearly when faced with foreigners who had customized and concentrated their rationality.

The rationality of the foreigners also led them to create complicated social systems that grouped together peoples of different tribes and nationalities, such that our singular tribal entities stood no chance against a well-oiled post-tribal people like the British Empire or the Arab sultanates.

Contemplating the weakness within a people, even if they have strong group experiences in the conscious / spiritual realm, has led me to question the usefulness of the collective consciousness itself. Could it be that the collective consciousness by itself has little value, unless it leads individual members to have a concentrated subjective consciousness? Could it be that having the strongest group consciousness, without individuals being rational, means that it is in vain? This reasoning can be extended to mean that understanding or living just by acknowledging that all our conscious minds are in union is useless in itself, unless you individually rationalize your mind. So I believe collective consciousness is only useful if a person is able to stay with a singular individualized mind, even if living in the sea of collective consciousness. If you are not individualized, then you reap little benefit from the collective consciousness. But if you are highly individualized, then you can innovate or actually come up with new collective consciousness for your group, e.g. the way religious founders and nationalistic leaders are able to forge a whole new collective consciousness for their people. Unfortunately, this individual effort can be for either good or bad; a really bad example is how Adolf Hitler was able to create an enormous collective consciousness around his personal identity, sucking in all Germans including all the intellectuals and the Christian leadership.

Tying the above reasoning to my Heri of Kesa, the bottom line is that being high on consciousness alone without understanding the laws of nature rationally and exploiting them (the way foreigners did with religions and sciences and technology) is not enough. Thus, for any one group's survival it needs to acquire a level of rationality that can be complemented by consciousness, not the other way round. Without that, a people are committing cultural suicide, because they have no chance when faced with foreigners who are versed in creating computers, nuclear weapons and missiles because they exploited the laws of nature as shown by the different equations of mathematics or physics.

The Heri of Kesa gives you a sense of looking at the world in a way characterized by a sharpened concentrated mind. One is able to grasp and indeed live fully within the realm of the wider existence. Which existence is governed by natural laws, which come from the Eternal Source, which all peoples and indeed all the universe must obey.

How the Heri solves the African's Eternal Dilemma

Of all the psychological effects of the three sins of Western and Islamic dominance, the dilemma is the biggest of them all. If we can solve this, all the others will go away subsequently. Another way of describing the African's eternal dilemma is the fact that, "The more advanced we get in rationality (e.g. education which is western by design), the more we get cut off from our traditional roots (which is the consciousness of our human spirit)." And just as no tree can grow very tall or reach far with shallow roots, our failure to integrate the tribal mindset into the modern civilization has left us lacking a lot of mental fortitude to be creative and proportionately contribute to the current world civilization.

The first stage of how the Heri of Kesa solves the dilemma is that it has intrinsic attributes of the four heris of the societies I discussed in the first book.

If one internalizes and manifests the Heri of Kesa, by definition the individualization of understanding the world means that that person engenders the "individual freedom" attributes of the Americans' heri. Also, since anything to do with individualizing how one gets to have world knowledge points to one exhibiting skepticism, the Heri of Kesa intrinsically has the hallmark of the scientific heri.

The individualization of knowledge capture also engenders a work ethic akin to the "German Protestant work ethic" because interpretation of phenomena to partake in creation means that the person is free to use their take on whatever society teaches or whatever they experience. Once someone truly owns the outcome of the experience or individualizes societal dictates, the creation from that person's labor should be unique and personal. Anything personal points to the fact that the individual doing it actually cares and devotes a lot of effort in its completion – which, if done perfectly, is the attribute of the Japanese heri.

The second stage involves combating what propagates the dilemma by internalizing the four pillars that propagate the Heri of Kesa. By now we should all know that as long as the analysis and diagnosis of our predicament is within the confines of the Western and Islamic cultural boundaries, we can't escape the objective fact that we Africans have been left behind in development in this modern era. We need to be courageous and go beyond these two dominant civilizations by standing on the four pillars of the Heri of Kesa and being able to truly understand the universality of the discoveries of modern science (modern science has no cultural or civilization boundaries; it is universal and treats all the facts and truths from all civilizations the same way). This will open our mind's eyes to see what indeed it means for Africa to be the cradle of humanity. Since Africa is the weakest link in so many affairs of the modern world (e.g. economics, education, health, military power and scientific research), and a chain is only as strong as its weakest link, it really means that all we humans have the same fate on this planet Earth, and we will be able to enjoy peace and universal wellbeing when Africa lifts itself up.

Indeed, it's true that our long-gone forefathers immensely contributed to ancient cradle civilizations, but currently we Africans (or black people) are disproportionately represented among the peoples who are contributing to the progress of the current modern civilization. There are a few of our people here and there, but when you look at the numbers it is astonishing. Take one example: there are more Africans alone on the continent than there are people in North America and Europe combined. However, when you consider the power wielded in this modern civilization by North Americans and Europeans, you might think they make up the majority of world population. And they have had that disproportionate power in world affairs since they first came to Africa and committed the three sins. In fact, it is very easy to compare countries in Europe with minute populations to the whole continent of Africa, and it is utterly disorienting to even compare. For example, a small island like Great Britain with less than 70 million people has more contributions in modern times in mathematics, physics, biology, religions, and industrialization, than a continent of one billion people. To begin with, it created the language that most Africans use to access modern knowledge. When you look at ethnic groups, a small group like the Jews with less than 15 million people worldwide (0.2% of world population) have 25% of all the Nobel laureates in mathematics and the natural sciences, yet our continent of a billion people has zero.

It is such obvious contrasts that lead people to say Africans are inferior or a primitive race. Even if many of our people counter this with all kinds of angry rhetoric, the silent fact remains in people's minds that we Africans have done very little to contribute to the current modern civilization. The long lost ancient civilizations, where people from Africa were advanced cultures, are no more. Being exploited by Europeans or forced to be labor in building the modern civilization does not count as much as actually creating the tools for the civilization.

Therefore, my in-depth contemplation about the disproportionately negligible contribution of Africans to the current modern world led me to the idea that maybe there is something derailing us despite the fact that we are equally educated as any other group in the world. There must be something that prevents many of our overly qualified peoples from being able to contribute adequately to the current civilization. I zeroed in on the fact that as long as we get cut from our core human roots by this current civilization, but at the same time keep holding onto them for the sake of identity but not knowledge, we end up standing on very shaky ground that leads us to excel in being copycats and proud consumers of things created by non-Africans; from religions, to political systems, to economical ways of thinking, we are comfortable copying outsiders. Socially, there is a gross hypocrisy and utter psychological malaise when you hear people proudly manifesting their allegiance to foreign religions at the expense of their afro-humanist teachings about morality, but in the same breath they turn around and politically abhor the effects of the European man and how he has contributed to the demise of our traditional ways. A very good example of this that hits home is the historical fact of how in the 1880s one of the Ugandan kings, Kabaka Mwanga, executed some of his subjects who had converted to Christianity and started to disobey his orders, which was akin to treason. However, more than 100 years later, our entire society celebrates the Christians who were killed as "heroes" or "martyrs," and the person who was fighting to protect our traditional ways is vilified as the bad guy. If that does not show you how upside down we are in our minds, then I don't know what will.

How on earth does such an African psyche, which is so violated and totally lost in the way it looks at itself regarding the religions that outsiders created, find a way to stand deeply rooted in its Africanness in order to contribute to the modern civilization? I for one say that it cannot. It cannot look at anything in the modern historical past to use as a basis. The only way we can escape from this diabolically disorienting dilemma is if we can create a totally different model of looking at our history and the two dominant civilizations that overwhelmed our forefathers.

So if you don't understand the gravity of this dilemma and appreciate my little effort in giving a small contribution regarding how we can approach this deeply-rooted psychological pathology, then you have not really sat down and pondered why Africa is the way it is in this modern civilization. My creations in all the three books are a quiet but bold proposal of specific ways that I believe can bring forth the much needed agency within our men and women. I truly believe that many of the creations in these three books can be used as concentrating agents that all our peoples – irrespective of tribe, religion or color – can use to progress our societies.

Given the dichotomy of consciousness and rationality, I believe even if many Africans climb the rationality ladder by getting advanced degrees, they still fall prey to the four ills, especially the dilemma, because their deepest consciousness is not in tune with the integration of the triple heritages. This state of mind is represented in the first Kamp diagram I drew in Chapter 10. The first Kamp diagram is in utter contrast with the developed societies because as I showed in their Naki diagram, their consciousness and core being is solid and rooted in their first heritage which acts as the springboard for creativity and development. In order for us to acquire a similar mental springboard, the rationality needs to be in sync with the consciousness, and they both have to be universal, not tribal or racial. The below Kamp diagram shows that by internalizing the Heri of Kesa, our people's rationality and consciousness can converge so that a modern mindset is born. Such a mindset has consciousness seamlessly synced with rationality.

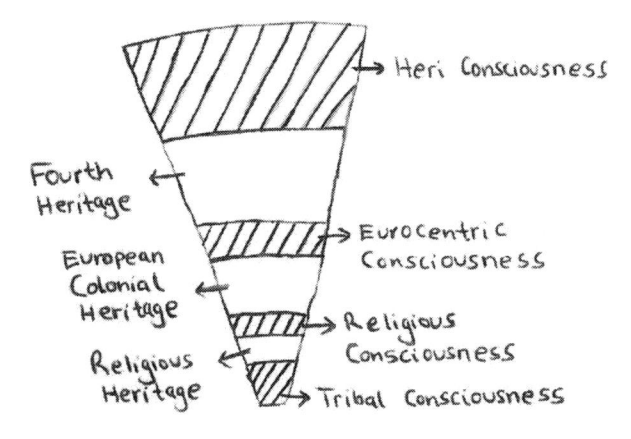

Figure 8: The Kamp Diagram Due to The Heri of Kesa

You can see that the first layer, the tribal layer, remains whole and intact – for someone only with a tribal mindset (without exposure to foreign religions or European colonial education) there is no psychological conflict between their tribal consciousness and the way they use it to understand the "real nature" of the world. It is just that they understand very little of the real world. The second layer (the religious layer) is no longer conflicted because by using the Heri of Kesa, someone is able to see the limit of the religious heritage in their reasoning and ably engender a religious consciousness that only builds on the positives in the tribal and religious heritages. The third layer (the Eurocentric layer) is no longer conflicted because by using the Heri of Kesa, someone is able to see the limit of the Western heritage in their reasoning and ably engender a worldview that only builds on the positives in the tribal, religious and colonial heritages. The result is that that person has a fourth heritage as their core heritage for any rationalization of the "natural world," and at the same time embraces the Heri of Kesa as the core consciousness with which to view the universe and its natural laws.

In this chapter I have discussed the thesis of my book, the main point of the book. It is the eleventh hypothesis of how to transcend our heritages of birth.

Hypothesis 1: The origin of all humans is in Africa.

Hypothesis 2: Even if the origin of all humans is in Africa, the Semites created the idea of one God as it is known to most of us and the Europeans created the modern world as we know it; the most important similarity shared by all humans is the collective unconscious.

Hypothesis 3: Even if all humans are similar, there are real differences and inequalities among peoples due to the differences in collective consciousness.

Hypothesis 4: Absence of evidence is not evidence of absence. Just because we don't have undisputed scientific evidence of civilizations before 10,000 BC does not mean that for certain periods between the creation of the Earth 4.5 billion years ago and 10,000 BC, there were no advanced civilizations (humans or other creatures) that inhabited Africa and other parts of the planet.

Hypothesis 5: The six cradle civilizations, i.e. Ancient Egypt, the Olmecs of Central & North America, the Andean civilization in South America, the Mesopotamian civilization of the Middle East, the Indus Valley civilization of the Asian sub-continent, and the Ancient China civilization were multi-ethnic, multi-racial civilizations that hold significance for all humans.

Hypothesis 6: After the collapse of the African cradle civilization of Ancient Egypt, the Greco-Roman civilization became the intellectual foundation to what we know now as the European Western civilization.

Hypothesis 7: During the European Medieval ages, between the fall of the Roman Empire and the Italian Renaissance, the Islamic civilization played a critical role of safeguarding the ancient Greco-Roman classical knowledge which was resurrected in what we call the European Western civilization.

Hypothesis 8: The European Western civilization is the current modern civilization and it is the first known civilization to unite the whole of humanity through individualism.

Hypothesis 9: The dominance of the Islamic and European Western civilizations led to their people committing three sins with worldwide implications: 1) slave trade, 2) genocide against native peoples, and 3) colonization.

Hypothesis 10: In this modern era, Africa has suffered greatly due to the three sins of the Islamic and European Western civilizations, but in order for the whole of humanity to find peace and wellbeing, Africa – inspired by its unique universal spirit that is not Islamic and not European – must rise up again to take its rightful position in human civilization. How high the human species goes in finding peace and wellbeing depends on how high Africa can lift itself up.

Hypothesis 11: In order to develop a modern consciousness and rationality that enables us to understand and contribute to the modern human civilization, we need to create and live by our own original heri. Personally, I achieved this through the Heri of Kesa.

12

A Case For Doubt

I started this book by talking about how I discarded doubt, and the confidence gained thereafter has enabled me to go through life in a very positive and somewhat successful way. I want to end my book by discussing the flipside of "doubt."

There is another side to "doubt" in that there are situations in which if you are lucky enough to develop "doubt" within your mind, then you get a golden chance to survive and actually continue to live life. This is the kind of doubt that creeps in your head when you think about going out alone in the dark when it is raining and there is no electricity in the whole city. Developing doubt might be what saves your life in such a situation.

I believe we need this other kind of "doubt" in order to confront and achieve the hope we need in the challenging world of today.

Personally, this kind of "doubt" served me immensely when my father passed away in 1995. If it wasn't for doubt, I could have lost my mind, if not worse. Before my father passed away in November 1995, it was a culmination of a long arduous journey that at times seemed unreal and other times it seemed dead right out of Hell. The previous year, my father had gone missing. For months on end we put out announcements about his disappearance on the radio, in the newspapers and all over the country. I was in boarding school at King's College Budo, so I did not participate actively in the announcements and searches, but as a 15-year-old boy I don't know what I could have done. Then somehow in mysterious circumstances, after almost a year, he was found in Kenya on the East African coast.

When he returned home, I never had any inquisitive conversation with him as I was still a young boy, but to say the least, a lot of things had gone wrong at home and in his businesses while he was away. Fast forward to a year later, he got very sick, and even though I was just 16 years old I managed to use my luck with friends in the city of Kampala to borrow money and find a doctor who agreed to admit him. I remember for some days I stayed with him alone in the hospital in Kampala, missing school, until my step-mother and other relatives came up a week or so later. After some time, he recovered very well, and I went back to King's College Budo. Shortly after my departure, he was discharged and taken back to Iganga. However, within days of being in Iganga, my sister called me and told me he had died abruptly. I left boarding school and went back to Iganga for the burial.

What transpired next is something that can fill its own book. As I mentioned in the first book, after my father's death the clan powers-that-be wanted me to stop using the name "Kesa" because to them it had no meaning. Instead they insisted I start using my given names, which were of special significance because they were for our clan patriarch who had died just before I was born. With my father not around to vouch for me that he allowed me to use the names I was using in school, I had to stand on my young legs to assert my identity. In my mind, I kept wondering why, if by the time my father died a lot of clan people were not treating him fairly, should I succumb to their dictates? Also, when my father returned from Kenya, he had picked up a strange religious practice of wearing a turban and praying in Swahili in the early mornings in loud voices. So by the time he died, I was not sure if he was still the Anglican Christian that he was supposed to be. In fact, I don't know if he had changed religions all together. Death is something that brings all relatives from near and far to converge, so I found that time very illuminating in our tribal cultural practices, because so many people were sharing so much about tradition and what death means in our culture.

During the fracas of being directed to agree to abandon my name Kesa, I had an "aha" moment. It dawned on me that maybe my father died not a Christian. Since I was a strong Christian, I doubted; maybe he was not in Heaven. But since according to tradition his spirit stays with me and with my family, it felt like he had not left us. For the first time, I doubted the existence of Heaven.

With an emboldened sense of defiance, I refused to give in to discarding my self-given name Kesa (it is my recollection of this episode that has informed the phrasing of the 12th hypothesis). We came to a compromise that I could still use it in school, but when I was in the village I would still go by the clan names. After that episode, when later on I was faced with the school fee challenges that I discussed in the first book, what kept me going and not losing my mind was the first belief that I was my father's son and he was with me beyond the grave.

When, 20 years later, I read Prof. Ali Mazrui's book in which he says, "The solution to Africa's war of culture must include the pronouncement that the ancestral is authentic," I understood it from the practical sustenance of my well-being that I got from my culture during the difficult time after my father's death. I internalized the fact that just because the written cultures have more power in the way they have built the Western and Islamic civilizations, it does not mean that the oral traditions of tribal culture are evil or that they have nothing to teach us concerning God, life and death. God is my witness, but I am very convinced my doubt about "my dead father being in Heaven" might have been what saved my fragile 16-year-old psyche from being ruptured by the entire emotional trauma that one goes through with the death of a loved one, especially a parent. I felt more than ever that I was my father's son. When I read the celebrated Princeton Professor Elaine Pagels – who is considered by many as an authority on early Christianity – say that she felt the presence of her dead husband and son soon after they passed, I completely understood what she meant. It is a very natural phenomenon – not supernatural – that as soon as a loved one dies, their presence can still be with you for a short while. And over time, it dissipates into the unknown (maybe to join the Eternal Source).

So it is true, a seed of doubt in your mind in the right circumstance could also be the best thing that could happen to you. But how do we know the difference between good doubt and bad doubt? The answer is in the fruits or the outcome of the decision.

By using what William James calls a pragmatic approach to life, one is able to find peace of mind in one's beliefs about God and religion, and at the same time work hard in this life so that you can have material wealth, to help your practical existence in this world. One does both with varied degrees of confidence mixed in with a dose of doubt here and there. The pragmatic existence that will help us build a truly human civilization involves three elements: ancient indigenous cultures, inter-religious harmony and rebooting our human identities.

Ancient Indigenous Cultures

As we struggle with the problems of this modern world and we try to find everlasting peace between the nations and harmony between the races or the different peoples, we should not forget that our current civilization is less than 2,000 years old. Before the Renaissance in Italy, there were the six agreed-upon cradle civilizations and maybe many others before them, and currently numerous other smaller civilizations or non-Western cultures all over the globe. Some became extinct by themselves, while others were violently destroyed by the conquering European and Islamic civilizations. But luckily enough, some of these non-Western, non-Islamic cultures are still around with us.

When you read about African tribes or South American Indian enclaves or the numerous Asian ancient peoples, those societies or mini civilizations still have a trove of knowledge for mankind that we should cherish and do our very best to harvest. There are cultures that I have read about in my random searches about ancient indigenous cultures, who have a totally different morality about how to achieve tranquility within a society. Our modern civilization should not be deaf to these members of the human family. The only handicap is that their knowledge is oral (not written down), so the bullying tactics of the written civilizations make us all erroneously think that "might is right."

At the very least, we need to ensure that languages from such peoples are preserved and well-guarded. Since these oral traditional peoples have their collective consciousness stored not in books but rather in a sophisticated generation-to-generation passage of human knowledge over thousands of years, we cannot underestimate the contribution we could get from them. Since languages are not only mediums of communication, but also are a complicated repository for people's sense of self and their souls, preserving languages would be a good first step to truly achieving a human civilization.

Let us not forget, the Western and Islamic civilizations are still juvenile in so many ways. We need to open up to the possibility, to doubt, that they are the best man can produce.

To underscore the above point, I remember reading about the Kogi tribe of northern Colombia. This is a tribe of less than 50,000 remaining members who are so removed from the current Western civilization that the Colombian government has forbade any person to encroach on their land and their remaining enclave. From a rare interview that the BBC did with them – they allowed the BBC access to their land for one crucial chance for us all to have a window into their unfathomable way of looking at life – we learn a totally different yet awe-inspiring outlook on life. For example, this tribe understands so well the difference between a collective unconscious and the collective consciousness that they do something totally unimaginable when a new child is born into the world.

At a very infant age, before three years old, the child and its mother are taken to a dark cave and locked up in total darkness for up to nine years. With each year signifying a month that the child spent in the womb of the mother, they go on to simulate the womb of the Earth (the cave) and communicate to the child in only imaginary ways, as he does not see the sun for nine years. Since the collective unconscious works with imagery and archetypes, this is an ingenious way for society to actually develop one's unconsciousness in a way never heard of in our current civilization. After the nine years, when the kid is coming into his pre-teen years, he comes out to see the sun and the world for the first time with his conscious mind. He gets to merge his overly developed unconsciousness with the conscious world that is before him. From that moment, for the rest of his life, there is no way his mind or consciousness can ever stray away from its anchorage in a well-cultivated unconsciousness of "the universality of all things" and "the universal brotherhood of all peoples" and "the indifference of the universe in regard to good and evil," and all these things he had learned for nine years in the womb of the Earth.

So you learn that the tribe believes that good and evil are in equal balance in the universe, and in fact people should feel free to commit small sins in order to safeguard the good. Evil balances the good. Looked at deeply, how different is that moral ethic from Jesus' eternal redemption of our sins? According to Christianity, no matter how much sin you commit, Jesus can always forgive you. How beautiful would it be if the whole humanity embraced such an ethic which relegates to irrelevance the ethnocentric stories of punishment of people, especially eternal punishment after death? I am mentioning this alternative universe of morality for us all to realize that whatever culture we are holed up in at the present, with its orthodoxy teachings about this or that, there are a million other ways that people could access the same morality but in a more peaceful and self-evident way. We just need to open our minds to doubt the infallibility of our modern civilization's teachings.

Inter-religious Harmony

No amount of rationalization will take away the fact that right now, the whole world is under the negative effects from the three sins of the Islamic and European civilizations. When I saw two innocent Japanese hostages being beheaded by ISIS, I could not imagine the profound sadness I felt for the Japanese people. Here is a people who have no idea about what the Abrahamic God is or what Jesus or Mohammad have to do with life on Earth, but they had been dragged into a conflict where one of them was beheaded like a chicken. Just think about it: the Japanese people have no inch of inclination that God supposedly revealed two holy books – the Bible or the Koran – and that they being from an island in the east of the planet are infidels. But there in front of our screens we saw images of the Japanese Prime Minister and the mother of the hostage being put through psychological torture along with financial extortion – the terrorists had asked for $200 million in order to spare the hostage's life. This incident should inform anyone who is apathetic about religion that whether you know it or not, whether you want it or not, what people believe in their religions can affect you. In fact, there were two other stories in Kenya where the Somali terrorists Al Shabaab boarded a bus and, if you did not have a Muslim name, they killed you. So your ignorance about Islam would not have excused you.

Another way of looking at the present world order is as if the Islamic and Western civilizations have us all held for ransom. We non-indigenous to the Western and Islamic civilization cannot escape the implications of their beliefs and disbeliefs. And particularly I am saying this because while the Western civilization has matured and many of its people feel remorse and guilty about the three sins committed by their civilization in the past, there is still propaganda within the Islamic civilization that portrays itself as the only civilizing force for us non-natives of Arabia – it is totally blind to its sins during the time of its dominance.

Unfortunately, even if religion has brought a lot of good and has been a civilizing force in the world, when we talk about the evil it has also brought about in the world, the main culprits are my own Christianity and Islam. It is mainly because these two religions are the only ones that claim – albeit independently – that they are the final religions from God Almighty. And what makes it complicated is that they also claim – again independently – that all humanity needs to follow them, hence they proselytize a lot. If it was not for their proselytizing nature, I would not have been born a Christian – the Europeans brought the religion to my country in 1879. Also the whole of South America would not be Christian and the whole of North Africa would not be Islamic. Other religions, e.g. Hinduism, Judaism, Shintoism and Buddhism don't go on to cause worldwide evil, because they don't proselytize. Maybe this has to do with the fact that they are not "the revealed messages from God via one man," but rather an accumulation of ethnic traditions and customs, which over time some people attribute to God, but other people have the freedom not to attribute to God.

So the biggest problem we face regarding religion, the reason that we have to debate religion, is mainly because of effects of the sins that the adherents of the Islamic and European Christianity committed around the world during their dominant eras. Since the whole world is now in the sphere of influence of these two religions, it is not a small matter that can be wished away. The hope for us confronting this problem is first of all to be honest about the facts. Three of the major facts are as follows: 1) the Islamic and Christian religions both claiming to be true yet independent of each other cannot be a true proposition, 2) both were spread throughout the world during the dominant periods of their respective civilizations, and as such they both committed gross evil to reach the ubiquitous privileged state that they now enjoy throughout the world, 3) we who are victims of either Islam or Christianity have a right to criticize anything and everything about these two religions. If not for our own sanity and well-being, then it is for the sake of the memory of our forefathers who were slaughtered or forcefully converted.

So while we advocate for tolerance and multiculturalism, this makes sense only when you are referring to ethnicities but not different religions. This is because no one has a choice about ethnicity, and even if one wanted, they can't change their ethnicity. That is not the same for religions. When it comes to religions we should not be talking about multi-cultural tolerance, but rather inter-religious tolerance. This is a very important distinction. It means the religions themselves have to take the bulk of responsibility to kick out the evil within their ranks, before society can embrace them. The various religions need to work together first, and find commonality and see the humanity in people of other religions before the wider society, which might be non-religious, can accept them as forces of good.

The only way these religions can be used to build the much needed universal human civilization is if they have inter-religious councils and inter-religious practices. It is not helpful that there are cities within the Islamic world where non-Muslims can't go. How harmonious is it that Muslims can build mosques in Rome (one of the most important Christian cities), in Jerusalem, in London, and in any Christian city, but non-Muslims cannot be allowed to visit Mecca and Medina let alone build churches? I am saying that, as a human being, I should be able to visit very important places like Mecca, because for the sake of human heritage don't non-Muslims have a right to understand very consequential religions like Islam? I think it would go a long way to building harmony among people if any human being had the right to visit any place that has religious significance. When visiting Notre Dame Cathedral in Paris in 2006, maybe the most important Christian church in France, it was a beautiful sight for me to see a pair of Muslim couples with one of the women covered in an Islamic head scarf, or hijab, touring the Cathedral. If these religions are truly universal they should act like it and let non-believers have access to them. Maybe the non-believers will convert upon visiting your holy site! Actually this issue once hit home when a relative I know who lived in Kuwait told me that her friend was burnt by acid just because she was found reading the Bible in that Islamic country. Our world leaders who happen to be Western countries and institutions have become too liberal and too progressive to have the passion to call out evil when the evil is non-Western. They are too quick to criticize themselves – as the issue of the Cologne rape scourge last year showed – but they can't raise a figure and demand that some non-Western societies need to open up and be tolerant the way "the civilized West" has become.

To further illustrate the difference between multi-culturalism and inter-religious tolerance, when two people from different cultures marry, the woman is not coerced to change her ethnicity. She is accepted as she is. In my family my mother is from a different dialect and clan from my father's, but we don't make her become part of our clan, the *Baise Nkwalu*, or inhibit her in any way from speaking her dialect with her siblings. But on the other hand, when one marries across religions, there is a lot of coercion for one party – usually the woman – to change religion. How dehumanizing that must be! Imagine that you grew up a Christian your entire life, but because of love, love that is supposed to be from God, you marry a Muslim and you are forced to change your religion. Religions need to categorically stop coercing people to convert if we really are to have a human civilization with religion playing a central role.

Therefore, if we are serious about bringing about a world of inter-religious harmony, below are my four suggestions of the changes needed in religions in order to create a human civilization that can bring about peace and happiness to this world. Without such changes, we are only kidding ourselves that we can achieve hope and optimism despite being under the plausible banner of religious tolerance.

First, these two proselytizing religions need to appreciate the convergence of both the oral tradition and the written tradition in the idea called God. The non-proselytizing religions (especially Buddhism and Shintoism) do a good job of accepting the spirituality of peoples who know God through oral tradition. Hence, you find that it is very natural for those religions to coexist with indigenous peoples all over the world. I met a Japanese woman during my travels in Mexico, who told me that Shintoism was not at odds with the native Indo-Mexican beliefs that were held by the people who built the Pyramid of the Sun at Teotihuacan, near Mexico City.

The main, seemingly unbridgeable, divide between the oral traditional people and the proselytizing religious people is the power differential. Because the proselytizing religions use rationality through their written tradition while the oral tradition cultures are all about consciousness, that rationality mindset has more worldly power than consciousness (though not more correct), so the proselytizing religions use their written culture to subjugate or coerce indigenous oral peoples all over the world. The movie *The Mission* with Robert De Niro examines this problem very well. This is what happened to us Africans when the outsiders brought their religions. There is no example in history where the oral-tradition-based people overpowered or imposed their belief systems on a literate people. So the onus is on the written-based religions to be humble and see the God in the oral tradition people and respect it. Remember the oral peoples acknowledge that God is unknowable, so they are not atheists or infidels. Actually, they have acknowledged God as unknowable for millennia, since the rise of *Homo sapiens* 500,000–200,000 years ago all the way up to today. Contrast that with the written-based religions which are not more than 2,000 years old. Today, when you visit oral traditional people in their tribal areas in the countryside or in the jungles of the Amazon, there is no way you can say that they don't acknowledge the God Source of the universe. People like us who have known both realities accept the convergence of rationality and consciousness in the idea of a Source God.

Second, the orthodoxy in religions – especially Christianity and Islam – needs to be rejected so that the scriptures and the practices are reformed for the modern civilization. Both these religions were started during the medieval or Dark Ages, around the Mediterranean coast, not in Africa where God created the first man, or in Asia which was more civilized at that time. It is no small wonder that these two religions are dismissive of the beliefs and God-given spirituality that was native to Africa, Asia and the Americas. Surely we all need to be humble and accept that the monopoly on God's revelation cannot be by a small slice of humanity living in a medieval time. To underscore how myopic their view was, and by logical extension evidence that they did not have the monopoly over access to God's knowledge, they wrote their scripture assuming that the world was flat, it had four corners, and that it was physically the center of the whole universe. So when they go into specifics like "don't eat pork," "kill the adulterer," and "only the people who believe in them will go to Heaven to be with the Creator of the universe," it all screams of total disregard for us all who are non-indigenous to the Middle East. We are also created in God's image and surely God can talk to us directly in our own languages and in the present.

If we objectively accept the non-universality of the scriptures from only one part of the world, then it is easy to see that the scriptures are not irrefutable and unchanging. In fact, that was the realization that Jesus and Christianity came to when they rejected traditional Jewish scripture and created a new one altogether. That is also what Mohammad did in the seventh century when he rejected the orthodoxy in Jewish and Christian scripture and created a brand new scripture altogether. Furthermore, that is even what Joseph Smith did in nineteenth century America when he wrote a new scripture called *The Book of Mormon* and started a whole new religion, Mormonism, which is now flourishing and growing rapidly throughout the world. To further highlight how scripture can be changed, more than 1,000 years after the Hebrews had written in their scripture that God commanded Abraham to kill his beloved son Isaac (the patriarch of the 12 tribes of Israel) instead of Ishmael, Mohammad was able to write a new scripture which says that God commanded Abraham to kill his beloved son Ishmael (the patriarch of the Arabs) instead of Isaac. So surely, God can talk to another person with different commands or corrections to scripture. If the Christian Bible was God's word 2.0, and the Islamic Koran was 3.0, I am sure God might tell someone else – hopefully from another part of the world and not the Middle East – to write 4.0.

The main takeaway here is that at each time in history, people are able to receive new revelation and write new scripture. So in order to truly build a human civilization with inter-religious harmony, religions need to be open and put more value on the present and future as opposed to history. Religions should be rebooted so that instead of looking into history and old scripture to get guidance on how the world is supposed to be now, we instead study the natural world now and maybe get updated revelation and we project the future from the present. If the revelation is not coming in the present, it does not hurt to understand the natural laws that science is discovering, which must also be the laws of God, if you believe in one. It is not enough, actually it is not convincing, for someone to say that, "In the beginning God created Heaven and Earth. He created everything in six days, and the world is about 6,000 years old." That is from history, and it is not accurate. Now we know that, "Based on natural laws, the universe came into being about 13.7 billion years ago (which points to the idea that if God created it, then he did it 13.7 billion years ago, not 6,000), and many societies have different calendars, e.g. the Yoruba have a calendar which has a week of four days, so the idea of God creating the world in six days is an ethnocentric perspective because at the time of writing, the writers were referencing the Mesopotamian calendar which had seven days in a week."

It would be far easier to convince all humans (not only Judeo-Christians) about God's creation and everything else if we start from the findings of science, because they are more universal and more majestic than any other written account of the physical world. For example, when you see the intricate composition of the human genome and what genes tell us about human qualities and traits, if you take that knowledge as coming from God, you don't need any historical scripture to learn about human qualities and traits. Just from studying the human genome you can know why black people are black, why certain people get certain diseases, why humans are different from birds but similar to chimpanzees, etc. It really does not make sense to say that God revealed his message only 2,000 years ago, and he cannot reveal new information in the present time which can replace all previous revelation. If religions are rebooted and written in a less superstitious way and given a more intelligent narrative, we will no longer have the need to argue about interpreting whether one day in God's eyes is equal to millions of years in man's eyes. That is not a good way to use our God-given human potential. Indeed, it is a waste of human brainpower to be preoccupied with archaic intellectual lines of reasoning.

One time the famous scientist Carl Sagan asked the Dalai Lama (considered by most to be the leader of the Buddhist religion), "What would happen to religion if at one time, science proves it to be wrong?" The Dalai Lama emphatically responded that if something is found that contradicts the scriptures, then one is meant to discard the scripture and go by the evidence in real life. If science proves that there is no continuation of the soul after death, he emphatically says then at that point Buddhism has to exit. If all religious leaders said such a thing, then indeed, religions would be on the way to being in tandem with science and whatever science can ever discover. In a way, the Dalai Lama was saying that Buddhism is actually the science of life ... when you find evidence, keep believing, if you don't find evidence, discard the old belief. And most importantly, him saying that the holy scriptures are from the past so they can be discarded if they become irrelevant is something that all other religions need to be brave enough to believe and teach to their followers.

If scripture and religion are looked at this way, they really can be used to build togetherness because they will remain part of society as cultural heritages, as opposed to immutable belief frameworks.

Rigid belief should not be as important as traditional customs. This is already present in the modern-day English Anglican, or its American equivalent, Episcopalian, religion where its members take their kids for baptisms, and families to go Sunday prayers occasionally, where they sing those glorious Christian hymns that are indeed a world heritage, but the people don't have rigid beliefs. Hence, they now accept women to be bishops, and in England they accept Muslims to have their separate Sharia courts. In general, as a religion, Anglicanism today is very open to other peoples and other beliefs. And it just turns out to be my religion of birth, so I am very proud of it. The openness within the Anglican religion creates inter-religious harmony, because people keep to the traditional customs but don't use the orthodoxy in scriptures to exclude other human beings from the Anglican society. It is this very forward-looking outlook on religion by the Anglican Church that allowed the Royal Society during the reign of Queen Victoria – who was the head of the Anglican Church – to bestow the Royal Medal on a man like Charles Darwin, whose theory of evolution seemed at face value to contradict the very tenet of Christianity.

Religious openness like that exhibited by the Anglican Church should be applauded, because in today's multi-cultural environment, many of us end up meeting people for the first time who can introduce totally alien belief systems that you might never have heard of before. Everyone should be at liberty to freely choose what they believe, without a religious backlash from their religion of birth. For example, every religion has a different eschatology doctrine, the part of religious theology which purports to describe the final events of history, or the ultimate destiny of humanity. Given that even the most advanced human minds put together from all nations and all time cannot say definitively how history will end; it is disingenuous for a religion to describe in great detail how history will end, only for that religion to excommunicate or banish any of its members who believe in a different eschatological doctrine. In fact, religious beliefs that prevent people from following their conscience in changing religions is the highest form of human rights violation I can think of. When you read that the punishment for apostasy (leaving one's religion) is death as evidenced in 2014 by the sentencing to death of the Sudanese woman Meriam Ibrahim who converted from Islam to Christianity, how can one realistically talk of multi-culturalism instead of inter-religious harmony?

In order to bring the multi-faceted human family together, we need to appreciate that, just like any other social taboos, religious taboos are to be followed only by the believers. So, if someone converts from Christianity to Buddhism, you cannot judge them using the Christian belief system. If someone converts from Islam to Christianity and starts eating pork, you cannot and shouldn't use Islamic belief to judge that person. This principle of religious taboos being like social taboos means that nothing in one's religion should be beyond criticism by people from other religions. Of course all religions should respect each other, but if one decides not to respect your religion, understand that they have a right to because they do not believe in your set of beliefs. I have gone to bars with Muslims who sit drinking soda as I am having my alcohol, and it is very edifying to know that even if they don't agree with my drinking alcohol, they acknowledge that social taboo does not extend to me so they accept me.

During the days when slavery was permitted in society, Christian preachers used their beliefs to say that God allows for the slavery of black people. The same was done in the Muslim world, where many Arab leaders, as recently as the late twentieth century, would defend their practice and go as far as calling the anti-abolishment European Christians infidels who don't know the real commandments from God. In both instances, supposedly having slaves was a religious right beyond criticism from non-believers. We should desist from handling with kiddy gloves tenets of beliefs within religions that may be used as pretexts to cause a lot of misery in the world, all under the banner of, "You can't criticize my religion." As mature adults, believers should have a thick skin. If you can't handle your religion being criticized, you are acting with a child's psychology. We should know that there are practices within our own religions that should be criticized, and people have a human right to criticize if their conscience so permits. I greatly applaud the Mormon Church's reaction to the Book of Mormon play, which I watched in London and can say that by all accounts it is a very anti-Mormon comedy. The Mormon Church defended their religion via an array of counter advertisements in newspapers and on TV instead of advocating for the censure of the play.

The bottom line with religious taboos as social taboos is that each human belief and activity should be judged by the standards of its time, or by its civilization. Whether you like it or not, there are things that religions permitted in the medieval era that cannot be permitted today. For example, the Roman society, as civilized as they were, permitted grown men to have sex with young boys; there is no way any society now can permit such acts. In the seventh century, Mohammad the founder of Islam married a nine-year-old girl; modern society will find it very hard to allow such a practice. During the Spanish Inquisition in the late fifteenth century, the Spaniards massacred Arabs and Jews with state sanction; now you cannot even think that there is any modern nation that can allow such a crime. Even during the eleventh and twelfth centuries, when the Pope sanctioned European Christians to wage the crusades as a counter offensive to take back "the holy land" from the Islamic Empire that had conquered them in the seventh century; such barbaric wars which had innocent people slaughtered cannot be sanctioned by the Pope in this twenty-first century.

Third, religions need to bring back feminine qualities into their spirituality. All the non-proselytizing religions and all indigenous peoples accept feminine aspects of God or spirituality in general. There are some minority accounts which point to the fact that initially the ancient Israelites in fact had femininity in their attributes of God in that Yahweh had a wife called Asherah. However, due to patriarchal power during the whole time of writing the Biblical books, all mention of female attributes in God were systematically suppressed. Zoroastrianism, maybe the greatest religion of ancient times, from which Judaism and Christianity copied many themes, used to have a balanced view of God in that God had both female and male attributes. Since spirituality is the deepest sense of humanity, without a balanced view of masculine and feminine in matters to do with the divine realm, the human soul can't be in balance.

When people present that the argument that God's words are allegoric, they are not to be taken literary, many times it is just an excuse by rationalizing religious people to avoid admitting that when you take God's word literally, many of it does not make sense or in fact seems wrong and possibly evil. However, if we can accept that God's scripture needs to be updated, then we have the golden chance to actually develop a belief dogma that is not culturally specific or gender biased, but in fact one that can truly unite all races of humanity. For example, such a belief would have major tenets like, "Traditionally, the Western religions refer to God as a man but since God is beyond gender, giving God a male gender is just for convenience." Such a general update of religion would free up people to refer to God as a female without being castigated by the status quo. This would make perfect sense now, because we have achieved a lot of female emancipation to the point that instead of apologizing for the evil done to women in the past because of patriarchal religious beliefs, we should give them back their power by allowing the usage of a female article "she" for God. I am saying give them power back, because most traditional views of God used to be asexual or feminine until the Western civilization created a male God who is even able to have a child (another male) without ever having sex with a female. Non-Western religions are comfortable giving female attributes to God, and since God is beyond human (neither male nor female), no one should be offended if God is referred to in non-orthodox ways as "she" or "it."

In the past, the Catholic Church did a good job during the height of European civilization to bring back the feminine image with the Virgin Mary and baby Jesus, but it was stifled by the all-male clergy who still run all facets of the Church. The Protestant churches such as the Anglican Church have now opened up and started having female bishops, but it is not enough. The real issue at the center of this problem is that the actual spirit of God needs to be seen as a balanced paradigm. Once the male and female is brought back into the idea of God, then human consciousness and rationality will easily converge and bring about spiritually balanced and emotionally healthy human beings.

Fourth, in order to foster inter-religious harmony, religious people need to appreciate that true religiosity is a solitary and contemplative journey. When it becomes a public affair, it gets corrupted. If religion is practiced the way it is meant to be, i.e. in contemplative sacred settings, it has the potential to bring about harmony in the human enterprise. The story of Jesus is a very good example of the good that a genuine spiritual life can bring to the world. Jesus is the most influential religious figure in this Western civilization and his followers make up the biggest religion worldwide, not to mention that the international calendar we use is based on his life and death. His story was the central inspiration that led to the propagation of the European Western civilization which is the first to cover all "four corners" of the Earth. The life of Jesus can be summed up as surrendering oneself to live a simple life, giving up attachments to all worldly things, and to love all humans like one's siblings (this last one is in line with the scientific finding that all humans are the same genetically – we are all brothers and sisters).

And by all accounts, Jesus lived a solitary life. He never married or had children and he converted only 12 people (you can't compare that with the millions of people that today's religious leaders aim to influence). Just in tune with the divine, and working in a very solitary way, Jesus was able to leave the most enduring religious heritage of any person born of man. For those people who are disillusioned with the corruption in the modern church, but still get inspiration from Jesus' life, it is important for you to understand that there is another way of following Jesus' example. When you consider that there is a non-Nicene tradition of following Jesus, maybe you need to doubt that what the Council of Nicaea agreed on was the only way to believe in Jesus. Before the Council of Nicaea sat in 325 AD to codify a specific creed to be followed by Christendom, there were contending views on how to believe in Jesus Christ. These other ways of believing in Jesus are more spiritual and personal, as opposed to conformist social organizations sustained by power and riches. You can find them in the gospels that never made it into the official Catholic canon of books, some of which are the Gospel of Thomas, the Gospel of Mary, and the Gospel of Judas. If you don't want to open your mind to this line of reasoning, then in effect all you are saying is that the Roman men who sat in Nicaea in the fourth century AD were the only ones with God's wisdom to accept or discard accounts about Jesus. This means that even if there were no women at that council, it did not matter.

Upon reading the Gospel of Judas – one of the gospels not sanctioned by the men at the Nicene Council – you get to know a totally different story about Jesus and Judas. In the Gospel of Judas, you learn that true belief in Jesus is about solitary living, and that salvation and resurrection occur in the spiritual realm, not the physical resurrection of the body. The gospel also gives a different account of what Judas did. Instead of him being a traitor who gave up Jesus, the account shows him as the true follower of Christ who Jesus commanded to give him up to the authorities – the way a leader can command a subordinate to do something against his will. Also, it suggests that the other 11 apostles were more preoccupied with worldly affairs and misleading people about the imminent literal resurrection of the body and judgment day. It is no small detail that the early church leaders said that, "The second coming of Jesus would be in people's lifetime." This has not happened yet, more than 2,000 years later.

You don't have to believe in the Gospel of Judas, but his account is also corroborated by the gospel according to Mary. The gospel according to Mary asserts that the traditional disciples, especially Peter, were jealous because Jesus loved Mary more than them. According to the gospel, Jesus entrusted his true unadulterated message with Mary, a woman, at the expense of the men because he did not trust them as much as he trusted her. During the early years of the Church, leaders were decreeing the destruction of any non-canonical narratives about Jesus, especially those that show him favoring Mary; maybe this explains the historical suppression of female leadership in the Church. The Gospel of Thomas can also lead one who is a follower of Christ to realize that the true spiritual way of following Christ is to see him as a living Christ within you. If your conscience can feel the living Christ in your soul, then there is no need for you to waste time with all the social and organizational routines which are more cultural than spiritual.

I truly believe that if religious people can start living true solitary, contemplative lives in their spiritual matters instead of agitating for public control, then even the non-believer will be able to see that religions have a net positive balance sheet, i.e. even if there is some evil done in the name of religion, the positives outweigh the negatives. This is because the leaders will take on the attributes of being "the light of the world" that lights up the darkness in the world, instead of being "the heat of the world" that tries to burn everyone into submission. This is another reason why "The Christ as the light of the world" is a universal theme, and I believe it can be adopted by all, even if non-Christians use different names or titles for a person who embodies the light of the world.

In summary, the real counteraction to the religious terrorists today is for us to build a type of new religious environment that encourages a solitary type of spiritual life. This is the true method of getting to the divine. And once that is encouraged, then on a personal level people will start having the true spiritual experiences of the divine. Through an authentic communion with the divine, individuals will start to expand their spiritual minds beyond the traditional orthodox creeds. That is when the seeds of doubt could be planted in the mind of a terrorist about to embark on a mission. If there is a way we can create processes and systems of religious discourse that could allow even one single potential terrorist to doubt that by blowing himself up he will go to a heaven and have 72 virgins, then we have hope of beating them at their own game. Since they have a proclivity of believing harmful things, let us work to induce them into believing something good. It is only when we ignite some doubts in the minds of the fanatical believers that they will be able to meet us at the public square so that we can start discussing a truly human civilization based on inter-religious harmony. To underscore the role doubt can play in the affairs of man, Pierre Abelard, the keenest thinker and greatest theologian of twelfth century Europe, praised doubt, saying, "By doubting we come to questioning, and by questioning we perceive the truth." This embrace of doubting is also in tandem with the heri of science, skepticism.

Rebooting our Human Identities

We need to doubt that history has brought us to the best possible way in how we identify ourselves. Whether as compatriots in a nation-state, or people who share a tribal identity, or people who belong to this or that race, we all need to think it possible that what we see on the surface isn't what it really is. We need to start doubting that the deepest personal identity for every black person is "his being black" or for the Germany is his "German identity." I have met black people who, for all intents and purposes, would fit in very well among white people. I have met Jews who would pass for gentiles if only they could undo the clock of nature. We need to doubt that every African is doomed to have an inferiority complex. In fact, even in the realm of gender, I have seen a strange phenomenon where some women can feel and identify themselves more with male gender dispositions than with traditional female dispositions. So even in biology, we need to be open to doubting the orthodoxy.

The human civilization started in Africa and it is my deepest belief that its future is still in Africa. There is a natural way of things, a cycle to events in the universe. What goes around comes around. To my fellow Africans, you need to open your mind to start doubting the historical narrative that we are destined to be eternal subjects in the story that the Europeans and Arabs have written. We need to doubt that we can't be great. Yes, in this modern civilization, Africa is the least developed, but don't forget there was a time before the modern civilization when people on the African continent would have looked at people in Europe as savages and primitive.

Will Durant once said that civilization is created by stoic peoples, but it falls when it reaches epicurean levels. This partly explains why some of the most enduring stories of human triumphs have been created by the oppressed peoples. For example, the Khabiru peoples who were slaves in the Egyptian and Mesopotamian civilization were able to create a mythic story of their origin and destiny that has been the cornerstone of the Abrahamic religions of Judaism, Christianity and Islam, and by extension, the Western civilization. Another example is the fact that Christian peoples were a small persecuted cult during the peak of the Roman Empire, and many of them were burnt alive or killed in genocides, but they managed to create a story centered on the life of a man they never even saw (Jesus). A story so powerful and inspirational that it went on to become the ethos at the center of the Western European civilization. Lastly, the oppressed black slaves of America, more than any other ethnic group, have been able to create an unfathomable trove of original music that is indeed the quintessential American soul, and the biggest contribution of the American heritage to world entertainment.

So it is not far-fetched that the next step in human civilization can start in Africa. Actually Jacob Bronowski said it in his masterpiece, *The Ascent of Man*, that given the moral decay in Western civilization due to the triumph of materialism, maybe Africa, maybe China, will take on the mantle of advancing the ascent of man.

There is something so fundamentally wrong with the world now that skews all world affairs to be seen only in the eyes of Islamic and Western lenses. There was human civilization before these two, and there will be a human civilization when these two fade away, the way Ancient Egypt existed for over 3,000 years before finally fading away. Even the mighty Roman Republic / Empire, whose grandeur for over 1,000 years is not matched by any of our modern infant republics that are only a couple of centuries old and can't even start to compare.

We need to doubt that as a human species we can't extend our consciousness to borrow from long lost civilizations or the six cradle civilizations, so that we can create a new human civilization that transcends the limits of the current Western and Islamic civilizations.

We need to doubt that someone can't get all his morality from ancient indigenous tribal sources. Or that one can't listen to a song like Dire Straits' *Brothers in Arms*, and get all his moral compass from there: peace not war, brotherhood, oneness in the universe, time and space – everything that cuts across different civilizations. In fact, we need to doubt that music alone can't be the universal song of the human spirit. Nietzsche once said that a life without music is a mistake; from my life's experience I would go further to say that a life without music is evil. We need to doubt the notion that man can't reach the sublime, the numinous, in non-Western or non-Islamic religious ways.

White people, or Europeans, have to doubt that their forefathers have committed sins so grave they are beyond redemption. They need to doubt that they are destined to have eternal guilt, and to be unable find it within themselves to be proud of the enormous contributions to human civilization that their forefathers brought to the world. Weak people can be evil too. Before we blame Christians for the evils of the crusades, we need to use the same moral compass to judge the Arab conquest of North Africa and the rest of the Middle East way before the European reactions via the crusades. In my first book I extensively wrote about the expansion of "the black people," we the Bantu from the Niger delta to the current situation where we occupy all of central, eastern and southern Africa – and it was no picnic for the indigenous bushman people that we encountered during those massive episodes of the Bantu migrations.

The human civilization has to be about transcending our individual civilizations of birth, but since all peoples of the world now are under the influence of the Western civilization, the human civilization I am advocating for is about extending the virtues while diminishing the negatives of Western Europe. Since this civilization is currently under a lot of strain and there is no longer a center holding it together (the way Christianity did during its peak), and the triumphant materialism in most of the Western world has created a spiritual vacuum, we need to look somewhere else for the inspiration that can create confidence while diminishing the boredom. This source of inspiration has to be created anew. It will spring from a blend of the best of the Western civilization – the imagery of the child wonder, the vulnerable virgin and all the virtues attributed to Jesus – and something else coming from Africa or the East. We need to look for this missing link. Since all you need to achieve in life is inspiration, the new source of inspiration from this missing link is what will truly create a human civilization. Even if you are a non-believer, and you are opposed or don't understand the idea of getting inspiration from the above virtues of Western civilization, it is okay for you to get your inspiration from science and the objective facts and merge them with the missing link. The bottom line is, for both the believers and the non-believers, we are all in this thing together, and we need each other.

On a personal note, after I had finished writing this book and proofread it twice, I was in the process of proofreading it for the third and last time before I gave it to the publisher, when about three weeks before my target date of submission I suddenly got an inspiration to change the entire book in its totality. I really wanted to ignore the urging, but I could not sleep. So I spent about three days working day and night, rearranging the whole book anew and cutting out about two thirds of the material I had written before. The result is this simpler and better organized book, as opposed to the complicated rambling longer version I was planning to publish. In fact, when I finally added the pieces about my learning of the cradle civilizations in primary school, I felt that this version, more than the first one, actually has all my life's accumulated knowledge. It was the book I was meant to write in the first place.

When I finished writing this book anew, I could see that I have actually tied my childhood imaginations of ancient civilizations to my doubting that I can be great. No longer am I that ten-year-old boy who used to be beaten in school because I couldn't write proper English; I have actually managed to write three books. If only my father was around, there is so much I would feel confident enough to teach him.

Looking back, it is unbelievable that much of this final book was not actually planned for months or years, save for that strange urging three weeks before submission. So it is another testament that all you need in life is inspiration. Where do you get your inspiration?

From advocating for a post-Western civilization new dispensation, we shall heal the world of the effects of the sins of dominance and free the former oppressors from guilt, while at the same time healing the former victims. It is obvious to anyone who cares to see that if we stay siloed within the Western and Islamic world views, a Muslim who eats pork or a white American who is a Muslim faces a lot of unnecessary resistance if not outright animosity within their traditional heritage of birth. However, if they embraced a post-Western, post-Islamic human civilization, it is feasible that even a true practicing Muslim could embrace the traits of peace from Jesus, and a European who is tired of Western materialism and decay could learn from the Islamic submission to God and the meekness of heart to quench a spiritual vacuum. In a truly human civilization, a non-believer will be welcome to partake in meditation and yoga, without feeling encroachment on his non-belief.

Moving towards a human civilization is equal to the reform of the Western civilization. And from my small vantage point of a kid born with the triple heritages, I have envisioned three pillars of such a human civilization: 1) personal identities akin to the Fourth Heritage, 2) post-tribal groupings of people akin to the Fourth Republic, and 3) a spiritual compass that can guide one to actualize the Heri of

Kesa, which is akin to rebooting your human identity the way that ten-year-old boy in Iganga Uganda was able to reboot his identity by creating Kesa.

This chapter brings us to the end of the discussion of how to transcend our heritages of birth. Thus, I can confidently give the last hypothesis for my thinking.

Hypothesis 1: The origin of all humans is in Africa.

Hypothesis 2: Even if the origin of all humans is in Africa, the Semites created the idea of one God as it is known to most of us and the Europeans created the modern world as we know it; the most important similarity shared by all humans is the collective unconscious.

Hypothesis 3: Even if all humans are similar, there are real differences and inequalities among peoples due to the differences in collective consciousness.

Hypothesis 4: Absence of evidence is not evidence of absence. Just because we don't have undisputed scientific evidence of civilizations before 10,000 BC does not mean that for certain periods between the creation of the Earth 4.5 billion years ago and 10,000 BC, there were no advanced civilizations (humans or other creatures) that inhabited Africa and other parts of the planet.

Hypothesis 5: The six cradle civilizations, i.e. Ancient Egypt, the Olmecs of Central & North America, the Andean civilization in South America, the Mesopotamian civilization of the Middle East, the Indus Valley civilization of the Asian sub-continent, and the Ancient

China civilization were multi-ethnic, multi-racial civilizations that hold significance for all humans.

Hypothesis 6: After the collapse of the African cradle civilization of Ancient Egypt, the Greco-Roman civilization became the intellectual foundation to what we know now as the European Western civilization.

Hypothesis 7: During the European Medieval ages, between the fall of the Roman Empire and the Italian Renaissance, the Islamic civilization played a critical role of safeguarding the ancient Greco-Roman classical knowledge which was resurrected in what we call the European Western civilization.

Hypothesis 8: The European Western civilization is the current modern civilization and it is the first known civilization to unite the whole of humanity through individualism.

Hypothesis 9: The dominance of the Islamic and European Western civilizations led to their people committing three sins with worldwide implications: 1) slave trade, 2) genocide against native peoples, and 3) colonization.

Hypothesis 10: In this modern era, Africa has suffered greatly due to the three sins of the Islamic and European Western civilizations, but in order for the whole of humanity to find peace and wellbeing, Africa – inspired by its unique universal spirit that is not Islamic and not European – must rise up again to take its rightful position in human civilization. How high the human species goes in finding peace and wellbeing depends on how high Africa can lift itself up.

Hypothesis 11: In order to develop a modern consciousness and rationality that enables us to understand and contribute to the modern human civilization, we need to create and live by our own original heri. Personally, I achieved this through the Heri of Kesa.

Hypothesis 12 / Triumph of the mind: **Imagine the whole of human civilization depends on you. Think so that you find confidence to go beyond any "doubt" that limits you, however, also be open to embrace "doubt" when it can preserve you so that you continue contributing to the enterprise of creation here on this Earth.**

End Notes

1 Naki Diagram is a diagrammatic representation of the order of dominance among the heritages of western, religious and indigenous heritages.
2 *sub specie eternitatis* means 'taking a universal perspective.'
3 An asymptote is a line or curve that approaches a given point arbitrarily closer and closer, but can never actually reach the point.
4 Scientific Method: The scientific method has four steps: observe something in the universe; hypothesize or give an educated guess of why things are the way they are; verify your assumptions through experiments; and theorize by generalizing your hypothesis to the whole working of the universe. If you do these four steps, any human being can pick up from "verification" and through their personal experiments, that person can get to know your proposal.
5 Cognitive dissonance is the psychological state of having inconsistent thoughts, beliefs, or attitudes, especially those relating to behavioral decisions. In a way it is the state of having psychological conflicts.
6 The frontal lobe is the part of the brain that is most advanced. It controls creative thought, problem solving, intellect, judgment, behavior, attention and abstract thinking.
7 South Park is a series of cartoon shows on American television created by Matt Stone and Trey Parker. The cartoons are for adult consumption as they use vulgar language and delve into a wide array of social commentary about sex, religion, politics and everything in between. One of their hallmarks is that they insult the bad tenets in everything including religion. Matt and Trey recently created a play out of their religious critique. The play, called *The Book of Mormon*, is showing in major cities of the world like New York, London, Chicago, etc. The play makes fun of the Mormon religion.

APPENDIX

AFRICA AND MODERN CIVILIZATION

This is the longer discussion on Africa in the modern civilization that I briefly allude to in Chapter 10. The discussion delves more into the enormous challenges of Africa and my proposed creative solutions on how to triumph over these challenges. Without recreating "our world," starting with our own psyches and then the national society, we Africans live in a mental state that Fanon refers to as a psychological pathology, and which others call "the inferiority and backwardness of Africans," but I describe it as, "Africans have a pre-modern mind frame."

A

Africa In The Modern World

Since the advent of the modern civilization in the Italian Renaissance, Africa and Africans have been thrust into this modern world, sometimes positively and other times negatively. In this modern world, Africans and people who originated in Africa can be found in all corners of the world contributing to modernity in small and big ways. In academia, it is important to note that since the foundational contribution of the Egyptian civilization to the study of mathematics and natural science and that knowledge's transit into modernity via the Greeks, Africans and people of African descent have had an everlasting impact on human intellect. Presently, you find Africans and people of African descent teaching and engaged in world class research in all areas of intellectual inquiry.

In the social, economic and political arenas, Africans and people of African descent are well represented and greatly contribute to the UN, Wall Street, religions, and of course politics (the most visible one being Barack Obama, "the leader of the free world from 2008 to 2016"). In the arena of sports and athletics, it goes without saying that every time the Olympics or the soccer World Cup comes up, Africa and people of its origin overwhelmingly occupy center stage.

In entertainment, besides Hollywood, the African contribution to world music is something that has baffled me while at the same time makes me really proud to be African. When you consider that "American Music" – the music that is pretty much the de-facto world music – is hugely from creations of Americans of African descent, it is no small matter. The blues scale with its ubiquitous application is the building block for most of modern pop music. The world-renowned American music genres created by African Americans range from rock 'n' roll, jazz, blues, gospel, rap, R 'n' B to the modern youth's favorite hip hop. Famous personalities range from the great jazz and blues maestros like Miles Davis, Duke Ellington, John Coltrane, Louis Armstrong and BB King to more recent artists like James Brown, Michael Jackson and Whitney Houston.

On the non-American world stage, I can't imagine the world without contributions of music from Africa and the people who hail from Africa. Whether it is a Zulu a capella serenade, a Congolese soukous dance, a Brazilian sensuous samba dance, a Dominican bachata dance (my favorite), or a Cuban salsa, Africa has truly blessed the world with the eternal food of the human soul. Even in far away parts of the world that most Africans don't even know about, like Peru in South America, the legacy of Afro music in all its forms is immense. I had the privilege of meeting the most popular Peruvian Afro musician Eva Ayllon at a concert in Santiago, Chile. I had fallen in love with her songs like *Toro Mata* and *Mal Paso*. I can vividly remember the subliminal feeling I experienced when she asked me in her Spanish accent, "Como te llamas?" and signed a big signature on the album I had just bought: "A mi carino Emmanuel."

Before I discuss the very important topic of the negative effect of the three sins by the dominant Islamic and European civilizations – see main section for details of this dominance – it is supremely important that the reader understands that there are aspects of our Africanness which did a disservice to us such that we were easy prey to the exploits of outsiders. It is the mindsets that were not and are not modern in nature that continue to make Africa the least modern continent. It is actually ironic that in Africa itself, people actually define modernity as European or American influences. Our mindsets made it possible that the Arabs and Europeans came to our land, exploited us, enslaved us and turned us into their images – images which sometimes are in conflict with who we are in our deepest spiritual sense. These mindsets are predominantly pre-modern and sometimes they are outright bicameral.

B

AFRICA AND THE PRE-MODERN MINDSETS

To understand the pre-modern mindsets, you need to understand the paradigm in which they operate, which is the wider bicameral paradigm. Jaynes proposes a structure of this paradigm. By bicameralism I am referring to the reversion to a form of mindset that is characterized by low or diminished consciousness as opposed to a precise active alertness that is the attribute of the modern mind. The paradigm has the following four aspects:

1: <u>Collective cognitive imperative</u> – a belief system that is culturally agreed upon by members of the group regarding specific phenomena in the community or universe, and the roles each member is to play.
2: <u>Induction</u> – ritualized procedure that leads the members partaking in it to narrow their consciousness and focus on a specific idea or item.
3: <u>Trance</u> – a response to the two above that leads to the diminishing or entire loss of consciousness, the loss of the analog "I" and resulting in a role that is expected and encouraged by the group.
4: <u>Archaic authorization</u> – this is the authority reference to which the trance is directed, usually a god / spirit or an authority figure (dead or alive) accepted by the group and who according to the collective cognitive imperative is recognized as the entity directing the trance.

If you have ever witnessed African traditional cultural ceremonies which other people call "ancestral worship" they squarely fall within the above paradigm.

1: In the African tribal traditions, the people (despite being Christians or Muslims) still believe that the spirits of the dead remain within the area of the clan. The people believe that the spirits manifest strongly immediately after the actual death of a person, but over time their manifestation dilutes until they totally disappear after years pass. Sometimes there are special shrines behind houses / homes where the spirits are believed to reside. I remember when I was young visiting my grandmother deep in Luuka village; I would witness people taking food to such shrines for the spirits to feast on. Don't ask me if the food was eaten ... your guess is as good as mine. There is a whole pantheon of spirits and their living counterparts or spiritual mediums who manage the cosmology of this belief system. In my tribe, the Basoga, our more than 100 clans have spiritual mediums called abaswezi who cut across all clans and have their spiritual head called Budagali (Bujagali in Luganda) which is also the name of the falls at the source of the Nile near Lake Victoria. Budagali the spiritual leader is a dreadlocked pipe-smoking old man who resides at the source of the Nile in Jinja. In my days in Iganga we used to hear stories that Budagali can float on a mat along the Nile.

If you watched the coronation ceremony of the current Kyabazinga (the cultural head of the Basoga) on the TV, you must have seen that Budagali came to the function, leading a big entourage of spiritual men and women (abaswezi) – some of them already in trances. He was accorded a special seat across from the King and after he blessed the occasion, he left the function with all his baswezi. Listening to the speech that was read on behalf of Budagali, I was a little confused when the speaker, speaking in Luganda (not in the local language Lusoga), mentioned that the whole entourage represented all the spirits from all the tribes in Uganda. To me, that affirmed the fact that the collective cognitive imperative of believing in ancestral spirits is indeed shared amongst all tribes in Uganda, it is not an isolated aspect just within my tribe – the Basoga. What makes it even more interesting is the fact that the spiritual mediums are called abaswesi, which is the name of the semi-gods who in ancient times ruled the Great Lakes region of Uganda, Congo, Rwanda, Burundi, and Northern Tanzania. Most of the Bantu tribes in Uganda claim direct lineage from the Baswezi, commonly referred to as the Bachwezi dynasty.

> 2: The second aspect is the occasional cultural rituals that take place in the clan setting during important events, like the death of someone or when the clan wants to consult "the ancestors" for something. The rituals consist of spiritual mediums educating the people who will be induced into trances about the different family or clan spirits and their characteristics. One specific oddity I remember is that sometimes the people who were candidates for the induction would have their hair shaved. This is a very peculiar detail that I picked up when Jaynes alludes to the fact that people in trances usually move their heads from right to left. Remember that the archaic bicameral consciousness resides in the right hemisphere of the brain. Shaved heads are easier to excite just for the simple reason that they are more sensitive to touch and also to other elements (e.g. breezes). It is for the same reason that hypnotists

usually touch people's heads during the induction process if the subjects aren't aroused easily. The actual moment of induction in the village involved men playing drums in a very hypnotic rhythmic way while they are joined by singing women. This induction stage is exactly the same as what is called "the mass" within the Afro-Brazilian religion Candomble, which was taken to Brazil by African slaves.

3: The actual trance starts when "the ancestral spirits" enter the bodies of the inductees. The inductees start by shaking their heads at the hypnotic singing and drumming, then their whole bodies, and ultimately they take on a different role, acting differently: e.g. they can talk in a different voice from their normal one, they can start acting physically in a way that their normal conscious selves would never act in. While they are at it, the baswezi or other elders of the clan keep re-affirming to the audience in attendance about the validity and behavior of the specific spirits.

4: The archaic authorization is the actual teaching that the parents pass onto their children or the instructions that the elders and the baswezi give to the people participating in the traditional rituals. When the baswezi or elders of the clan interrogate the spirit, they would do it in a loud and public manner which re-affirms the authenticity of the spirit; while at it, they make all kinds of referential dialogue with the "spirit". The entranced person acts in a very abnormal manner which makes anyone present realize that the person is not themself – the person no longer has their normal consciousness.

I remember some people would be induced with animal spirits (hence the term animism) and would act exactly like the animal whose spirit they have. For example, if a snake spirit possessed someone, that person would crawl on the ground effortlessly like a winding snake. Or a lion spirit would possess someone and they would act strangely with roar-like voices, lion strength and all.

At the end of the session, there is a specific way the person in a trance gains their normal consciousness. They shake their head in a reversed way from the initial side movements, and then they would raise their hands before bowing their head, and just like that the person automatically regains their normal consciousness. After the trance, the person does not remember anything that they did or said. And if they got injured during the trance, it is after regaining their normal consciousness that they start feeling the pain and wonder what happened to them. If the trance took a very long time, e.g. hours, it is at that time that the person starts feeling thirsty or hungry.

My recollection of that loss and then the eventual regaining of consciousness after the session is what made me connect the dots between our tribal practices and the hypnosis in my American university and the trances I saw in the Afro-Brazilian religious practices.

In the Brazilian Candomble and Umbanda Afro-religious ceremonies, people get possessed by Pretos Velhos or the spirits of African slaves taken to Brazil, and also by the Criancas which are the spirits of dead children. The ceremonies and activities among those Afro-Brazilians are the same as we have in our villages. When I realized this phenomenon, I kept thinking to myself how many people back home in Africa know this fact. I researched it from so many angles, e.g. historical, cultural, political, and theological, but the real satisfactory answer I got was in Julius Jaynes' theory. There is something about an archaic consciousness that is still at play in the people who take part in such rituals.

Julius Jaynes extensively describes similar bicameral mind frames in Greece and the Middle East thousands of years before the modern era in which people used to be possessed by spirits. Young women called "oracles" would be the transmitters of ancestral knowledge to the community and the land was littered with all kinds of prophets. In fact, Jaynes gives concrete examples of how the ancient civilizations like the Olmecs, Mayans, Egyptians, Incas and the Mesopotamians were bicameral kingdoms in which the King was worshiped as God on Earth – not different from the way the Japanese worshiped their emperor as God on Earth before 1945. After defeat in the Second World War, the US forced the Japanese to change their belief by way of the Humanity Declaration. Through this declaration, the US forced the Japanese Emperor to issue an imperial prescript denying his divinity. It is this proclamation that led to the separation of religion and state and ushered in the birth of the modern secular Japan of today.

Jaynes shows how the creation of a new Judeo-Christian theology around the start of the first millennium violently introduced a non-prophecy belief system, one that transcended bicameralism (the fertile ground for prophecy and oracles). He gives accounts of massacres of people who called themselves prophets, because the new religious order was turning away from any form of bicameral spirituality purely to book-based literate ways of understanding the divine.

Consequently, the Africans' adoption of the written monotheistic Christian and Islamic faiths played a crucial role in the breakdown of the bicameralism found in some of our tribal practices. Our embrace of modern science has further progressed our place in this modern civilization of post-bicameralism. Nonetheless, there are six examples that illustrate how many of us are still engulfed within the remnants of the pre-modern paradigm: 1) many people still have a porous type of mind, 2) religion in Africa still takes on bicameral practices, 3) most Africans have a herd mentality, 4) everything is supernatural, 5) many Africans lack the notion of spatialization of time, and 6) most Africans lack agency.

1. A Porous Mind

I have discussed in great detail the four vestiges of the bicameral mind in Chapter 8. I believe such vestiges of the bicameral mind manifest themselves today in people whose minds are susceptible to influencing by outside factors. Even if I have discussed that the spectrum of the mindset has three sections, there are two types of mind that people can have: a concentrated mind and a porous mind. The bicameral and pre-modern minds are porous minds, while the modern mind is a concentrated mind.

In as much as both types of minds are human, they live by seeking patterns in the ways of life and in the universe generally. A porous mind finds pattern in the universe primarily by belief because it needs and seeks certainty in life. As such it is prone to superstitions. On the other hand, a concentrated mind is very comfortable with the inherent uncertainties in life and does not fall for superstitious beliefs. A concentrated mind cannot be read by another mind, e.g. hypnotists, traditional healers, or sensationalist preachers. Only a concentrated mind can grasp the modern findings in science like the cutting edge theories of quantum physics which show that at the very fundamental level of the universe, everything is uncertain – everything is measured not in absolute certain positions, but rather as levels of potentiality.

Porous minds can be extremely sensitive, which means they are susceptible to being manipulated or controlled by people with strong / concentrated minds. The way to turn a porous mind into a concentrated mind is first and foremost by reading books. Not one book or books of one type over and over, but books of various types. It is similar to food; you are not supposed to eat one type of food over and over. For example, if you eat only carbohydrates, you end up sick, if you eat only proteins, you end up sick. With regard to books, one needs to feed one's mind on books in the four major categorizations I listed in *The Fourth Heritage*: books about tribal / spiritual knowledge, religious books, books about school subjects (mathematics, science, geography, etc.) and personal books (e.g. sports, biographies, etc.). If one reads from the balanced diet of the four types of books above, it becomes easy to grasp the concepts in the Heri of Kesa thesis and over time, one develops a concentrated mind.

A concentrated mind easily leads to the best knowledge, i.e. knowing yourself and at the same time having an objective understanding of the nature of the universe - what Spinoza calls *sub-specie eternitatis* knowledge. A porous mind on the other hand leads to wrong knowledge, i.e. not knowing yourself and having only a subjective understanding of the universe - what Spinoza calls *sub-specie durationis* knowledge. The main downside is that the porous mind is a slave to its environment and other people's interpretation of the workings of the universe.

In my first book, I mentioned how twice I volunteered to be hypnotized at my university, but to no avail. I have also mentioned that throughout all the traditional rituals in the village, I could not get in a trance the way my fellow relatives would easily get induced into trances. I want to discuss below a near-miss incident that almost got me over the edge into manifesting a porous mind. I am African, so I am highly susceptible to this type of mind, largely because of the social settings I find myself in sometimes.

The following narrative is a classic example of how I almost fell prey to a mind-altering and consciousness diminishing experience.

In 2007, while I was living in Austin, Texas, a friend of mine invited me to a conference in Dallas, Texas. Supposedly, it was a business conference; I later found out the business falls under what is called a multi-level marketing business (MLM). I won't mention the name of the company partly because it has changed names a lot due to multiple lawsuits brought up against it, and also because I don't want to give it free publicity. MLM companies are sometimes called direct marketing companies because they use your network of family and friends for you to sell house products. Their rallying cry is that you can get rich in a short time if you sell products by word-of-mouth to a network of friends and family members.

The conference in Dallas had tens of thousands of people from all over the US. And most of them fit in three demographic categories: Indians from Asia who had settled in the US, black Christians from all over the US and lastly conservative white southern Christians. I am mentioning the demographical composition because of the important role the collective consciousness plays in the manifestation of a cognitive imperative.

The weekend conference proceeded along two general procedures:

1) People who had been part of the business for a long time would come onto the stage and talk very charismatically and enthusiastically about their fortunes got by selling simple products to networks of friends and family. At the end of each speech, the people ended by drumming up interest for some other leader within their business segment who would come to inspire us even more.

2) Flickering lights and interlude music, which I can now characterize as a hypnotic setting. The music would swing between loud and low sound, but it was the type you would call inspirational Christian music that serenades believers in an overnight prayer session. The lights would flicker on and off in very mesmerizing patterns.

There was so much testimony about how people got rich and how happy they were, and a very repetitive message of how they could help all of us get the same fortunes. As dozens of speakers kept coming to the stage, one gripping narrative was getting clearer and clearer: there was someone totally out of this world, who would come to give us The Message about becoming rich beyond our wildest dreams. By the late hours of the second night, it became clear that the biggest of the senior leaders – someone whose initials are BB – would come to close the conference.

By the time BB came on stage way in the wee hours of the night, trust me, we were all so exhausted from lack of sleep and ready for the taking. As soon as BB appeared, many people (I now think it might have been stage-managed) came running down the aisles to the front to have a glimpse of this guy and many stretched to touch him. Definitely he had been billed as a "messiah" and he did not disappoint.

He talked very inspirationally about how the Bible commands that people should be rich, he quoted many verses from the Bible, and then went on a diatribe about the Holy Land Israel and how Jesus was about to come back and there will be a final battle where all Muslims will be killed in the Holy Land. He played so well to the beliefs of the majority Christians (black and white) and the Hindus in the audience, he must have had a degree in knowing what collective cognitive imperative can lead to. There was total hysteria between the loud speaking of BB, the synchronized music, the flickering lights and the loud affirmative responses from the audience. He would randomly go into prayer mode – very similar to the charismatic televangelists we see on TV – and I remember seeing people around me praying, shouting and some fell down in total loss of consciousness. I saw people being taken out of the building on stretchers. I did not know what was going on, but all I knew was that I was sold. I started imagining who of my friends I would contact as soon as I left the conference, and how to set up my own person-to-person business so that I can start on the road to be like BB.

Immediately after BB's world-class act of preaching and inspirational business talk, ushers led us to places where we signed up our names to be partners of the business. Right after the signup, it was almost morning time and I just got into the car to drive three hours back home to Austin. On the way back, I kept excitedly calling up my friends to tell them the awesome good news of how we would grow a multimillion dollar business in just a couple of months. As I went through my list of friends, I reached out to one who worked on Wall Street in New York. Being the smart finance-savvy person he is, he straight away saw through what I was trying to convince him to join by citing Economics 101 and some simple product, price and market matrices that made it impossible for a strategy like mine to create so much value that within six or 12 months (those were the timelines in which they said we could get our first million dollars) I could be a rich man. When we discussed the cost of labor for the products, the value I would be putting in – in terms of time and money, it became obvious there was no way I could make such big margins in a short time. It would require margins even bigger than Wal-Mart – the wealthiest company in the world at the time.

If I was not purchasing things which were made at a very small cost of production and selling them at a high price, or if I was not selling in volume (person to person is not about volume), the way big businesses are, then I was up to something stupid. For the first time I realized I had been duped. For the first time I developed doubt about my belief in "the good news of this MLM business venture." It is the personal recollection of this incident that led me to coin the message in the concluding chapter to this book, which is that "doubt can be a good thing sometimes."

Just like that, I instantaneously snapped out of my new-found ecstasy of owning a personal business and gained my rightful mental orientation. I realized I had been manipulated somehow. I got very upset at myself for not knowing that I was not thinking straight. As I went on to think about what had happened, it dawned me that the loud music, the flickering lights, the lack of sleep, the fundamentalist Christian belief talk and lastly the constant promising of the ultimate business leader (the messiah figure) had all played a part in decreasing my cognitive faculties to such a point that my diminished consciousness gave way to me acting in a very irrational way. I had signed up for something that I would never do in my normal senses.

Looking back to that event with the bicameralism paradigm in mind, I can vividly see how I fell prey to my diminished consciousness. Manipulative motivation speakers like BB know this and they use it against unsuspecting victims. I did a lot of research about the company and BB and found out that actually BB was an east coast conman who was divorced and in a lot of legal troubles with business partners and his ex-wife, from whom he swindled business money. The company was exposed by an NBC Dateline investigative team for conning the public. There were dozens of lawsuits by former business members who lost vast personal wealth; some had lost everything including houses. Such lawsuits meant great legal and financial pressure and it forced the company to change names at least three times by 2007.

So in just one life experience, I came very close to doing something totally out of my normal mind, because my mind was porous to outside influence that capitalized on my diminished consciousness. On so many occasions in my life I have witnessed my fellow Africans easily succumb to being manipulated in such a way just because they need to believe in a certainty about life or religious teachings. In such instances, the poor Africans have no doubt at all about the message their inspirational leader is preaching, and exhibit a classic porous kind of mind. If this point is unclear, read the next section to understand the implications of a porous mind.

2. Religion is Largely Bicameral

The way religion is practiced, specifically the way people behave in many of the new churches in Africa today, is a strong indicator of people having a porous mind. These are lots of charismatic revivalist churches characterized by congregants singing and clapping, wailing, and drumming in rhythmic ways that create an atmosphere of induction within the collective bicameral paradigm. On many occasions I have witnessed congregants eventually lose their consciousness while singing and wailing in churches. The subtle difference is that they attribute the loss of consciousness to religious spiritual authority as opposed to family spirits. Nonetheless, the concept of 'seeking authorization' is the same.

Let me show you how such churches are functioning within the bicameral paradigm. One, they tell their members and the members deeply believe some form of the Western idea that God can come down from Heaven to control them (a collective cognitive imperative is drummed within the audience). These churches engage in hypnotic singing and rhythmic drumming that leads to the lessening of people's consciousness (inducement), and some people go into a trance exactly like the one that tribal people undergo. They do all this attributing it to an all-powerful celestial entity (archaic authorization).

For most of us who are born with a traditional tribal heritage stamp, even when we drop the traditional way of believing, and turn to practice Western religions, the mindset remains 100% tribal. In as much as that is the case, we end up behaving from a vantage point of a pre-modern mind frame in our newfound religion. I have noticed a reversion to bicameralism in many churches I have attended in Uganda. I have also witnessed it in Ghanaian and Nigerian churches I see on TV, and definitely I saw it in some of the black churches I attended in the USA. I have seen many people being taken out on stretchers from mega public services called Christian crusades.

In fact, I have talked to people who go utterly bicameral and say they have seen visions of Jesus. Before I left Uganda for England in October 2015, I attended a church service where the leader said he saw Jesus the previous weekend. All of us in the audience sat attentively as it was said that, "Just like a man sits with another man, Jesus visited this Ugandan man." Now most modern people will straight away dismiss this story and say, no, that person did not see Jesus. However, knowing what I have learned about consciousness and the bicameral paradigm, I believe that that man really saw Jesus, the same way that some Catholics see the vision of the Virgin Mary, or some people see visions of their departed loved ones, or the way schizophrenic people see visions of other people – in as far as the person's reality is concerned, the vision is real (watch the movie *A Beautiful Mind* to see this phenomenon at display).

The only question I would have loved to ask that Christian leader was, "What color and physical attributes did the Jesus you saw have?" It is more than likely he would have answered that the Jesus he saw was a tall white man with blonde hair and blue eyes. I am saying "more than likely", because throughout our life in Uganda we grow up with the image of Jesus as a white man, tall and with blonde hair and blue eyes. This is our collective cognitive imperative that forms our collective consciousness. It is within the realm of possibilities that this black church leader would have said he saw Jesus as a black man, but this is very unlikely. To show you how unlikely this is, many of us Africans or black people shout to the top of our lungs when a black person achieves something great in this world. Just read the news of how we reacted when Kofi Annan became the first black Secretary General of the UN or when Barack Obama became the first half-black President of the US. Trust me, if Jesus – the God of the Universe – appeared as a black man to that Ugandan church leader, we in the church would have been told about it. But because bicameralism works within a specific collective cognitive imperative, in order for that Ugandan church leader to have seen a black Jesus, the whole paradigm of Christianity in Uganda would be turned upside down. Until that happens, we in Africa are still 100% living within a Jesus paradigm that the European culture created in the Middle Ages.

Within these African churches, sometimes in a loss of consciousness or diminished consciousness the people start "speaking in tongues." Growing up in my fundamentalist churches in Entebbe, Kampala and even at school at King's College Budo, I used to consciously speak in tongues.

Jaynes dedicates some considerable analysis to this "speaking in tongues" phenomenon, which is psychologically termed "glossolalia". Glossolalia is defined as the condition when someone with a diminished subjective consciousness starts speaking in unintelligible languages. In Christianity, Glossolalia is a phenomenon that is attributed to the apostle Paul, the person who more than any other was most instrumental in spreading the story of Jesus Christ and building the early Christian Church. Other than Jesus himself, Paul is the most significant man in the creation of the religion of Jesus. He wrote 14 out of the 27 books in the New Testament of the Bible and brilliantly wrote a message whose central theme was targeted at spreading Jesus' story beyond the Jews, hence he is called the Apostle of the Gentiles (non-Jews). Without Paul, it is very hard to conceive how the message of Jesus as Christ (the good news) would have been palatable to non-Jews like me. Even if early Christians in the Middle East and Europe "spoke in tongues," nowadays it is practically dead in those regions. This phenomenon is remnant now largely in the new charismatic movements in Africa and the Americas. It finds fertile ground in Afro-centric churches.

In my "The Spectrum of the Mindsets" diagram, glossolalia falls squarely in the transition points into bicameralism. Jaynes shows that glossolalia happens when the subject's consciousness diminishes so low that archaic language areas of the right brain are activated. He even analyses the unintelligible language that the subject speaks. Through modern neurological studies of the Wernicke's and Broca's areas in the brain, science can point out the specific nature of the grammar and sentence construction of the unintelligible language spoken by the subject. To my knowledge no real negative effects have been found for people who undergo this phenomenon. As a prime example of the vestiges of bicameralism in modern man, it is a natural, neutral phenomenon. However, the point I am making here is that the modern exacting mind in its health form cannot experience the phenomenon of glossolalia.

Because many of our people can easily revert to bicameralism within their religiosity, no wonder some preachers take advantage of them. I have been to churches where preachers dupe their congregants into giving the little they have to the church with the hope of getting rich due to God's blessings. I have known people who have lost their variable properties because they believed that if they take their TV or refrigerator or a lot of money to the church, they will get more blessings. It is truly disheartening, but this phenomenon would never happen if people were not living porous minds in a bicameral paradigm. I have heard the practice of giving lots of money and valuable things to the churches is called "sowing the seed." When you sow lots of seed, eventually they are supposed to grow and have you harvest a lot of riches and other good things in this worldly life. Through a collective consciousness that preaches this practice, people feel guilty if they don't sow a lot of seeds, and the renegades who oppose such practices are labeled non-believers or people with little faith. As a Protestant Christian I feel revolted by such beliefs among my own Protestant people, because the whole reason "Protestants" protested from the Catholic Church during the Reformation era was because Martin Luther said, and we are supposed to believe, "You don't have to do anything to gain favor from God." Our going to Heaven, or our salvation, is 100% purely based on God's grace, not on anything we do.

Last year, I read three high profile stories which illustrate the African's porous mind engulfed in bicameralism more than anything else you can imagine. They were stories of two pastors in South Africa and one from Kenya. One South African pastor, Lesgo Daniel of Rabboni Centre Ministries, told his congregants that in order to follow God's word they had to eat grass, because God can make the impossible possible. And of course a multitude of his members were caught on camera eating grass like cows. And while they were at it, the TV showed him walking over their bodies while they were on the ground. Supposedly his weight could not break their bones because it is God's way of making the impossible possible. The other preacher also from South Africa, Prophet Penuel Mnguni of End Times Disciples Ministries, went even further to convince his congregates to eat live snakes. Of course many of them followed suit. I saw images on South Africa TV of people with small snakes in their hands. The last I have read about this snake pastor is that he is now in jail because an animal rights organization sued him for cruelty to animals. Can you imagine – instead of a human rights organization guarding the public, it is the animal lovers that came to the public's rescue!

In Kenya there is one Njohi, the pastor of the Lord's Propeller Redemption Church, who reportedly refers to undergarments as "ungodly." He ordered female members to come to church without underwear, so that the Holy Spirit can easily enter them. You guessed right, there were images of dozens of these female believers happily showing off their removed underwear.

Earlier this year just before I finished editing this book, I read another story that clearly illustrates the schizophrenic nature of some of the behaviors that our religious people exhibit. A Christian leader who calls himself a prophet (remember prophecy is deeply rooted in people who have astute bicameral dispositions), Alec Ndiwane, heard the voice of God command him to charge a pack of lions in the Kruger National Park. He left his church members in the car and ran towards the pack of lions because the Holy Spirit had commanded him that "beasts would submit to him." As he was reaching the lions, the lions also decided to do what was in their nature, which is to go for a free lunch with him. Supposedly when he gained his rightful consciousness and started running away, one of the lions bit his buttocks and at that time the park rangers came to his rescue. In our African bicameralism, many religious people actually hear voices and see visions of images ingrained in us by the Christian collective consciousness. It is very hard to convince such people that the images they see or the voices they hear are not universal phenomena but purely because they have grown up in a spiritual envelope developed by non-African theologians, who created their own religious narrative and we Africans just consumed it. The Japanese or Hindus who did not consume the European Christian collective consciousness cannot hear voices of the Holy Spirit or see images of Jesus, but rather they can also see images of their gods and hear commands from them. The gist of this discussion is that we Africans need to realise that we have allowed ourselves be enslaved to a religious paradigm that very few of us have the mental faculties to transcend.

I cannot exhaust the list of pure buffoonery that goes on in many – not all – but so many churches in black Africa. It is easy to see that for many of these so-called preachers and their followers, the churches are no longer sacred places where one goes to have communion with the divine, but rather they are now profane places.

A very telling phenomenon about this whole saga is the victim's reactions to the outright abuses and criminality by these leaders in our African society. When you extrapolate from the bicameralism paradigm that people with a pre-modern mindset have a quest for authorization e.g. in gods, spirits, leaders, etc., it becomes clear why so many victims of these misdeeds in our African society go to such lengths actually to cover up for the perpetuators or indeed to defend them. While it is very easy for non-African leaders who engage in such buffoonery to be exorcised by the community or brought to justice by the law, in our African settings even if the law seeks to bring such people to justice, the community doesn't. For example, the people who were made to eat grass all came to the pastor's defense, saying that they actually are healthier and feel more powerful with God's spirit. There are stories of some male preachers who have been accused of raping young boys and men in their congregations, but the congregants passionately support them even when there are videos and images that suggest inappropriate behavior by these leaders. Indeed, the mind is a terrible thing to waste!

3. The Herd Mentality

By "herd mentality," I mean group mentalities that I referred to in my first book as "groupthink." By virtue of most of us being born into groups called tribes and spending our time whether in Africa or out of Africa with tribal affiliations, many of us internalize this identity and develop a closed mentality. The "herd mentality" can take the form of when someone from our social group, e.g. tribe or class, takes a stand about something, all members of the group are supposed to follow suit. When someone says that we, tribe X, don't believe in this or that thing, if you come out opposing that belief, you are easily castigated and labeled anti-tribal.

I remember seeing a video on the internet that showed a group of sheep – a herd – walking toward a cliff. When the first sheep fell off the cliff, the rest of the herd continued walking forward and all of them one by one fell off the cliff. Now I hope you grasp the vivid imagery of what it means to have a herd mentality. A person with a herd mentality cannot be a free person with personal agency – for whatever is accepted by society is what that person also accepts. As such, most of our people live lives dictated by how society expects them to be or behave, and not based on curiosity about life and the limitless desire to keep learning and changing as life unfolds.

Herd mentality is different from the notion of team spirit. In modern societies, people have a team-spirit mentality as opposed to a herd mentality. Team spirit allows people to argue and compete and be different in thinking, while remaining part of the group. But in our societies, because of the herd mentality, people rarely argue with "important people in society" and competition or diverse beliefs and thoughts are discouraged. So in a way, people are captives of their prevailing cultures, and hardly participate in innovative ways to move their cultures to modernity.

Many Africans may give herd mentality a positive spin and call it "brotherhood, protecting each other or standing up for one another" but because it is not "team spirit mentality," whenever their little brotherhood is infringed upon even by their own black people, we get all kinds of violence, which passes for black on black killings. If you have a true team spirit, which means you protect each other and stand up for one another, there is no reason to kill one of your own just because he hails from another part of town or another country.

People with a herd mentality will go to great lengths judging people and forcing members of their social grouping to live within group stereotypes and diminish any individualism that would be counter to the group attributes. I want to contrast the herd mentality with the individualism identity which you find in modern societies. Individualism has been ushered into the modern society by way of the European enlightenment and the protestant reformation, and currently is based on schools of thoughts that advocate for certain outlooks on life which take on terms like secularism, progressive religions, one man one vote democracy, respect of persons, freedom of conscience, and general liberty for each person to have the opportunity to think what they want to think and believe what they want to believe.

In traditional African settings, society is built up to guard against strong individualism and people go to great lengths to prevent others from concentrating their minds on issues that are not understood by the collective. Fanon observed this about black people / colonized people when he said, "When one of us tries, in Paris or any other university city, to study a problem seriously, he is accused of self-aggrandizement, and the surest way of cutting him down is to remind him of ... where he is from [or what tribe he belongs to]" (Fanon, p.24). For example, when I started my initial writing, there were friends and countrymen who discouraged me. Some would say it jokingly, others would allude to the fact I might be acting European, others would humbly advise me that writing would sabotage my settling down and having a wife and family. There is one who innocently told me that he thought I had lost my mind, maybe there was something wrong with me.

I am sure most of you have heard about the joke in many of our African settings to the effect that, "If you want to keep knowledge from a black person / African, keep it in a book." At first I would take offense to this characterization, not by non-Africans or white people, but all the time by my fellow Africans and fellow black people. I kept wondering: is it because there is no writing traditional culture in our history that people internalize things like that? And it is worse when even learned people utter it in passing. It is because of such frustrations that I took a highly individualized approach to write about what I think – not what my tribe or religion say I should think. When I commenced writing my first book, the audience was meant to be close friends and family, but since then my writings have caught a wider audience. I have since opened them up to a wide audience but still refer to them as "my personal view." Let it be known that these writings are my highly individual view, irrespective of what my heritages of birth might prescribe.

Now I can look back and agree with Fanon that many – not all – of our people cannot understand or appreciate someone who can devote an immeasurable amount of time to concentrate on one task. In my perspective, that is what great works are made of. In my first book, I allude to Charles Darwin being famously referred to as a genius and a great man of history and science, yet he devoted more than 26 years to crystallizing his theory of evolution. If we had just a handful of people in our countries who could be left alone to concentrate on a task for 20, or ten, years, we would have many great works such as his from our people. While you read about personalities from outside Africa, e.g. those Europeans who devoted their entire lives to their works, and never even got a chance to have children or marry, it is rare to find many Africans (even though very gifted) who devote their life's thinking and probing to one task, without relatives nagging them to fall in line and be like everyone else in the community. So by such cultural expectations, we have left this task to people in Europe, America and beyond to keep doing the studious work of researching and writing about the world and how the world should be, while our gifted people are preoccupied with obtaining money and luxuries in society and living comfortably to consume whatever comes out of the European man's brain.

Will Durant and his wife spent their entire lives from 1920s till 1988 writing one book about civilizations which ended up being 11 volumes. To dedicate such time you can't have a herd mentality, because issues to do with extended family or social circles will keep pulling you away from your commitment. I remember one of my friends in Uganda has always expressed concern about why our people never seem to work and finish many big projects they start.

There is a general tendency for our people, whether educated or not, to be very short-sighted and only do things that bring quick rewards. And I keep telling my friend, it is because our society is largely built on a herd mentality; people can't be left alone to devote long spans of time on a task. Social obligations will come up, and, being good Africans, they can't say no to those social obligations.

While modern mindsets are characterized by strong individualistic psychologies, many Africans have strong social psychologies. Because the group makes the individual, the African individual is always ready to abandon individuality for the sake of the group. This is different from the modern mindset. In modern societies, an individual with a concentrated modern mindset forges the group into being, not the other way around.

Africans are hyper-social creatures. If we live within the limits of the tribal heritage, we get our morality in group form from elders and ancestors. The modern person gets his morality from reading and subjectively choosing what is right, based on sound ethical theory. If we live our lives within the limit of the religious heritage, we blindly get our morality from God's command as taught by the European colonialists and Arabs – the same people we accuse of slavery and exploitation. If we venture out beyond our tribal and religion heritages, then we start expanding our minds and take on some universal views of morality that emanate from reading about secularism, agnosticism, atheism, and other alternative ways of thinking that could be used to access morality in this modern world. It is only if we can go beyond our traditional heritage of birth that we can embrace the type of morality I described in my first book, "which combines universal human love with an unflinching scientific judgement."

The hyper-social traits also make our people highly functional only within their environment or among people of their kind. Put the average African in a foreign land, and they will be out of their comfort zone in behavior if not utterly non-functional. In my first book, I gave an example of how this happened to me when I left my village in fourth grade to attend school in another part of the country and also how I spent my first year in the US living out of my comfort zone, to the extent that it affected my education, social life, concentration and general personal achievement. This trait of Africans being functional only within their environment or among their own people is the same reason that few of us can venture out on solo trips across the world, or venture out into remote areas within our countries solely for the thrill of adventure and discovery. Have you ever wondered why poor or average people from modern societies spend their life's savings to take trips around the world – many coming to Africa – yet many kids from super-rich families in Africa rarely take trips of self-discovery or adventure around the world? Getting a first class ticket from Africa to New York or London does not count. You need a modern mindset in order to travel to remote areas in a foreign land like Patagonia or middle-of-nowhere Alaska, and have subliminal experiences as you spend days just soaking in the wonder of nature and appreciating foreign indigenous cultures.

To further illustrate the herd mentality, even the most educated among us sometimes look at our race "the black people" as if it were a tribe. We tribalize being black and force a groupthink on other black people in case they behave in ways that are different from "the group." The latest example of this herd mentality is the recent "black people boycott the Oscars" social buzz that was all over the news. Without even thinking it through, some privileged black people are able to use the English language to criticize something initiated by white people as being unfair to black people, and yet they attained their privileged status by struggling to be treated without regard to race. I was so happy to see some black individuals like Janet Hubert say no to the herd mentality of "all black people must think the same" and actually boldly say no to groupthink.

The tribal collective consciousness remains with people even when they move beyond the tribal boundaries or even when they go to foreign lands. Herd mentality like "black people don't do that, why are you doing it" hit home for me one day when I was living in Utah. I grew up in Uganda playing soccer, running, and doing track & field. When I decided to pick up skiing, a sport suited to the cold snowy environment I was living in, there were many people who told me, "Black people don't ski." If I had not created The Fourth Heritage and cultivated the Heri of Kesa, I would have caved in to peer pressure and gone back to playing "soccer like other black people" instead of doing what I felt like doing depending on the environment.

I have actually met people living out of Africa who in all ways want to identify with being African as one big happy tribe. Accordingly, they coalesce and demand equal rights within their new homes in the West, with some getting into politics, and indeed many end up making it really big in America or Canada as ministers and politicians at the highest levels. However, when you hear their rhetoric concerning politics back home in Africa, they coalesce to keep out any non-natives e.g. white Africans or Asian Africans from politics, based on the fact that they are "not truly African." Such hypocrisy comes about because of our pre-modern mindset, because if you are really modern, the same vigor and universality you fight with for equal rights for us in the West should be the same vigor and universality you fight with for non-natives' acceptance into the general African society as equals.

On a personal note, when I returned to Uganda in late 2011 after living in the US for 13 years, I fell prey to this herd mentality in a way I did not envisage. I engaged one of my relatives to undertake works for me for pay. After the works were done, he informed me that he had put his own money into the works. At first I thought he was joking. But he kept insisting. I was perplexed; he never at any one time informed me that he was putting his own money into the assignment, and I knew for certain he had no job or any other source of income, which is why I involved him out of the desire to help a relative. Long story cut short, we had a big argument and I involved the police and lawyers. He, knowing the mindset of our people better than me, instead went to all the neighbors and all the relatives of our clan telling them that I was taking advantage of him. In the end the relatives decided to call a massive clan meeting and decided that I should give him more money because I was the one giving a bad name to our family and clan. In order for him not to continue tarnishing my name by telling everyone that I stole his money, which in turn tarnishes our family name, I had to give him more money.

If you are an average rational person with a modern mindset about laws and fairness, there is no way on Earth you can comprehend such a dynamic. But when you genuinely appreciate that many of our people indeed have a different mindset – which I am calling pre-modern with the characteristic of a herd – and one of its characteristics is that it yearns for authorization (in my case my relative knew that the large community has more authority than the lawyers and police I was so naively employing), you realize that the problem we have in Africa is 100% a mental problem. It is not colonialism, or white people, or slavery, or any of those things which are mere excuses to cover for our pre-modern mentalities. We have to conclude that the average African's mind cannot be judged with the same standards as modern people who go by the rule of law as opposed to social hierarchies. No wonder, even if on paper our constitutions could look like those of any modern country, in practice the law is hardly respected and when push comes to shove, the government can easily corrupt a few dedicated members of the political class and trample over the laws of the land without any accountability. The overbearing tendency to follow the herd, as per my example, also inhibits us from acting in authentic ways. In my case, because I could not stand up and rebel against my own mother, siblings and the entire clan structure – which could have been at a great rupture of the social order – I ended up acting in a very inauthentic way by accepting something that I knew was unfair and unethical. If we were living in a modern setting, I would not have had to commit to such a costly defilement of my sense of being.

This can explain why even many of our educated people, who adopt modern religions and understand modern science, still fail to fully internalize modernity – often using the excuse that, "It is not African," or "It is not for black people," whenever they want to get away with anything. This is usually the case when our dear political leaders say, "Human rights is a Western creation, it is not African," only for them to turn around and plead for the protection of the UN or an international human rights organization when they are deposed and are being persecuted. Our core being is still deeply rooted in the pre-modern mind frame.

By advocating for a Fourth Heritage and a heri (like the Heri of Kesa), I am hoping that young people in our African communities will start developing the confidence and courage to be independent in their thinking and in their way of searching for purpose in this life, without being enslaved to a tribal "groupthink." No one can quantify how much we miss out on as a society by having stringent expectations of people to blindly follow cultural norms that might not be in line with their deep-seated sense of how they want to live their own lives. We don't know how much we lose by expecting our women to play traditional roles without independent career aspirations. We don't know how much we lose by expecting young girls and boys to get married at very early ages, when they could have had an inclination to spend their 20s and 30s or even 40s deeply researching specific knowledge gaps, e.g. a mathematical problem that could turn out to be a breakthrough for the whole of humanity. We should not have to keep reading about Europeans and Americans who sacrifice so much in devoting their lives to science or religion or research, while we Africans are content with just benefiting from their hard-earned discoveries.

It should not be a social taboo for Africans to be independent or live solitary lives. I remember wondering when I had first gone to the US how some people opted to stay behind alone in public areas like the cafeteria or even movie theaters. Each time I offered to go join them, they would politely tell me that they were having "me time." These same people would be seen on other occasions mingling with groups of people and socializing when they felt like it. Over time, I learned that it is okay to step away from the crowd and have some solo quality time when you choose to. In fact, all of the findings in modern research or even in religion happened when people lived solitary lives.

A deep look at the lives of Jesus, Isaac Newton, Einstein etc., leads one to realize that these people were comfortable living solitary lives and it is from their solitary enclaves that they sprang to create or reveal knowledge to humanity. I believe the African cultural emphasis on collective thinking and community living prevents many of us, despite our advanced education, from venturing out on solitary missions and proposing new theories or offering independent ways of looking at society. This collectivism causes us to be hyper-social creatures – a psychological trait which leads people to value their social standing and how they are viewed by other people more, rather than how they think internally and wish to live. This hyper-social mentality can help explain even the most mundane of practices in our societies. For example, it explains the unfathomable high spending for weddings where a poor couple can borrow huge sums of money from the bank so that hundreds of people can attend their wedding. It also explains why ghetto people steal money to buy Rolex watches to impress others in their community, or why poor people spend their little earnings on clubbing, spending money on friends. In fact, it also explains to an extent the degree of nepotism in African governments. Nepotism is largely caused by people wanting to please their relatives.

4. Everything is Supernatural

Because of a porous mind, the herd mentality and having a bicameral religiosity, most Africans cannot comprehend many natural phenomena, but instead tend to accord them supernatural qualities and origin. This is because of what I have discussed earlier: people with a pre-modern mind frame cannot understand the real laws of nature (see my discussion of the two limits of tribal and religious heritages).

For example, when I was growing up in the 1990s, there were many deaths around Uganda due to the HIV / AIDS epidemic. Every family in Uganda lost at least one member due to this epidemic. In my small town, I remember whenever the dead person was not from one's family, people would naturally understand and acknowledge that the person died of HIV / AIDS. However, in many incidents, when you would talk to someone within the bereaved family, they would say the dead person was bewitched – supposedly they were killed by the enemies of the family. Even within my family and clan, many times when someone died, you would hear the same story line.

Another example is that in almost all cases when people are mentally sick and reach the stage of schizophrenia, the belief is that the sick person is plagued with evil spirits. Consequently, family members take such sick people to witch doctors and spiritual mediums to seek healing. If not acting in such a tribal way, some owing to their religious mindsets will opt not to take the person to hospital but rather to churches for prayers. There is no real diagnosis in our traditional and religious culture to view people with mental health objectively. Only a modern mind can understand that there is something called "a sickness of the mind" that has nothing to do with spirits or the work of the devil.

Yet another example is of course the issue of possession. I have described in the section on the origin of consciousness how possession has been studied and found to be a severe form of alteration of consciousness within the bicameral paradigm. However, when people in Africa still participate in rituals that induce people to be possessed by ancestral spirits, the collective cognitive expectation is that the supernatural world can intervene in our daily lives.

Furthermore, there is the issue of many Africans finding spiritual meaning in everyday objects or occurrences. There is a famous pastor in Uganda who gives his congregation "holy water" for various things. One day when I asked a member of his congregation who had obtained a bucket-load of this water how it becomes holy, he told me it was actually normal tap water that the pastor blesses with his holy hands. With thousands believing this "supposedly godly act of the pastor blessing the water with his hands," every weekend morning you will find people lining up in their hundreds or thousands with big water containers eager to get portions of the "holy water."

Lastly, I will mention the issue of out-of-body experience and prophesy. All over Africa there are modern day prophets and people who out of their heightened consciousness can experience out-of-body experiences and also read other people's minds. Jaynes discussed all these in great detail, and I have personally witnessed some of them. Jaynes gives examples of where some people who lose their consciousness in accidents have been able to wake up days or weeks later with their consciousness not in their body but in the ceiling or in a specific part of the hospital room or in a part of the body that is not the head. When the consciousness comes back in another part of the room, e.g. the ceiling, it is true that that person can even see his lifeless body lying down. For prophets or time travelers, these are people who are gifted to be able to return to the bicameral consciousness. I call it a gift, because it is natural although rare. It is just like the natural and rare music gift where some people with eyes closed can tell you 100% any note that you play on the piano. Similarly, there are people who because of their attuned consciousness can "read" other people's minds as long as there is a big enough differential between their concentrated minds versus the porous mind of the subject. This is the process that enables cold reading techniques used by modern day psychics, hypnotists and illusionists. Cold reading is a set of techniques by which people we call psychics, fortune tellers, illusionists or spiritual mediums imply that they know much more about the person they are reading than they actually do. There is nothing supernatural or anything to do with God regarding cold reading abilities.

Concerning prophecy and out of body experiences, people within the religious paradigm will use confirmation bias (a type of logical fallacy) to ascribe divine attributes to them. People who see the future or prophets always do those things within their own religious paradigm. You have never heard of Christian prophet seeing visions of Islamic or Hindu figures, and consequently Hindu sages don't see instances of the future as described by the Bible. On the other hand, people within the secular rational paradigm, e.g. scientists, might discredit out-of-body experiences or cold reading because within their modern mindset disposition they are not able to comprehend such events. Nonetheless, as we modernize our dispositions we should not be arrogant enough to dismiss naturally gifted people who could have extra-sensuous abilities like intuition or abilities to use their consciousness to see beyond their locality in space.

If you have a concentrated modern mind, you can study all the above examples given and understand them for what they are: natural phenomena. It is just that some people can manifest these phenomena while others can't – nature is random, not all people can have the same degree of mind.

5. The Lack of Spatialization of Time

All traditional Africans and most of the modern educated Africans too lack the modern mindset that allows people to grasp the spatialization of time. By this I mean literally the mental exercise of placing space or events in their specific temporal location.

Jaynes asserts that, "History is impossible without the spatialization of time that is characteristic of subjective consciousness." Have you ever pondered the fact that everything that happened before the Arabs and Europeans brought their calendars to Africa is not marked down in any traditional way? Instead we use the European and Islamic calendar to mark events. The only exception I know of are some peoples (Coptics and Ethiopians) who use a calendar based on the Ancient Egyptian calendar of 13 months (12 months of 30 days each plus a thirteenth month of five or six days). Other than those few exceptions, many of our African communities had to create or change their time demarcation to fit the Gregorian calendar, and we have months and days of the week that refer to the Gregorian calendar.

You might think this is trivial, but given the negativity people give to colonialism, it is a surprise that no African movement has ever come up to create a calendar that has relevance to Africa. Without a robust set of cultural devices such as written language and original post-tribal grouping, calendars act as the specific concentrating agents that a society uses to anchor their collective consciousness on. Every civilization has had its own calendar. The most recent one is the Islamic calendar which the Arabs created only, 1,400 years ago, which references the journey of Mohammad from Mecca to Medina as year one.

We don't have any indigenous calendar sophisticated enough to map out events that occurred over the thousands of years that passed before the Europeans came to Africa. Even when we refer to events that were not a direct narration by Europeans, we talk about them in general vagueness of their actual time of occurrence. For example, most tribes in Uganda refer to their origin as the Chwezi Dynasty, and many oral stories tell of events and great rulers of that dynasty, but their existence on a time scale is never given. So we are left with the option of using a European calendar to mark something so central to our psychological and physiological being. Owing to the fact that for hundreds and thousands of years our ancestors never created a time scale and calendar system on which to attach our collective consciousness, even the most sophisticated Africans have problems keeping time or respecting time in the modern era. You might have heard of the derogatory saying "He is keeping African time," whenever someone is late. The psychological explanation of our laissez-faire attitude to time is because deep down in our mindsets, we don't have an innate realization that an event happening at specific orientation of time is very important, especially for civilizing.

When I would talk to my grandparents or even my parents, I quickly learned that they did not have an exacting sense of time. These are my immediate forefathers, but if you consider their ancestors hundreds of years preceding, the situation is even worse. For example, my father died in 1995 but up to now I don't know the exact month or date he was born. Regarding his year of birth, it also started off iffy, but after many years of pestering him that I needed to write down "a date for my father's birth" on school records, we settled on him being born in 1944. For consistency purposes, I did choose April 15 as his date of birth for my official documents, but never told him. Recently when I went to view my grandparents' and great-grandparents' graves, they all had "general" dates of birth and death. Specifically, they all had inscriptions of "born and died" January 1 of random years, e.g. 1933. One elder told me that during those days, when people died there were no written inscriptions on their graves. It is only in recent years that relatives of deceased persons wrote on the graves. They usually wrote January 1 and the year of death (the years of death could easily be remembered due to the advance in colonial rule between 1930 and 1960). For date of birth they simply wrote January 1 and an approximate year calculated backwards from year of death. This practice might seem trivial to some people, but multiply it hundreds of years and see how our collective memories as indigenous Africans can easily turn to vagueness and its psychological counterpart is a non-concentrated mind.

Another example that shows people's lack of internalizing the spatialization of time is that in many parts of Africa when people talk about early morning or late evening it is a general categorization, not an exact hour of the day. It is no small matter, that by default when it is announced that an event, e.g. a burial, will be at two o'clock in the afternoon, it will actually happen sometime between 3 and 6 pm. I have been to some events where people agree to come at a certain time, but eventually show up late and feel no need to apologize. And this problem is not only in villages or among the uneducated people, it is equally among the vast majority of degree holders, even those who have lived and studied in modern countries. Of course there are always a few who have internalized the importance of keeping and valuing time.

I remember the last event that concreted this realization for me was a book event I organized last year. Even if several dozens of people showed interest, 17 ended up confirming attendance and some of them even paid for the attendance fee. The organizing committee and I worked for over five months to book a very expensive venue and we sent out monthly emails about the preparations, the agenda-making and all details about the day and times for the different events. However, on the day of the event, half of the organizing committee showed up and none of the rest of the people came. A few of the people called to say they had to change at the last minute due to pressing family emergencies, but the vast majority did not call or even communicate that they will not come.

I kept asking my two colleagues who showed up how on Earth we could explain the turn of events. Plans change in life, but not even to communicate that you can't make it? I had to console the main event organizer because she kept feeling guilty about the fact that I paid half the money for the venue more than five months in advance, and it was all going down the drain. Instead of having the event, we ended up chatting amongst ourselves about the shock we experienced, but I told my colleagues that it was a blessing in disguise. The turn of events and the conversation we had gave me the final confirmation about how we Africans have no sense of importance of our own and less so other people's time. There is no internal compass in a typical African about how important time is. If you think I am exaggerating this story, sometime later I met some of these people, and guess what they told me: "By the way I could not come for the event because something came up." Of course I smiled and told them, I understand – and in all seriousness I did understand – I understood our mental composition.

A friend tried to explain it away that maybe those people were just not interested in the book – you know Africans don't read – however I reminded him that these were people who had actually read the book, and they responded to me via email that they would attend. In fact, people like them and me are "the future leaders" of our society. That friend further told me that you know if you had turned the event into a social event with music and maybe brought in a local singer, people would have showed up. He told me Africans are hyper-social people, they will show up to events – even book events – if there is a social angle to it, e.g. free food, meeting girls or dancing. Following the "real world" example of that event, I finalized the formulation of the two aspects of the African's pre-modern mindsets: the lack of spatialization of time, and the herd mentality. The herd mentality has to do with the fact that had the event been a social one as opposed to a serious book event where we had to study the book, people would have told many other friends about the food, music etc. and the venue would have been filled.

6. The Lack of Agency

The last example of lack of a modern mindset is our inability to act with agency – a robust agency. Because of our hyper-social lifestyle and an overbearing bias toward group mentality as opposed to individualism, you find that many Africans live life without strong sense of agency. By agency I mean a personal will to decide how one lives their life irrespective of the social dictates. By agency I mean an individual having independent thinking so that they decide without coercion what to reject or accept from society. Having agency is a very important aspect of having a modern mindset, and the earlier you can have it the better for your development.

Personally, I first exercised my agency when I was about 8, when I decided to change my birth name for reasons you can read about in the first book. Since then, I have lived almost 30 years of cultivating and nourishing my agency. By the time I was 22 I had matured my agency regarding every facet of my life – from the belief / non-belief in the religion of my birth to my personal sense of morality. I was lucky; my father and mother as early as I can remember gave me the impression that I could do anything, I could believe anything. So I grew up with the protection of my mother's love and with a mindset that was open to the world and at the same time very free to think as I pleased. Of course because we have to live in society, my elder sister and teachers did a good job in shaping me into the creature they wanted – my sister's role in regard to my Christian religion, and the school teachers in regard to cultivating discipline and the interest to pursue a wide spectrum of knowledge.

In my writings, it is when I contemplate the limits within the three heritages of my birth that I feel I can offer a framework on how our collective society can bring forth children who can have agency in the way they live their lives. Because many of our children progress in life without agency, no wonder our African countries end up ruled by people who are okay with us not having agency collectively. How else do you explain the psychological reasons that make most of our

African leaders settle for mediocrity by accepting most of what the colonialists left behind as our so called "African state," or by badly copying Western models without improvements or customization?

Most of the structures of the African state are overwhelmingly in the way that Europeans created them for their own understanding of "nation or state," and there is no single African country that has remade itself in any original way that is independent of the county that colonized them. What I am saying is that if many of us (Africans) grew up with agency about many aspects of our lives (including religions, names, statutes, etc.), this collective mindset would show on the national level such that we would have conversations about how "the African state should be" instead of copying American ideas of presidential systems or the British idea of parliamentary system. When you look at a typical African model of statehood, it is a badly appropriated version of how Europeans think societies are supposed to be arranged.

I believe the major cause of lack of agency in us as a people has something to do with the absence of what I called "concentrating agents" in our society. Concentrating agents are what lead people to develop "concentrated minds." I discussed earlier that the rise of civilization has to do with the development of two concentrating agents: writing, and a post-tribal social grouping. All modern peoples now have very advanced systems of writing and also a very robust social grouping structure that is not based on tribal affiliations. The advanced culture of writing enables modern people to communicate using their language to a much wider audience, and this communication goes into the future for thousands of years. So modern peoples can concentrate their minds by reading about their religions, history, art and general cultural institutions that have existed for hundreds if not thousands of years. Through this vast market of ideas and stories, some contradicting one another, but others edifying and building peoples' sense of being, each individual is able to exercise their brain and in the process concentrate their mind.

The modern person's mental recollection can stretch thousands and even millions and billions of years. By reading a written language I can get lost in imagining myself in Ancient Greece during the height of the Greek civilization, or I can picture details of how an Ancient Egyptian group of slaves building the pyramids worked and prayed. I can't do this with a lack of spatialization of events, no. I can image the different years that a dynasty ruled and what month a war started ... multiply this exercise a hundred times because I have read hundreds of books, and the result is that I end up concentrating my mind.

Unfortunately for most indigenous Africans, concentrating our minds through reading and writing is a recent phenomenon, and it is still a strange thing. I remember I used to be ashamed because my parents could not read my report cards due to their illiteracy. By the time I was in Primary Five / fifth grade, I could not pronounce basic English words like "porridge" or "protractor" because my brain had not developed enough to distinguish English spelling from what my tribal language would inform me about sounds of words. I always envied my friends at school who could read books called "novels" like *Hardy Boys* and *Nancy Drew*, because they learned greatly about reading and writing from such books. Now I interpret such an activity as an exercise of concentrating one's mind. Personally, I was more drawn to mathematics, science and non-language-intensive books. It is only when I went to the US in 1998 that I really immersed myself in concentrating my mind via reading ancient literature and history. In Uganda if you are deemed good at mathematics and science, you can go through your entire education without learning English literature. I remember in the winter of 1999 while in high school in New Mexico, I spent a week in the library of Santa Fe reading everything I could find about Ancient Greece and some English Shakespeare plays, *King Lear* and *Julius Caesar*.

People also get their agency from the sense of identity and inspiration they get from long existing and robust post-tribal grouping. This is because as I have shown, these groupings are one of the concentrating agents for civilization and children belonging to them grow up with lots of mental images that help the development of their minds. It is not the same as tribal peoples who grow up mainly with mental images of the village or their extended kinship. In early developing years, mental images caused by written religions, national flags, national anthems, national literature, etc. play a big role in shaping the concentrated mind of modern individuals. And in turn, when one feels community beyond blood relation, it helps to strengthen the collective consciousness of the society.

CONCLUSION:

It is not hard to see that when the modern peoples had developed beyond the bicameral / pre-modern mind frames, through developing a collective consciousness from writing and post-tribal groupings (nations and written religions), the advantage they had was way up the scale when they came face to face with our ancestors who were still bicameral / pre-modern with oral animist belief systems. What enabled the outsiders to develop beyond the archaic animist beliefs is that because of a writing culture, and all the mental flexing that comes with it, over time the left brain matured to be equal to the right brain or even surpassed the right brain. Since the left brain is the one concerned with rationality and preciseness, once consciousness took root in the left brain, their minds became more rational and they stopped believing in irrational things of the right brain, some of which are superstitions about ancestral spirits.

When you see that practices like child sacrifice are still happening in some parts of Africa, remember that the same used to happen in Europe and elsewhere thousands of years ago. Because rationality brings brain power which leads to social power by way of civilization, no wonder that when a few dozen Arabs and European people came to Africa or the Americas, millions of our indigenous ancestors could not match them and offer any formidable resistance. Just like a deck of cards, a few dozen Arabs and Europeans were able to convert millions of us into Islam and Christianity, and set up "post-tribal communities" called countries, which were in their image of how society should be organized.

In Africa, people have great talent and gifts, but very few great works. Look at our engineers or scientists: many of them are world class, but in the end they leave hardly any great works for our society to draw from. Why? I went to school in Uganda with some pure geniuses, but how sad that when I look at some of their lives now, they have settled into our African mediocrity and not used their genius to propose paradigm shifting innovations in our society. Contrast this with average kids in the US who drop out of school – sometimes because they are not smart enough – but are able to concentrate their minds and bring forth world class works and inventions in computers, business, culture, literature, etc. More important than family or relatives or the pleasures of this world, we Africans must strive to do some great works for our people. Doing great at our jobs is not good enough.

Unlike the people from modern societies who sacrifice so much to leave great works, many of our gifted people are preoccupied with getting money, status in society, and having big families. It is very humbling to realize that some of the great works we enjoy in physics, medicine, music, etc. were done by Europeans or Americans who sacrificed so much – some of them even made the ultimate sacrifice, e.g. Ludwig Boltzmann, who committed suicide, and many others made social sacrifice by not marrying. Men like Immanuel Kant put the whole civilization of mankind on their shoulders as they labored away all their entire life "thinking about the human condition" that they did not have time to marry or have a family. But now we all celebrate their genius and benefit tremendously from the great works it brought to mankind.

A man like Boltzmann ended up committing suicide, yet the entire humanity benefits from his genius contribution to physics, and the understanding of the laws governing the universe. Boltzmann is the Austrian man who unveiled a deeper understanding of the entropy natural law in the universe by developing a mathematical formula that shows that there is more disorder than order in the universe. Also, he proposed an unpopular model of the atom for which he received a lot of backlash and outright animosity from his fellow scientists in Vienna at the time – but years after his death, it turned out he was correct. He withstood tremendous psychological strain and great resistance from the established scientists who at one time exiled him from his native Vienna. How can we not give eternal credit to that army of great Jewish physicists of the early twentieth century (Einstein, Max Born, Eugene Wigner, Bohr, etc.) who, during a difficult time when their own countries wanted to exterminate them, were able to push humanity ahead by their discoveries in nuclear physics – discoveries that all peoples enjoy, even those who hate Jews?

And I can't forget how I get emotional every time I think about the young lad in seventeenth century Amsterdam by the name of

Spinoza who was excommunicated and banished from his community just because he expressed views that were not held by society at the time. Spinoza's simple but unique writings about religions and God can only be marveled at as the apex of moral courage, for he was risking his life, and after the excommunication he lived a poor man and never even got a chance to marry and have a family. However, 300 years down the line the whole of humanity is able to read his writing and many consider him as one of the most influential European philosophers ever. Just a kid was able to courageously write something so great that the religious leaders who excommunicated him had to issue such a vile decree as I quoted in Chapter 11 under my discussion about God. The insight that Spinoza brought to the world concerning issues of God and religion stand the test of time to the point that even Einstein said that he believes in Spinoza's idea of God.

Spinoza's story is very humbling because there is nothing my direct ancestors (some of whom grew up to be mature men with big families) left behind in terms of written knowledge that can influence me just 50 years since their death, yet a young European of about 24 years at the time is able to influence me 300 years after his death. As Africans we have to ponder why such a young European boy of the seventeenth century can influence modern times, yet many of our "great ancestors" stop only on DNA influence. The story is also edifying because it shows you the amount of moral courage such a young person had. He knew his ideas could lead to his death, but due to his conscience, he felt a strong personal duty to write what he deemed right. I am lucky that however much I write sacrilegious ideas about my tribe or my religion, no one is going to excommunicate me or banish me from my tribe. There is no one with authority in my tribe or my protestant Christian tradition that can excommunicate me from my two heritages of birth. In that way, I am lucky that I was born to parents who were from a tribe and religion that allows me the liberty to feel free in my thoughts. I know there are religious heritages where people can still be excommunicated (or worse, sentenced to death) for believing ideas contrary to the traditional dogmas.

In our effort to leave great works for the benefit of our communities and the entire human race, we Africans need to dig deep and have courage in our convictions. Once we have the conviction, then we need to sacrifice whatever it takes to make sure that unlike our forefathers, we leave behind something that is written down.

C

OUR PSYCHE WAS DISMEMBERED

At the time the Islamic and European civilizations reached Africa, they found our ancestors in such a poor, weak and inferior state because of what I have explained previously: our ancestors were deeply rooted in a pre-modern mindset and all the disadvantages that come with it. In other words, it was very easy for the Arabs and Europeans to be dominant and subjugate our forefathers, forcing their religions on us and committing the three sins of 1) slavery 2) genocides and displacement of our peoples, and 3) colonization. The result is that our collective psyche was permanently dismembered.

At the time of our contact with the outsiders, they had already developed a modern mind frame that gave them so much power through understanding the natural world by way of objective scientific knowledge, harnessing of technology from that science, which technology was used to create industries and weapons they used against us. Also they had evolved past the tribal stage of social development (I earlier discussed how tribes are just a stage in social development, not a final arrangement of society) by creating religions based on written books. See the sub-chapter "Origin of consciousness and the modern mind" to understand how the creation of writing was the first stage in the breakdown of the archaic non-subjective mind.

The outsiders committed the three sins and in the process, they created our societies in their own images. This reality has caused us a lot of seemingly irreparable damages. I say "seemingly" because it is what one concludes when you see the cultural confusion and underdevelopment in much of Africa.

The Four Psychological Ills

There was a general psychological dismembering of our peoples, such that up to now many people are conflicted about who they are or what they believe in and have signs of a psychological makeup that borders on a mental malaise.

To understand the psychological effects or malaise due to the outsiders' sins in Africa, I will start by invoking the anti-colonialism black Caribbean writer – later turned Algerian freedom fighter – Frantz Fanon. Fanon was one of the foremost anti-colonialism writers in the 1950s and 1960s who influenced most of our African independence freedom fighters, and played a great role in instilling a Marxist anti-colonialism ideology in them. Even if it is not clear if Fanon was a straight-up Marxist, he espoused similar views as Marxism. The list of African anti-colonialism freedom fighters who embraced Marxism because of Fanon's advocacy for revolution and violence through "creating a new man" to shake off colonialism is very long. It ranges from Tanzania's Julius Nyerere, Mozambique's Samora Machel, Cuba's Che Guevara to the Algerian freedom fighters. Even our very own Museveni, who wrote his university thesis as an analysis of Fanon's 1961 book *The Wretched of the Earth*, was greatly influenced by Fanon. Anyone who advocated black consciousness, e.g. Steven Biko of South Africa, or Malcolm X of the Civil Rights Movement in America, had read his books. Fanon devoted a great deal of his short life and his books (the first one, which I believe is the most important of them all: *Black Skins, White Masks*, was written when he was just 26 years old) to study both the psychological aftermath of colonization and the societal dysfunction that faces all colonized people. It is amazing how you straight away realize how much the world has changed when you read Fanon's book 50 years after colonialism ended. He is famous for saying, "Each generation must discover its mission, fulfill it or betray it."

In his writings, you can clearly see that our colonized forefathers really faced psychological issues and societal issues that we cannot even imagine right now. I don't want to go into details of these astonishingly cruel things that our colonized forefathers endured. We should be thankful that some of our forefathers were brave enough to fight against the monster of colonialism. Those freedom fighters did their part in the history of mankind. They fought and succeeded in physically liberating our societies. For that, we, the current generation, have to say thank you and be eternally grateful.

But with the same token and taking note of what Fanon said, surely our generation's struggle today is not against colonialism. When Samora Machel says *A Luta Continua* (The Struggle Continues), I believe it is not the struggle today of waging war against colonialism. Our generation's struggle is not about pointing fingers to Europeans and Americans. No. Now that you can go live and work in Europe and America, and even have a child who can grow up to be the President of the United States, surely you and I need to realize that our struggle is very different from that of our forefathers. The verdict is still out there, but from my point of view, our struggle is these things I am writing about in my three books. We need to snap out of the dualism of attributing our shortcomings to outsiders, and instead start looking inside ourselves to answer the question: what did we do wrong to find ourselves on the losing end of history?

Our struggle does not involve accusing some white people who happened to grow up in Europe or America, saying all our problems are because of them. Our struggle is more about our internal thinking processes. Our struggle is more about creating things to add to this modern human civilization. Our struggle is about ensuring that no child grows up in our countries only to be hindered in society because he was born in a small marginal tribe, or in a tribe to which some of our past dictators belonged. Our struggle is to develop an education system where we can internalize the theories and tenets in mathematics and sciences, which were started in Europe, but are really universal. Our struggle is trying to come up with a way of thinking so that our people can stop calling every white man "muzungu" which has connotations of rich person, foreign person, superior person, basically "master." Our struggle is about that deep internalized psychological marking that makes our people look at their black skins as ugly. And our struggle goes beyond black consciousness: our struggle is creating ideas, processes, ways of thinking and innovation in knowledge and society generally for the benefits of all human beings. Being conscious that you are black is irrelevant given what needs to be done for our people. Is it enough for you to comfortably settle down into your black and beautiful existence? You need to do the hard work of searching for knowledge so that you can participate in the process of co-creation here on Earth.

More specific on the psychological angle, the mental pathology (disease) that the Arab and European outsiders brought is at the core of our ontology. According to Webster's dictionary, ontology is a type of metaphysics or philosophical thinking concerned with the nature and relations of being. It is a way of thinking about the actual existence or reality of something. According to Fanon (*Black Skins, White Masks* p. 83), the colonized black man has no ontological resistance in the eyes of the colonialist. Our customs, and the sources on which our ontology was based, were wiped out because they were in conflict with the European civilization that we did not know, and that imposed itself on us. Since our whole being was discredited and forced not to exist, the result is that we grew subservient, became "yes-men" to the

European, gave away our names in favor of European names, forgot all the spiritual compasses that had sustained our forefathers for thousands of years in favor of holding Eurocentric Bibles or Islamic Korans and using them as the reference point for a metaphysics that has our image on the losing end. Because our forefathers were not developed in as far as the modern mind frame is concerned, our "state of being," or ontology, was recreated because referencing the written narrative of the Bible or the Koran proved more dominant than our ancestral oral references.

Fanon further contends that since the world is Eurocentric, a normal African who grows up in a normal family and environment turns abnormal the minute he encounters the outside world. For example, when I was a little boy I remember being totally overwhelmed and out of my element when I encountered the first Europeans – unlike other African countries, Europeans did not settle in Uganda so it was not common to see white people. Even as recently as last year, when two of my European friends visited me in Uganda and I took them to my village, the way the kids in the village followed them around and kept giggling and murmuring things to my friends, was a very poignant illustration of how we black people grow up with an abnormal view of white people or the Eurocentric world. From an early age, society plays a big role in cultivating in us the view that Europeans or white people are superior. From the books we read, to the programming on TV to the social colloquialism we use toward white people, it is very hard to grow up normal and seeing a white person as your equal. In fact, I have heard grown people tell young Europeans visiting our country to give them some dollars or pounds, yet clearly some of these black people actually might be richer than the Europeans.

A white friend of mine told me a very sad story that will illustrate this psychological malaise clearly. He visited a village in Uganda to assess what his organization's funding had done for the local people. The organization had built a classroom in the village and children were being taught under roofed structures for the first time. When he had a meeting with the local area elders, something happened that dumbfounded him. One of the local chiefs, a man with hundreds of cattle, thanked my white friend for the roofed structures, but begged him to help the students with the provision of pencils. To say that my friend was disgusted is an understatement. He wanted to shout out, "What the f&$^ is wrong with you, you have more cattle than I can ever buy, and instead of you selling one of them to buy pencils for the whole village for years to come, you are asking me, a foreigner, just because I am white?" He did not say the preceding sentence, but from hearing the tone in his voice, he wanted to say it. When I keep hearing stories like this, even if it is not politically correct to say people with such dependency mentality are primitive, I must say, and with no apologies, that we as represented by such people have a pre-modern mentality. Just because we were colonized by white people, somehow our society internalizes a mentality of looking at white people as our saviors in the way we should think, the way we should govern ourselves, and as I have shown, even in the way everything should be provided to us. Such psychology borders on pathology. I hope by the time you read all my three books, you will be able to open your mind's eye and forge a mental framework on how to heal this devastating malaise.

Another very vivid example of how our psychology was dismembered is in the area of language. Fanon contends that:

> The Negro's adoption of a language different from that of the group into which he was born is evidence of a dislocation, a separation. ... The Negroes' inferiority complex is particularly intensified among the most educated, who must struggle with it unceasingly. Their way of doing so ... is frequently naive: the wearing of European clothes, whether rags or the most up-to-date style; using European furniture and European forms of social intercourse; adorning the Native language with European expressions; using bombastic phrases in speaking or writing a European language; all these contribute to a feeling of equality with the European and his achievements. (Fanon, p.14)

The area of language is so vital in understanding our mental dislocation that Fanon adds:

> Every colonized people – in other words, every people in whose soul an inferiority complex has been created by the death and burial of its local cultural originality – finds itself face to face with the language of the civilizing nation; that is, with the culture of the mother country. The colonized is above his jungle status in proportion to his adoption of the mother country's cultural standards. (Fanon, p.9)

Growing up we were beaten at school for speaking our native languages, and the measure of our educational development was and still is by way of how well we speak the English language. I don't advocate a rejection of speaking this English (see my second book on this issue), but the argument I am making here is we need to know the potential pitfall that comes from it and our policy makers need to craft a way to mitigate the negative psychological effects that come with it. Unfortunately, I don't see any remedy within our political system, religious system, or social system right now that is working to prevent the negative psychological effects we get from being dislocated from our mother languages. I hope that the readers of my three books will be able to see a solution that I believe can bridge this gap.

There are four specific psychological ills that befall us as a result of the dominant Islamic and European civilizations making us into their own images: 1) we develop a victim mentality, 2) we develop an inferiority complex, 3) we are eager to consume foreign things, and 4) we develop a complex I am calling "The African's eternal dilemma".

1: The Victim Mentality

Because our ancestors had been left behind in the modern civilization, and because the Islamic and European civilizations that colonized us wiped out the cornerstones of our tribal cultures, the overwhelming majority of our people psychologically internalize the feeling that they are victims to history. As such they blame all their shortcomings on the colonialists or white people, yet as I have shown, indeed the white people / Europeans and Arabs found us when we were already lagging behind as far as modern consciousness is concerned. Contrast our reality with how the white people did not manage to transplant their image onto the Japanese people. Even if the Europeans and Americans came to the small island of Japan, they failed to colonize it and more importantly even if they managed to influence it in many ways, they failed to impart their religion (Christianity) on Japan. Up to now only about 1.5 % of Japanese accept the Western religion of Christianity, yet for my country we are almost 100% either Christian or Islamic. As I argued in the first book, this dynamic meant that the psyches of the Japanese were never dismembered like ours; their social development was never sabotaged. They still remained with their core social organization around the Emperor who was God on Earth, and as I illustrated in the Naki diagrams, they were able to choose only the good from Western civilization and retain their ontology based on a dominant "indigenous" heritage.

For Africans it is different. It is sad to see our leaders going to great lengths and expending enormous energy (which could be invested in coming up with objectively fair solutions) to give speeches explaining away the unexplainable or blaming the colonialists for all our problems. The real question is "why were we colonized?" The answer is an inconvenient truth that cannot find its way into this politically correct social environment of today. We grow up in a society where there is tremendous social pressure for us to keep pointing figures to the outsiders. Why are our economies small and undeveloped? Supposedly, it is because our wealth was stolen by colonialists. Why are our schools so backward? Supposedly, it is because of colonial legacy of bad education. Really?! If the colonial education system was so bad, why don't we devote all national resources to change it? Another excuse that will be given is that the problems are due to bad past leaders who were used by foreign interests. If you believe an iota of this mentality, you must be a current leader who is not driven by foreign interests! But how can we verify this? Everywhere I look, especially in my country, you have a leadership that will bend over backward to give all kinds of special incentives to any non-black, non-native person who comes as an "investor." In the early 2000s, a whole factory was given to a Malaysian "group of investors" at $25. The list of excuses as to why we are backward is endless. And it all emanates from the fact that we are socialized to blame outsiders, which cultivates a mentality of victimhood in our brains.

I remember another classic example to illustrate this absurd eagerness to blame outsiders. It was the war in Congo in the late 1990s which drew in Uganda, Rwanda, Zimbabwe and Angola, each fighting on a different side of the conflict. Unconfirmed reports say as many as two million people might have died. When the international community got concerned and started naming the countries that were pillaging and looting the mineral rich country, many of our African leaders did not blame each other. That was too hard to ask for. Instead they blamed the Europeans and Americans, saying that the war was a result of a new colonial conspiracy to disorganize Congo using proxy weak African leaders.

We need to stop preaching this victimization of our lives! And until this happens, our children will keep growing up thinking that Europeans / Americans owe us something. No, they don't. If they did, should they also ask for us to give back the positives that they left in our countries? I can think of a few ... we are using their language (if it is so bad and colonial, what effort have we made to develop our indigenous languages to replace the European languages?), we are using their model of statehood, we are using their theories in mathematics, science, economics and even in politics, to mention but a few. The anti-European bashing can get really absurd. The positive reaction should be to do good with the positives that colonialism left behind.

Until we face the naked truth that we were colonized because our forefathers were weak and poor in the mind, we will not be adult enough to take responsibility for our shortcomings presently. I hope the reader is able to see in my three books, especially the sub-chapter about our pre-modern mentalities, that as a people, we were quite behind in a lot of things before the colonialists came to our continent. There is no strong evidence that colonialism, which lasted a mere 68 years in my country, is to blame for shortcomings we had for thousands of years before they came. Our not having a writing culture – which is step number one for modern consciousness – has nothing to do with the evils of colonialism. I have given examples of non-African countries that were also colonized but are not in the dire state of affairs that we find many of us in. We need to realize that we have to start creating original ideas and ways of looking at life, which will translate into our peoples developing mental fortitude that can cultivate modern mindsets. It is only when we reach such a time that the victimization mentality will be lost forever and then we shall be counted as equal partners on the table of modern civilization.

The close cousin to victimization is the lack of personal responsibility by many members of our society. I have heard stories and also witnessed to some extent how some of my fellow countrymen treat their bosses differently if it is a white man versus if it is a native. It is unbelievable how when the boss is a white person, people will always come to work on time and attend all the meetings when he is around. The minute he is not around, they come late to work and start not showing up for meetings. On the other hand, if the same position was occupied by a native, people don't show up on time and they start arguing against the importance of meetings. Not all, but many native Africans will despise one of their own in leadership position, but not do the same when a white person occupies that position. When the person is working hard to impress a white boss, it is not that they are hardworking or responsible employees. Left alone, that same employee will not show a sense of personal responsibility irrespective of who the boss is. So it turns out people have a psychological complex about white person that they don't have about their fellow black people. Generally, in so many examples, when there is no supervisor at the workplace, many people will slack off and waste a lot of time on the internet or actually not do the work. But the minute the supervisor is around, people concentrate on their work. This is a lack of awareness that it is your personal responsibility to work whether the boss is there or not.

2: Inferiority Complex

In psychology, a complex is a system of interrelated, emotionally-charged ideas, feelings, memories, and impulses that is usually repressed and that gives rise to abnormal or pathological behavior. As such, the inferiority complex that Africans have cannot be understood by non-Africans, but the consequences are in the open for everyone to see.

Personally, I had this inferiority complex towards whites, Europeans and Asian peoples for most of my development years until I formed the ideas that I have written about in my three books. The inferiority complex Africans have manifests itself in so many ways; here are just a few of the multitudes of examples: 1) culturally, most of us look at our cultures as inferior to European / American or Asian cultures because they are not written traditions, 2) spiritually, we look at our age-old ways of relating to the divine and the scared as primitive compared to the Islamic and Christian religions, 3) emotionally, people feel better when they are associated with European / American things, ideas or people, 4) behavior-wise, most people feel deferential towards Europeans / Americans to the extent that they can even harm their own people just to please a European / American, 5) physically, most people look at European skin and features as more attractive and they socially make fun of dark skin or features that are traditionally African, 6) in the socioeconomic arena, people give favor to Europeans / Americans to occupy positions in our societies because they are viewed as smarter and better than our fellow Africans, 7) in education you have whole systems of education that teach anything and everything European / American to the exclusion of teaching our kids about African things in any detailed way, and 8) regarding the political economy, our leaders copy systems verbatim and transpose them onto our societies to the detriment of the growth of indigenous systems of economic and political thinking.

For example, I once discussed this with a World Bank land consultant who informed me that there are many studies that show the benefits of traditional land ownerships in African societies. But the majority of governments on the continent study and implement ownership systems that are native to Europe or America. When you look at the architecture and building of cities, they are copies or appropriations of European and American architecture and designs. There is no localizing for indigenous ways of living due to our lifestyles being different from European and American lifestyles. A friend of mine reminded me of how the idea of the modern house, where the front door leads directly into a living room and the set-up of the living room is so European / American that does not mesh with our traditional ways of homesteads and living space. A better design more suited for African living would be more like the Togo's Tamberma people's design, which has the living room as a meeting space not with four corners but open space, with the rest of the house to the side or lifted by a column. This would be more in line with African living lifestyles because we are a communal people; when a visitor comes to someone's home he is not tucked away in one room, but is rather sat in an open area where he greets everyone and also interacts with the rest of the environment.

Another example is that most African traditional homesteads have domestic animals and birds at their homes, but nowadays modern city homesteads in the cities are carbon copies of European / American ones, not catering for small scale rearing of animals and birds which is very traditional for us. It is because we put European and American designs on such a pedestal that many of our traditional people feel inferior and out of place when they visit the cities. We could design cities to be inspired and informed by our indigenous ways.

Contrast the above discussion with Japanese society. In Japanese homes, the living room is not a Western one, with sofas and tall chairs, but rather in line with traditional norms it has seating cushions on the level with the floor, or sometimes, the living room table is a dugout into the floor. This accentuates the Japanese traditional way of sitting and allows for a comfortable place for meditation as per traditional customs.

In the language area, most African societies favor the speaking of European / American languages over traditional languages. In Uganda, you cannot get anywhere in public life or attain any education if you don't speak English. If our people in the villages equate speaking English with "scholarly advancement" and all power is in ministers and a president who conduct business in a language that majority of our old population does not understand, you can't blame them for feeling inferior to someone who speaks the language really well. There is a strong correlation between speaking good English and having money and power in society. Again, I am giving this example not as a call to shun English in our countries, but for us to understand the damage it caused our people and consequently be sensitive enough to come up with solutions that alleviate the psychological malaise in our people.

Our inferiority complex is a mental pathology caused by us Africans having to live in a Eurocentric world and not doing enough to create a different world-view where we are at the center. I have contrasted our situation with that of other non-white peoples who are developed; they were able to adopt only the good within Western civilization but built their world view with them at the center. The Japanese created their world view, ontology and spiritual outlook squarely with them and their emperor at the centers, such that there is no Western philosophy or religion that displaces the Japanese from their spiritual centeredness. As such, they do not have an inferiority complex towards the white people the way we do.

Before colonialism even if our peoples were weak and poor, I don't think they exhibited or manifested a complex. Yes, they could have felt weak, but not borne a psychological complex that any serious observer (e.g. Fanon) is able to call a mental sickness. You can still witness this reality with our old peoples in the villages who have not had serious contact with the European world; they are psychologically normal, they are not conflicted the way we who have encountered the Eurocentric world are. In observing some of our elders who have not had a direct impact from Europeans / white people, you find that there is not an inferiority complex but rather a kind of humanity that is so open, accepting and universal, not necessarily a feeling of inferiority. Such people will treat a white European or a Chinese or any other black person from another country as "special" and offer privileges to that person. They are intrigued by "otherness" or "foreignness" in a very innocent and naïve way. But it is not pathological. It is the same with the Japanese society; they will bow their heads to foreigners not as a sign of inferiority complex but rather as a normal gesture that is in line with their tradition of respecting others. For us, even when we don't specifically bow down and physically act deferential to white people, still it could be out of a complex as we may instead unnecessarily act emotionally aggressive to them.

The inferiority complex might be camouflaged among us, the educated elites (though you can see it if you are keen), but not so for the uneducated Africans. They wholeheartedly verbalize this complex while having no idea or shame that they are willingly putting themselves in an inferior position with relation to Europeans / Americans.

Our languages are littered with phrases that when spoken portray anything good or beautiful to be white, American or European and anything bad or ugly to be African. I remember this happened to me many times, and I am sure it still happens to other people to this day. When I would spend a lot of effort studying after school hours or during school vacations, random people would say things like, "You read too much, you might become European," or, "You have performed so well, you might even be better than the Europeans." We have instances where a woman who is beautiful is referred to as "being akin to a white person." There are so many sayings within the local languages that work to propagate this deep seated psychological paradigm. And at the same time, people are comfortable looking at something bad or unbecoming and derogatively term it as "real African."

I remember when I started playing golf with some of my white friends, the Ugandan caddies would pass me by and run to pick up the golf bags from the white guys. It would take many visits before I would be treated equally like the white people. Or consider another example that a white former World Bank executive in Uganda told me: in the 1980s, he once visited a top government official, and as they were having a chat seated under a tree, a bird pooped on him. The government official – mind you, he is one of the top senior people in the country – apologized profoundly, and was very furious. Months later when this same World Bank executive visited again, he found that the whole tree had been cut down. When he asked the host what happened to the tree, the host apologized and said he did not want the bad misfortune of last time to happen again when he is hosting important guests. A whole tree was cut down just because our dear leader found it embarrassing that something as natural as birds pooping might have gravely offended some white guy. Such a way of thinking is a result of a complex we develop toward the Europeans / white people because of our history of being dominated by them. Trust me, if it was just another Ugandan who was pooped on, the official would have suggested that they shift to another place, but not cut down a whole tree.

Another very vivid example that has institutionalized inferiority complex in our society is the practice of indigenous tourism. This is where communities and countries allow tourists to come from all over the world to "tour" where our indigenous tribal peoples live. Basically, we perceive the traditional people in our societies as objects in the eyes of foreigners who are largely Europeans or Americans. We have a legitimate tourism industry propped up by our own governments and whose basis is for people to pay and look at the backward ways in which indigenous people like the Karamojong or the Maasai in Kenya live. Until the nineties when the Uganda government forced the Karamojong people to start wearing some clothes, you would read reports of "tourists" being amused by these people who used to live their entire lives naked. When I drove through Karamoja in early 2015, there were still remnants of those who don't wear clothes.

Usually the tour guide companies and the government that allows this kind of debasing tourism, actually have a vested interest in keeping these primitive people in that state – because it earns big dollars. It might be good financially, but psychologically do you know how much it perpetrates backwardness among our own kin and kith? Don't you see that if you would put yourself in those peoples' shoes – the people who are mere objects – you would internalize a weak sense of self, and in fact you would feel inferior to the touring Europeans? And to say that this has been enabled by your own governments – the same governments that complain about the evils of colonialism – is disturbing. Have you ever thought about why even the richest among Africans don't publicize the touring of "indigenous European communities"? This problem is not only an African problem. When I visited Rio de Janeiro, I found a massive tourism industry that takes Americans and Europeans to see the poor people (usually black people) who live in the 600 ghettos in the city. We as educated Africans and black people need to do everything possible to plug every hole that the inferiority complex sips into our psyche. And stopping "indigenous tourism" would be a good starting point.

Sometime last year I drove a white friend of mine to her apartment which happened to be next to the presidential house in the city. I did not know the exact house of the president, as I never grew up in the city. Because we parked in the road and not inside the gates, some army personnel came to confront us. When I told them I was going to drive off, they refused to let me go and starting accusing me of potential assassination plans. If it were not for my white friend, those guys would have roughed me up or worse, thrown me in a truck and taken me to some unknown secret prison. My little young white friend was able to talk to these men who were already fuming and shouting at me, and was able to calm them down and save my head that day. When I drove off, I kept wondering, what is wrong with our African minds? Why couldn't those guys treat me civilly and with respect the way they treated my white friend? If it had been just two Ugandan people, there is no way those army officers would have shown the restraint they showed us. It is very frustrating, but it is episodes like that that inspire me to write that our problems have nothing to do with the way Europeans or white people treated us, but more to do with the psychological malaise we have internalized. And the inferiority complex toward white people, while denigrating our own people contributes to us not having a modern mentality.

The inferiority complex towards Europeans or white people is so mind boggling, I am not aware of strategies in our society to combat it. Even without a European doing anything or saying anything, most of our population accords them superiority. So you find that problems like racism against black people, which is what happens when Europeans act negatively towards black people, are not as much a problem as the fact that we feel inferior to Europeans and constantly want to get approval from them. Racism is secondary compared to the Africans' willingness to treat Europeans / white people as superior. If this was not the case, how can you explain the fact that Europeans enjoy better and easier lives when they live among us here in Africa, due to the politicians, other leaders and our fellow colleagues offering favoritism with regard to them in so many spheres of life? I know for sure a white person without any degree or qualifications can come to Uganda, put on a suit and walk to any locally run bank, and would be able to get a big loan from a bank which many qualified black Ugandans can never dream of. Why? That has nothing to do with the Europeans themselves but everything to do with the way we feel inferior to them.

The last example I want to give about this subject of inferiority complex is what happened to me at the Entebbe Airport sometime in early 2015, as I went to board a flight to London. As we were standing in line to have our passports checked before we entered to scan our bags, I noticed that the guy checking was letting the white American guys pass him without showing their passports. I thought it was odd. And as you would guess, when it came to my turn, he asked me for my passport. I asked him why he was asking for mine, yet he let about five guys in their early twenties – ripe age for potential terrorists – go without checking their passports. You won't believe how incredibly stupid this guy was; he told me, "I use a method called random checking, you would not know about it." Dah, I wonder how I would ever be so privileged as to comprehend such a complex method!

To cut the story short, for the first time in my life I lost my cool in a public place by getting into a verbal exchange with this fellow. I could not stand it. If this is not a classic example of mental sickness toward white people by us Africans, then others will call it backwardness or primitivism. I had had it in my own country, my own people behaving like total servants, if not slaves, to non-black people, at my expense. I asked for his name and badge and also the name of his manager. However, when he told me his manager was over there – the manager was looking on all the time we were exchanging verbal attacks with each other – I realized that actually the manager also did not see anything wrong with such behavior. I just gave up. I had a plane to board. The only good thing that came out of it is that the next group of Americans behind me were asked to produce their passports just like me.

To me, examples like these are worse than racism. On my flight to London, I furiously wrote this sub-section about inferiority complex with a lot of clarity. For the life of me, I know that no matter what the colonialist did in our countries, the biggest problem we have is our mindsets. Everything else is a lot of excuses or people running away from personal responsibility. If you think racism in Europe and America is bad because black Africans are disadvantaged while white people are privileged, you have no idea how much worse the situation in Africa is. At least in Europe and America racism is widely acknowledged as a social vice and people of all colors fight it. In Africa we the black people ourselves give undue privileges to white people at the same time as we hate and discriminate against our own people. So even before I think of problems like racism in Europe and America, the bigger elephant in the room is the favoritism we show white people at our own expense. So when I read about black people in South Africa killing other black people because they were coming from different parts of the continent, to me that was just another manifestation of this psychological malaise.

To conclude this section, I believe that the Europeans have an immense advantage in that their history is characterized by their ancestors having written books for thousands of years, which tradition has translated into them developing a strong collective consciousness which gave birth to modern mindsets. Our people, on the other hand, due to never transitioning to a literate culture, have remained in a pre-modern collective consciousness that even the most educated among us can't escape. In fact, when you see that for most of world history it is as if Africa did not exist, for example Africa is always talked about in regard to which Europeans colonized it and the effects of colonialism, there is some truth to it. It is as if we came into existence only when Europeans started writing about Africa. And since someone once said, "Whatever is not written, does not exist," in the long history of the world, our thousands of years of oral history is basically non-existent. Because it was never written, our people's minds can't reach out far enough in history and feed on mental imagery that causes a strong collective consciousness (see the first part of this book concerning my discussion on collective consciousness). So "the inferiority complex" is just a complicated symptom of the absence of a strong collective consciousness. And if we want to try to chip away at it, the ideas I hint at in my three books are a good starting point to debate in the public square.

3. Our Eagerness to Consume Foreign Things

Growing up in Uganda or Africa, in general, it is very easy to take for granted how much stuff we comfortably consume from outside of our countries. As a people we have consumed so much from foreign countries to the point that it distorts who we are and definitely it stifles our creativity. Although we ourselves don't see the absurdity of it all, to a foreigner it is very shocking and easy for them to observe our dependency on foreign things. I started seriously thinking about this reality during my first year living in the US when some white American student curiously asked me why I was a Christian. I thought what an idiot; of course I am a Christian because Christianity is the only true religion in the world.

However, when we chatted and I understood his point of view, it shook me up. In his mind, he could not have the understanding that in this modern time there are Africans who still hold onto the colonialists' religion. He was genuinely expressing apologetic acknowledgment that the "white European Christians" had used religion to placate our forefathers with a docile mentality of holding onto a hope for a glory in Heaven despite the hardship on Earth. At that time I did not know it, but many post-colonial African leaders have concluded that, "The Europeans came to Africa with their Bible and found us with our land, but they took our land and left us with their Bibles." It is from that time in 1998–99 that for the first time my mind's eye was opened to the fact that we in Africa just consumed a religious product from Europe. And the other section of our society had consumed the Arabic religious product Islam.

Moving from the religious sphere, one can look at the general society or political sphere. Mainly because we use a European language for our public business in Uganda, with it comes all the ideas that the people in England created. A language is not merely a tool for communication, but also embedded in it are assumptions about life and beliefs, and of course words actually inform how our minds develop. If you grew up in Japan where you have no word or idea of what "Satan" is, when you come to live in a Christian country where people talk of Satan, however much you try, it is impossible for you to internalize what a belief in Satan does to a Christian's psychology.

The cost of using the English language in our public affairs is that we have replaced most of societal / political ideas that were created by our ancestors and in our languages with those created by Europeans. For example, the whole structure of government in Uganda, i.e. the whole idea of three branches of government, democratic mandate, and common law statutes cannot be understood without using English words like "president," "precedence in law," and "separation of church and state." In most cases we copy 100% from England or America without much infusion of indigenous innovation or original thought on how these facets of life should be tuned to the African condition. It is amazing how more than 50 years after colonialism, our leaders still board planes to attend seminars in England or the US about how society should be structured, and I have never read a story of Americans or British politicians coming to learn from how Ugandans structure their society.

It is pretty sad that there is nothing our political system can point to as an idea from any of the 56 tribal groups that has informed the national political structure. I am sure there are one or two things that nationally we could adopt that were created by a specific tribal group. For example, the idea of a council of elders that worked for many tribes can be modernized and applied on the national stage. Or the idea of putting emphasis on "compensating the victim," as opposed to "punishing the offender," which is a hallmark of African justice, could be incorporated into our judicial system instead of badly copying English laws verbatim. When I read that in Rwanda, after the genocide, the perpetrators and victims were brought together in a process of reconciliation through the local Gacaca courts, which have nothing to do with European ideas of justice, I was so proud that such a small country had the pride and vision to understand that appropriating our traditional ways into the modern world is the only sure way to make us Africans assimilate while contributing to this current modern civilization.

In the material world, how is it that more than 50 years since independence we import more than 90% of the goods we have in our houses and offices (from clothes, electronics, cars and planes, and machinery to minute things like safety pins, needles, and match sticks)? I once spoke to a business man who was making a lot of money importing match sticks from China to Uganda, and I wondered: how on Earth does a respectable country operate and be proudly independent when something as simple and easy to make as match sticks cannot be economically made in Uganda?

The main reason for our slavish consumption of foreign goods and ideas is that non-Africans have produced goods and ideas that are either more superior or we view them as superior. But worse is the fact that we have failed to engender a culture that can enable us to create similar goods and ideas that we can live with, and also, more importantly, export to other countries. Surely, if our leaders understood the magnitude of this problem they could assemble national resources and ensure that at least we have a factory that produces match sticks; it is not so hard a thing to ask for. Why is it that our leaders don't see the psychological dependence that is perpetrated in our minds when we see that almost everything is imported from other countries? In my three books, I am trying to answer this question, by saying that I do not care what the status quo is, I am going to create my world in my head, and, God willing, it could come to manifest one day. If it does not manifest in the real world, that is okay, for in my mind I am already at peace thinking differently. Usually when I hear what our leaders and people we call important in society say ... things that are so off the mark, I usually just switch off and go back to my computer and get lost in my thinking by way of writing.

4. The African's Eternal Dilemma

This is the gravest of the four psychological ills; please see the main part of the book where it is discussed in detail.

D

SOCIAL DEVELOPMENT WAS SABOTAGED

Besides the four previously-mentioned psychological ills due to the three sins, our societies also experienced what I call "arrested development." The social evolution of our society was sabotaged.

Fanon contends that colonization destroyed our tribal foundation of existence and blocked the natural way to the future. The flipside of this is that maybe without colonialism there would have been enough time for one tribe to conquer the rest of the other tribes and institute one language and one "nation" that could have been strong enough to repel the colonialists. I mean, perhaps over time, we could have started writing our languages and been able to write down the story of our existence, so that we wouldn't find ourselves in a situation where we have no idea what happened more than a mere 100 years ago unless we use what the Europeans wrote or said. I mean that maybe at some point our people could have reached a point in history where in fact they received revelations from God about what Heaven is, what Hell is, what salvation is, what judgment day is, instead of outsiders coming to tell us the message from God. It is still a paradox, and no religious person has satisfactorily answered this question, since the African peoples were the first human beings (see Chapter 1) – I would suppose that means God created Africans first, so why is it that no ancient revelations from God were given to any African?

The list of what could have been is endless. Nonetheless, one thing that is for sure is that whatever could have been was sabotaged by the Europeans conquering our forefathers.

As I have mentioned, it is true that our forefathers were so weak and poor, they did not stand a chance against the Europeans. For our current leaders to demonize our pre-colonial leaders as sell-outs, or claim that they did not do enough to preserve our independence, is unfair and outright wrong. Our forefathers tried their level best, but because they were weak, ignorant and did not have a modern mind frame, they lost to the dominant civilizations. In fact, if you look at it critically, our leaders currently are doing the same, if not worse. At the present time, our leaders go to the same schools as the Western leaders, they speak the same languages, and in so many ways they seem more qualified than some Western leaders, yet we are in the same predicament, if not worse, in that we are dependent on the West both in spiritual and economical terms. To whom much is given, much is expected. When the colonialists came to bring their religions and ways of looking at the world, many of our leaders back then fought and many of them were killed or banished from their lands (in Uganda we have examples of Mwanga and Kabalega who were banished to the Seychelles Islands in the Indian Ocean).

Contrast that with today, where our leaders don't object much to foreign spiritual imperialism. Otherwise, how can you explain why it is so easy for many foreign religions to come and harvest the souls of our uneducated people, while our leaders just look on, if not encourage it? Nowadays, our leaders are the ones who invite foreigners to keep drilling away at our core being, as new foreign religious leaders are given a hero's welcome and there is no substantial home grown movement to define "who we are" and "how different we should look at the world, because we are not Europeans or Americans."

One chilling example of the above dynamic is a story I read in Uganda's leading daily newspaper *New Vision* in 2006, in which a Danish artist, Kristian von Hornsleth, had over 300 villagers in

Uganda adopt his last name, and also change the village name to his last name after giving each person one piglet. This story caught national publicity and some journalists ridiculed it, but there was no serious condemnation or indeed repudiation from our duly elected national leaders. They underestimated the magnitude of the psychological damage such an act can cause to our collective sense of being.

The actions of our current leaders are worse than those of our forefathers because, in this day and age, our current leaders know 1,000 times more than what our forefathers knew. To whom much is given, much is expected. It is expected that our current leaders would fight stronger and establish our independent ways of thinking and independent ways of organizing our society. Why is it that we spend millions of dollars every year for our leaders to go learn from Europe or America, and do not devote the same level of resources to encourage indigenous innovation and ways of thinking? Even if democracy as practiced in our nation-states originated from Europe or America, now we do have enough educated people who can synthesize democratic ideas and solutions that are in sync with indigenous ways of thinking, so that instead it is the Europeans and Americans who would come and study how differently our democracy works.

Last year, while in Kenya, I had a conversation with a friend about their new constitution, and we realized it was an almost carbon copy of the American structure of government: from separation of the three branches of state, to cabinet members being called secretaries, to having two chambers of parliament, to the president having a running mate, to counties being like American states with county assemblies; the list goes on. Even the South African republican model whose constitution is billed as the "the best liberal constitution in the world" – which translates into "the best modern constitution" – is a mere hybrid of American and British ways of governance, with some French semi-presidential system aspects thrown in. It is not original or non-Western, the way Gaddafi's Libyan republic was, or the Iranian Republic is. The point I am making here is that there is no African country that has organized itself politically in such an original way, that I can be proud to say that this is an African model of nationhood, that outsiders can study and maybe emulate.

I can't believe that however much the brightest in our countries think about governance and society, it has to be within the paradigm of British or American ways of thinking about society. Is it that there is nothing within our traditional ways that could have inspired an African people to structure their nations with two or four or five branches of government, or generally structure a society that is not in line with trying to appropriate Western models on us? Western models have meaning only in their societies, because they naturally evolved up to those societal structures. I believe however perfectly we copy from America or Europe, their systems cannot solve our essential problem, which is that the uneducated masses deep in the villages don't understand and have not internalized looking at the world through European or American lenses. Such a way of thinking is a privilege only for a select few of elites like you and me who have been taught in European languages to internalize Western models of thinking. Hence, the majority of our people are totally left out in the real national debates about our societies, and they are bewildered in such a way that their minds become fertile ground for the two invisible problems I discussed in the first book – indigenous culture domination, and the lack of a heri.

Surely, given the way our societies are badly-copied Western models, we can't be so hard on the average African when they are infested with the four psychological ills discussed above!

Unlike our forefathers who fought and many made the ultimate sacrifice, our current leaders willingly let foreign ideas of looking at the world determine every major structure of our political thinking and structuring. Our current leaders schmooze with their Western counterparts over cocktails in New York or London and end up thinking that they are equal partners, however those Western leaders look at our leaders as an unsophisticated bunch of people who at best are copying their systems yet hypocritically preaching independence of African states. If you don't think this is the verdict out there on our leaders, how do you explain the fact that most of our anti-colonialism leaders ascribed to the Marxist ideology (which is a European ideology) and in fact after getting into power, some of them tried to rule our African societies using that European ideology? For those that did not, they used the American ideology of capitalism. Do we have any example of another alternative? Even if there is no alternative that we can pick from, who has said we can't create a third alternative? It is from this cardinal thinking that I was inspired to write *The Fourth Republic*.

By our current leaders letting foreigners fund our education systems – partly because our government officials embezzle the little money that our countries have – it is no wonder that we continue being taught about the superiority of Europe and America, and their models of development, without any serious initiative on indigenous ways of thinking. What has education got to do with the fact that for four years of my studies I was taught about the Tennessee Valley Authority, the St. Lawrence Seaway, the Rhineland countries, and wheat growing in Canada? What have those studies got to do with a proper education? Nothing! They don't teach us how to think or give us any knowledge. Any person who can read can pick up the details of those "studies in development" without wasting our parents' meager resources by teaching us such mind-numbing Western idolatrous topics. I can't forget how embarrassed I felt when in my first year in the US, I was the only one who had memorized all the 50 US state capitals, only for the American students to remind me that that is a waste of my memory space. Memorizing facts is not the same as being taught knowledge. We need our leaders to create syllabi that teach us how to think and how to learn knowledge, instead of how to memorize facts – especially if those facts are American or European.

We need a new crop of leaders in our societies with fundamentally different ways of thinking, so that they scrap away all that colonial mentality education, and redesign new syllabi that will indeed enable the African child to grow in his intellectual knowledge and henceforth contribute to this modern civilization in an authentically African way.

Am I the only person who gets embarrassed when I read that some of our current leaders are shameless enough to take their families to Europe for simple medical checkups or to give birth, just because they did not invest in our countries to have world class medical institutions and the best doctors? It does not take a rich country to design a medical system that works. Look at how a poor little country like Cuba has done it.

I keep wondering what could have become of our peoples had the Europeans not come! Of course not everything would have been better, but it is a mystery we have to keep thinking about. Would all our 56 tribes in Uganda have evolved into different nations, or would Bunyoro or Buganda have conquered the rest of other tribes to make a super-tribe that would have become one nation? Would our traditional customs of God have developed to be like the Japanese traditions, so that instead of thinking about "one God" and "going to a place called Heaven" or "to Hell in eternal damnation," we would have preserved our family-oriented spiritual customs to have our spiritual lives tied to nature and a practical universal consciousness without alluding to the Western teachings of an abstract afterlife? Would we have developed a legal system that is based on the African Obuntu Bulamu – common humanity, that is more about compensating the aggrieved as opposed to the Western system that is largely about punishing the wrongdoer?

Would we have evolved to have a government structure that is not based on the American Presidential three branch governance system, but rather something else maybe like what Gaddafi was trying to instill in Libya – a people's republic with people's committees stretching from village level up to the highest level, or would we have had original political scientists who could have created a system based on two branches, or four branches of government? Or could it have been that somehow many tribes could have forged themselves into one super-country stretching across the colonial boundaries from the Indian Ocean to the Atlantic Ocean, the way the American nation purposefully pursued the destiny of being a country stretching across the North American continent from the Atlantic Ocean to the Pacific Ocean? All these questions are hypothetical, but I truly believe in the present time we have enough educated people who can think outside the box about how to socially arrange ourselves in an innovative way, divorced from the burden of colonial imprint or wanting to copy American or British systems.

There are numerous ways that our societies were cut off from evolving naturally, and it would be a sad day for humanity and history for us to be here in 2016 and think that the systems that the colonial masters left behind have to remain that way forever. As I said in one of the ten assumptions in *The Fourth Republic*, "History does not consist only of heroic acts by great people who arranged things for a long span of time, but rather history is made by you and me coming up with new ideas and creations in the present time." It would be really sad indeed if our young men and women are not allowed to think outside the box and create new systems for our society. Only we can understand the soul of our people, and even if we get western education, we can make it into something we can own. Something that speaks to our soul as stored in the unwritten stories we grow up with, and which is in the eyes of the uneducated grandparents who are so powerless in this modern society because our pseudo-modern African nations have turned into entities that they can't relate to culturally.

I have written all the above because after attaining Western education for all my life and living and working in the Western world for more than 15 years, I have arrived at a sobering fact: there are specific aspects about "Western development and progress" that cannot, and should not, have been exported to non-Western peoples. The fundamental assumption in the West, which is also shared by many of our African leaders, that the West represents the final form of society for human existence, is grossly flawed. I have come to deeply believe that the Western institutions of nation-state and judging democracy by a show of regular elections cannot just be transplanted into non-Western societies.

I have come to believe that the Western models are not the final forms of stable social structures that a uniquely different society like the African society has to aspire to. It is clear that when our brightest minds attain Western education and try to implement accountability, representative governance and a just society based on the Western models, the best is a dislocated state akin to the African "not-so-success stories" like South Africa, Kenya, or Ghana. I say this because the West bills these countries as doing well because they have regular elections and Western companies can do business in them. However, a close look at those societies shows a clear divide between the majority poor uneducated masses, and the few elites who are living in Western-type cities but largely bewildered with their Western mentalities that can't mesh with the ordinary person, whom the state is supposed to serve. Even as the middle class or the capitalist class keeps growing in Africa, the fundamental reasons why we are "the scar on the conscience of the world" are not being solved by this class.

Therefore, from my little humble way of looking at the world, we have to intellectually challenge the idealized image of the Western state as far as we African peoples are concerned. For crying out loud, we were on this planet for hundreds of thousands of years before Europeans came with their colonial states. There has to be something within our ontology or sense of existence, within our soul, that the European man cannot comprehend, which should inspire us to think anew, to recreate our countries in a way that truly speaks to our uneducated masses – not in a cheap populist rhetoric, but rather in a deeply authentic spiritual and cultural way.

The only way the Western models can work is if we are to recreate the conditions that facilitated the West's economic progress between the sixteenth and twentieth centuries. And as we all know, those conditions were characterized by an endless exploitation of valuable resources and its accompanied mass suffering and desecration as whole communities were killed, subjugated or enslaved.

E

SOLVING THE PSYCHOLOGICAL DISMEMBERMENT

We need to find a way to reject the colonial mental state and restructure our psyche or who we are. This is our struggle. Our struggle as stated earlier above is not about colonialism – that was our forefathers' struggle. And it is not about the white man or the European – that is a mere excuse. As Fanon stated, "Long ago the black man admitted the unarguable superiority of the white man … Have I no other purpose on Earth, then, but to avenge the negro of the seventeenth century? [or the negro of the slave trade?] … I have no wish to be the victim of the fraud of a black world. My life should not be devoted to drawing up the balance sheet of Negro values." (Fanon p.179). No, the white man is no longer a colonialist in Africa. Where he is still exploiting us in Africa, it is squarely because of the pact that our leaders willingly make with him. In such instances, our own leaders are co-conspirators in our exploitation, and they deserve more of the blame.

The proper question we need to ask ourselves is, "What have we done with our way of thinking, and our sense of who we are since the white man left?" When you consider that a country like Uganda in the early 1960s had better functioning industries, cities were better organized and planned, sports facilities like golf courses were well-maintained in most of our towns, the fact that today's Uganda is a cluster of confusion and unplanned urban development has something to do with how we think. For the congestion in the cities and the falling dilapidated buildings have nothing to do with age – I have seen buildings in London that are 500 years old that still look decent compared to some of our buildings that are a mere 50 years old. In the 1950s, Uganda's Makerere University was the envy of Africa in that it was a well-organized world class institution, which attracted the best from all over Africa, like Tanzania's Julius Nyerere and Benjamin Mkapa, Kenya's Ngugi Wa Thiongo and Mwai Kibaki, just to mention a few, but currently it is falling apart both physically and academically. The problem comes down to the way our minds are structured.

In *The Fourth Heritage* I give a personal suggestion about the first step in changing the way our minds are structured, which in turn will start the remedying of the psychological effects from the three sins. I stated that many of us Africans expend a lot of energy trying to figure out who we are, especially who we are in this Eurocentric white world that it ends up depleting the mental energies we could have put to use in being creative and engaging in activities that develop our communities. When one devotes so much inner energy struggling with "whether my tribe is more important than my religion," or "whether I should speak my tribal language more than I speak English," or "whether black people are automatically my true comrades in life or is it possible to really trust white people," or "whether I should date only black people or it is okay to date non-black people," or "whether it is okay to speak English with a British / American accent or to speak it with my broken African accent," we end up spending an astronomical amount of mental energy in trying to get to a comfortable position vis-à-vis who we are and what we really want in life, that we are left with so little mental energy to spend on things that could bring about advancement to ourselves and to our society.

So my suggestion is that the first remedy to all psychological malaise is to first and foremost develop an integrative identity combining only the positives from the tribal, religious and the colonial heritages. The celebrated Nigerian novelist, Chinua Achebe, once said that, "Nobody can teach me who I am. You can describe parts of me, but who I am – and what I need – is something I have to find out myself." In *The Fourth Heritage*, I describe who we are in regard to the triple heritages, which all Africans inherit at birth whether we know it or not. Also I discuss that what we need in order to develop is a phenomenon I called "a heri." Without a heri, we cannot be original in our creativity, and we cannot develop as a community. This book's in-depth discussion of my personal heri is meant to challenge all of us to bring forth originality in thought and realize we can make our world whatever we want to make it.

It is fair to say that in writing my three books, I have spent most of my thoughts on answering the question of who we are (principally in the first book), and how we should think (especially in the third book when I bring in my take on rationality and consciousness). So the remedy to our psychological dismemberment is in each individual struggling to forge an independent fourth heritage. For I believe if each of us can reach a comfortable individualized sense of "who we are" in regard to the triple heritages, the rest of our troubles in this world will be conquered within a generation, or maximum two, after.

Without reconciling the identity issues we have, many of us fall into a mental state that is perturbed and we work below par. For example, a friend of mine who left Africa to study in the US was quite successful academically, but could not find his footing in the American workplace. He decided to come back to Africa. However, because of the separation during his stay in the US, a lot of things had happened back home that he found himself a stranger to. He encountered lots of family struggles, neighborhood communal problems, and he was about to lose his mind amidst all these psychological struggles. With a thinking that fits in well with what I call the fourth heritage identity, he embarked on a mission to reconcile his Western educated mind with the teachings of the elders in the village. He was smart enough to understand and pick only the positives. After he took part in some rites-of-passage customs, all of a sudden all his psychological troubles in life and work cleared away. He has gone on to forge a very successful life both in his private living and his workplace. There are millions of Africans who don't get to reconcile their heritages the way my friend did, and as long as they remain in that psychologically unstable state of mind, we as a people lose out immensely because these are very smart and talented young people who could add a lot of value to our communities.

It is important to understand that since we have abandoned all rites of passage practices, when our young people reach adolescence and face psychological conflicts and contradictions, they end up falling in a permanent mental state of disarray. The religions do a good job of filling this gap and reconstruct their psyches around the foreign-born religious ideologies, but at the expense of them forgetting their traditional ways which are the cornerstones / foundations for their being and creativity. There should be national projects or efforts to recreate rites of passages for our youngsters, by amalgamating the good practices from our different tribal rites of passage and customizing from the Western religious heritages – not blindly copying and pasting. I am sure there are some tribes that undertake wonderful rites of passage rituals in isolation all over our country. We need to have a national effort to mobilize the cultivation of such knowledge and practices so that we have a nationwide envelope in which individuals can work to achieve their fourth heritages.

The Cure for The Four Ills

Whereas the Fourth Heritage is the remedy to our general psychological malaise due to the three sins of the Islamic and European civilizations, the Heri of Kesa is the cure to the four specific psychological ills of; 1) victim mentality, 2) inferiority complex, 3) Africans' eagerness to consume foreign things, and 4) the African's eternal dilemma. As I mentioned in the thesis chapter, the Heri of Kesa is, "The authentic individualized interpretation of one's experience of phenomena so that one grows a consciousness and rational mind frame that actualizes the understanding of the fundamental laws of the universe and one's duty to contribute toward creation here on Earth."

If you change your mindset as per the Heri of Kesa, by definition you cannot be victim to the four ills. But how exactly do you go about changing your mindset? Personally, it took me over 16 years to complete that process. Looking back, the beginning of the changing of my mindset was in Primary Two (second grade) when I was about 8 years old (1987). That was the time I started fighting with the school boys who would tease me at break-time about my name and, as I wrote about in my first book, this dynamic caused my first psychological conflict vis-à-vis my tribal heritage. I managed to make the first big mindset shift around 10 or 11 when I was transferred to another school in another town, at which point I changed my name from Yowasi Kampala Emmanuel to Kirunda Emmanuel Sunlight Arthur (KESA). Changing a name comes with a lot of psychological rebooting. So as an 11-year-old kid I managed to have a rudimentary change of mindset. I was lucky that I had parents who let me do that. If I did not have the mother and father that my parents were, maybe

I would not have changed my name at such an age, and that means maybe the Heri of Kesa would never have been created.

Over the years, I went through several religious conflicts until after my first year in the US when I got a mental framework that no longer is prey to any conflicting or contradicting tenets in my Christianity. I wrestled with the baggage of colonialism for many years until January 30, 2003 when I went through a mental paradigm shift that has found itself formulated in this book as the African's eternal dilemma. So all in all it took me about 16 years from 1987 to 2003 to change my mindset within the tribe, the religion and western confluences. I know it is hard work, which requires a lot of internal reflection and moral courage. But we Africans have to go through this, if we are to end up on the side of history that can see us truly make a contribution to this modern civilization.

In his masterpiece *The Ascent of Man*, Jacob Bronowski says that the fact that human beings have a long childhood (about 18 years or 21 years; elephants, who are the closest, have 8 to 10 years) makes us very special. He says in fact, "We are concerned in our early education actually with the postponement of decision. We have to put off the decision-making process in order to accumulate enough knowledge as a preparation for the future." So, seen in Bronowski's lens, my 24 years since birth until 2003 when I decided to start writing what has come to be these three books was a long drawn-out postponement period. So even if I am writing all these ideas as an adult now, it indeed encompasses more than two decades of observing and making conjectures about life and my place in it. In those 24 years I went through all the absurdity of life, the good and the bad, the positive and the negative, I got to know what being innocent / holy means and what being a sinner means. All that experience was preparing me to play my part in creation here on Earth.

The journey that started by me fighting and resisting other people's insults of my name has taken 16 years to result into me attaining a mindset where I can confidently smile at all insults directed at my person. However, I believe that journey has the potential to take as little as one day if one has a strong enough flash of consciousness. For example, the main founder of Christianity, Paul the Apostle, changed from being a non-believing persecutor of Christians, called Saul into a crusader for Christ, just in one day when he was on the journey to Damascus. Similarly, I believe anyone born of the triple heritage could have a strong enough epiphany that can alter their consciousness and leapfrog them from a tribal / religious closed mindset to a universal heri-based mindset. And when that happens, then by definition you are beyond the reach of the four ills.

1. The mentality of victimhood

The key to curing the victim mentality is to internalize personal responsibility. This starts with each individual taking personal responsibility to integrate the triple heritages by picking out only the good and shunning the bad. Personal responsibility means that each person has to realize that they have the power to struggle and chart a course of life they want to have. Irrespective of the poverty or the bad history – you have no power to change history – you have 100% power to change how responsible you are concerning your actions.

While you are at it, collectively we have to create a model African nation-state that is not a bad carbon-copy of American or European ideals of organizing society, but rather one that can proclaim, as Ali Mazrui said, that the ancestral is authentic, but people have to transition their mindsets from the tribe to the whole human race, from the village to the world.

If you internalize the Heri of Kesa, then the personal duty it entails should inspire you to create things, ideas or processes that can replace the source of victimization from the outsiders. If you feel a victim of history, then realize that history does not mean that men (usually non-Africans) arranged things to be in a certain way for ever. Rather, history is what you can decide to do today. What you do today will be history in 100 years. You can use this thinking framework to achieve power over anything that is the source of your feeling like a victim. If you feel victim to something that you cannot physically change, then remember the first part of the Heri of Kesa is individualized interpretation. You can decide to interpret something to your advantage. The interpretations given to things by outsiders are not objective or universal; they are always within the outsiders' cultural lenses. You have the power to interpret anything, any phenomenon and any idea the way that is beneficial to you.

2. The inferiority complex

How can we get rid of inferiority complex among our peoples? It is by ensuring that they get a new reference point. Not a reference point to history in which our society was weak, primitive and victimized by the dominant Islamic and European Civilizations, but rather a reference point that is of our own original creation. One that is powerful, in line with universal scientific findings, and not contradictory to our African soul which is indeed the human soul when you consider that all humans come from Africa. A very good beginning for such a reference point is the creation of The Fourth Heritage, The Fourth Republic and the Heri of Kesa, and all the concepts and models within the three books.

Fanon's anti-colonialism is in line with the above assertion, because he says that, "There are in every part of the world men who search. I am not a prisoner of history. I should not seek there for the meaning of my destiny. I should constantly remind myself that the real leap consists in introducing invention into existence." (Fanon p. 179)

Inferiority complex to Europeans or white people is partly because of colonialism, but as I have shown, even if colonialism did not happen, not having a modern mind frame would still have resulted in a similar mindset. So the cause of the inferiority complex has more to do with the pre-modern mindsets than any other historical dynamic. So if one internalizes the Heri of Kesa and truly engenders a consciousness and rational mindset that understands the fundamental laws of nature, there is no way a trace of inferiority complex could exist in such a person. More telling about this, and I know this from firsthand experience, is the fact that the vast majority of Europeans or white people don't feel superior per se, it is us who habitually and routinely lower ourselves before them.

3. The African's eagerness to consume foreign things

We are eager to consume foreign things in three categories: spiritual things, intellectual things, and material things. The cure has to target all three.

For the spiritual cure, it starts with each person acknowledging the validity of the first hypothesis in this book. When your mind's eye opens to the truth (the objective fact, not some kind of ethnocentric story), that humanity has its origin in Africa, then it leads you to realize how the highest form of human consciousness anyone can have starts with Africa and then goes outward to all the other places and peoples of the world. Unfortunately, most people know spirituality through modern religions (Christianity and Islam, which are not more than 2,000 years old), which both start from out of Africa and then spread or expand into Africa. This thinking is backwards. If you reverse your thinking about the trajectory of consciousness to be from Africa outwards, then you will be able to understand the real universal God (not a man-made God) and indeed you will bear a universal cosmological spirituality. You must keep in mind that just because no book was written about spirituality from the time of the rise of *Homo sapiens* in Africa 500,000 to 200,000 years ago to just a few millennia BC, does not mean that God and the human spirit were not abound on this planet. If you don't understand this section, then you have never authentically interpreted life's experience of all phenomena that have ever happened on this planet using only your consciousness. And if indeed that is the case, then you should use the best of your rationality to interpret the Heri of Kesa regarding spirituality.

For the intellectual cure, it starts with each person understanding the basic principles of the pinnacle of human intelligence, i.e. mathematics. But since in practical terms mathematics manifests itself in the world and to the average person through the natural sciences (biology, physics, chemistry), then the cure has to start with understanding the major laws and theories of the natural sciences. As I have alluded to in various parts in the main body of the book, all the various civilizations that have ever set foot on Earth have done some sort of mathematics. From the Ancient Egyptians, to the Olmecs, to the Indians, to the Chinese, and to all modern peoples currently. Universally we know what numbers are, what counting is, and what the basic mathematical principles are, e.g. 2 + 2 is a universal sentence. There is nothing in mathematics and the natural sciences that was discovered by any person or group of people and speaks only to that person or group of people. True mathematics and true natural sciences speaks to and is indeed for all human beings. To underscore the universality of mathematics, once the great Greek mathematician Pythagoras (whose name the famous theorem of right triangles is named after) said that mathematics is the language of God, and he taught his students that once you understand the principles of mathematics you can understand the principles of life and everything. That is the reason why I anchored the Heri of Kesa on the mathematical principle of "the fundamental concept of limits." When we take to heart the gist of the Heri of Kesa, all the principles of mathematics and the natural sciences will be accessible to us, and from that all the other subordinate intellectual pursuits like economics or religion will be within our domain of creation. And when that happens, we will not be slaves to consuming foreign intellectual creations.

Materially, we will start to cure this psychological ill when there are enough communities of people who have internalized *The Fourth Heritage* and The Heri of Kesa, and they come together to create *The Fourth Republic*. It is only in an environment akin to The Fourth Republic that each person can truly live so freely, and with enough inspiration centered on their true selves, that production of superior material goods that can be proudly consumed by our people will begin. That is when our peoples will unleash a creative energy to innovate material things that are world class and can even be exported to the rest of the world. Already there are some great innovations by our young people in IT and modern technology, e.g. internet apps, the Kira Vehicle, etc. But those innovations are happening in a very hard political, economic and social environment akin to a car running in gear one. If we are to have a Fourth Republic, those same things will happen in an environment akin to a car running on a turbo engine beyond gear four.

I repeat, I have not seen a social or political model anywhere in Africa that can fight this psychological ill. Not even Mandela's South Africa diagnosed this psychological ill and offered a solution that can be applied by all Africans. Otherwise you would not have South Africans killing the same black Africans who sacrificed so much to make sure Apartheid was defeated. In the end our people are gazing without a clue and seeing any idea or anything from "outside countries" to be superior and desirable, and we have to think outside the box in order to arrest this psychological pathology.

4. The African's eternal dilemma

This is covered in the main body of the book.

F

SOLVING THE SOCIAL SABOTAGE

The remedy to the second effect from the three sins of the outsiders is for us to reject the colonial political state by reconstructing original models of our societies. This is in line with what Fanon says: "I should constantly remind myself that the real leap consists in introducing invention into existence." My personal humble contribution to this "introduction of invention into existence" to remedy the social sabotage is included in my second book *The Fourth Republic*.

Throughout history you realize that social enterprises based on ethnocentric or religious heritages have resulted in a lot of bloodshed and destruction. You can think of the Arab Muslim expansion into North Africa and the Mediterranean, between the seventh and fourteenth centuries, in which whole cultures were wiped out if they did not convert to Islam to the extent that now the whole North Africa is almost 100% Arab. Or the counteroffensive by the Christian kingdoms at the request of the Byzantine Emperor in the eleventh century – who barbarically slaughtered people on their way from Western Europe through present-day Turkey, all the way to Jerusalem. Or the Bantu migrations we study in which my own ethnic grouping migrated from the Niger Congo delta and expanded to occupy almost the entirety of what we know as central, southern and eastern Africa. In *The Fourth Republic*, I advocate for and structure a social enterprise that is beyond one's specific sense of ethnic or religious heritage. We need to have a social structure that is based on everyone's human heritage characterized by a post-tribal and inter-religious identity.

The current problem of how our society is badly organized is no longer a legacy of colonialism – with more than 50 years since independence, we have had enough time and opportunity to recreate our societies anew if we wanted. If our politics are bad, our economies are small and not modern, our healthy systems dilapidated, or our education system not producing world class inventions, it is because we have failed to organize our society in a way that is in line with who we are and in a way that brings out the best from us.

The reason that some of us give, that it is the West impeding our development since independence, is just a lame excuse. There are societies that don't hold this lame excuse and have developed and recreated themselves against all odds. You cannot tell me that Uganda is sabotaged by the West so much more than the way Cuba has been sabotage physically by the US! In more than 50 years the American trade embargo has prevented Cuba from importing any cars, machinery, doing trade with Europe and most of the world, has imposed an arms embargo, declared the country a national sponsor of terrorism – all these to cripple and destroy the nation of Cuba. They have managed to cripple it, but the Cuban people have survived and they are proud of their independence. Cuba is a country with only one third of the Ugandan population, but it has been able, against overwhelming odds, to be independent in the way it organizes its society, in the way it ensures all citizens are educated, in the way it provides universal healthcare to its citizens, in the way it has world class cancer treatment and is one of the few countries in the world with 100% literacy level. In fact, unlike any African country this small country of Cuba, which is only 90 miles from the US, was able to fight off an intervention from the mighty US in 1961, and it won. Even after the end of the Soviet assistance in 1990, following the collapse of the USSR, the country has survived another 26 years with a fierce and proud independence.

Cuba did not use any excuses to manage its own affairs. It used its meager resources to recreate itself and become a proud independent nation. In fact, it is an open secret that when many of the Uganda NRA victorious soldiers came into power in 1986, many of the officers had AIDS. They were taken for treatment in Cuba, which was decades ahead of the treatment the West was providing to our hospitals. All these achievements by Cuba are more impressive when you consider that it has been under a trade embargo by the only remaining super power for more than five decades. How could such a small poor Third World country do it against the sabotage from the most powerful empire in existence today?

The explanation is that its people understood who they were (see my attempt at this exercise for Uganda in *The Fourth Heritage*) and created a society that is not pro-America or pro-Europe but pro-Cuba (see *The Fourth Republic* for my attempt at this). We have more potential in Africa than in Cuba (e.g. in Uganda we have more arable land, more minerals, oil, more people for a bigger market, no direct sabotage from America – in fact, America gives us a lot of aid instead), but why have we not been able to develop indigenous ways of doing things that can make us really independent and proud citizens? It is not because of colonialism or the effect of colonialism. It is a combination of many factors, many of which existed before colonialism and continue to plague us even after colonialism, and this book is my final chapter in getting to the root of this problem, diagnosing it and offering a specific arguable solution. In fact, when I visited Cuba in 2015, I also realized that, unlike African countries that have abandoned our own indigenous cultural belief, the Cubans have preserved our own African culture such that 70–90% of the Cubans follow an African religion called Santeria – which is dominant over Christianity in their society.

I created *The Fourth Republic* to give a suggestion on how an original way of looking at our history and society could ignite the creative powers in our people and produce a nation free from tribalism and one that can enable us make a mark on the world stage. In fact, one of the reviewers of my book Dr. Daniel Kawuma said that:

> *The Fourth Republic* stands out as one of the most original works rendered towards lifting the weight of tribalism and groupthink off the shoulders of a static and stagnant society … [the author] offers a sweeping viewpoint by creating a well thought out "Chwezi nation." *The Fourth Republic* is an extraordinary book with a detailed roadmap that if followed and implemented can procure Ugandans a more effective system of governance. The propositions offer each Ugandan citizen the "Chwezi dream." This dream has a foundation rooted in clearing the path for prosperity for each individual, shaped by the promises of their imagination. The "Chwezi dream" promises to liberate Ugandans from the shackles of tribalism, poverty, ignorance, religious divisiveness and cultural conflicts. My hope is for this message to reach every Ugandan and African, particularly those leading or aspiring to lead our nations in the coming years.

When you read *The Fourth Republic* you will see that whereas primitive practices like human sacrifices by witch doctors are entertained in society, the nation-state, as constituted now, cannot fight them. There is no political or cultural will to wage war against such backward customs in our society, because our psyche is largely tied to the way people think about things like these. The current nation-state cannot wage war against them, because "the elders" or "cultural leaders" could revolt. But I believe I was able to offer a surgical solution in *The Fourth Republic* that can deliver us from self-sabotaging customs like those.

The Nigerian writer Chinua Achebe writes in his masterpiece book *Things Fall Apart* that, "The white man is very clever. He came quietly and peaceably with his religion. We were amused at his foolishness and allowed him to stay. Now he has won our brothers, and our clan can no longer act like one. He has put a knife on the things that held us together and we have fallen apart." We need to grasp the fact that for the African / Ugandan, the tribe has never been and cannot be the civilizing force. The foreign religions as internalized by many have tried to civilize us but as I discussed in my first book, that civilizing came at a psychological cost that up to now we have failed to truly overcome. This psychological cost manifests supremely in the "African eternal dilemma" I discussed in the main part of this book.

So I concluded that the nation-state has to be the civilizing force that we need to use as Africans, not the tribe and definitely not the religions as they are foreign creations. The way we structure our nation-state should speak to who we are (we are humans but not Europeans or Americans, our model of a nation-state can't be American or European. God created us Africans for a reason). More importantly, the new African nation-state needs to take into account our special place in history as the continent that is the cradle of humanity, as stated in my first hypothesis. No other peoples can claim that unique privilege. As a Ugandan, I feel special that my country sits right at the beginning of the Nile, that river that birthed Ancient

Egypt, maybe the greatest nation-state in all ancient times. We can draw inspiration from that to create another great modern nation-state. No need to blindly follow American or British theories about society. We need to diagnose our problem and offer a solution that at its deepest level is tasked with transforming the African beyond the tribal mindset. That is the only way I can see we will rise above being a mere "scar on the conscience of the world."

One of the major building blocks of my theme in *The Fourth Republic* is the inspiration I received from reading about Ancient Egypt, which has special significance for us as Ugandans because of the Nile. The civilization of Ancient Egypt was able to stand for thousands of years because the people had a unique way of seeing themselves and their place in the world. The greatest nation-state currently, the US, has been around only for 240 years.

According to the Pyramid texts, and the Giza Plateau Complex, the reference point for Ancient Egypt was the legendary Zep Tepi (about 40,000 years BC) which is referred to as "the first time." This is based on a legend just like our own Chwezi legend. Archeologists give a different timeline that does not go that far. Egyptian legend has it that semi-god people, the Shemsu Hor, reputedly ruled Egypt and instituted all the principal elements comprising Ancient Egyptian dynastic civilization. Throughout all of dynastic history, Egyptians said that all their rituals and ways of kingship derived from the Shemsu Hor. In a similar way, I use the greatest legendary history we have in Uganda or East Africa – that of the Bachwezi (who were demi-gods and ruled over vast expanses of land before they disappeared in the underworld) to anchor our nationhood and everything that we can be. If we build a nation-state referencing something as original and which is so much "us" and not America or Europe, I believe the result is not only a strong and robust country, but it would be the beginning of a new African civilization that can pull the whole continent with us.

In modern countries like the US where I spent my formative years, you find that even the most illiterate of people would have a very solid grip of what their nation is. If there was to be abuse by the military or police, those illiterate people can allude to the constitution and find their reference point in struggling for their personal liberty. They can even recite in satisfactory fashion their fundamental right like the first or the second amendments – even if they have never read the document. Those are the illiterate ones. Now, for the literate ones, they will argue day and night about universal civil rights and literally fight in elections about what the constitution means. However, since the law is the law, not one resorts to force or to killing opponents when they lose elections. It is not okay that in our countries, even the educated elites cannot refer to or trust state institutions and definitely not the constitution to invoke their rights successfully.

In 2006 there was a case in Uganda where the Supreme Court granted bail to a political prisoner, but the army was able to enter the court forcefully, and take the prisoner away to military jail. If the highest leaders in our country can dismiss the constitutional independence between branches as clearly outlined in the constitution, who am I to belittle myself that the structure of the nation-state of Uganda is something for me to be so proud of that I should feel inadequate to comment on?

Now for the illiterate masses or people in our villages, there is no knowledge of the constitution or the laws made by MPs to safeguard people's rights. The only state institution that most point to is the President or the MP when they come to campaign and dish out sugar or salt in exchange for victory during elections. The state for these people is the person of the President, or the MP, and not much else.

Whether the President is good or bad, in their perception, is translated as a good state or a bad state respectively. When the President gives a bribe in broad daylight, people shout and say long live the state.

The Fourth Republic tries to argue for a change by suggesting the creation of a model that can be referenced to by an illiterate person in a village, and people will be able to truthfully know their rights within the state. The Fourth Republic is a model state that fully integrates the simplicity of indigenous ways of knowing with the sophistication of the modern world. I wrote the book out of frustration upon reading one of our President's books, *What is Africa's Problem*, in which he says, "There is something fundamentally wrong. The main problem is that our leaders did not find time to define the issues confronting them. They borrowed foreign ideas and superimposed them on their countries: This could not, and did not, work. If you examine the scene in Africa, it is quite difficult to find a model solution." (Kirunda, p.29)

In fact, I have always wondered why we spend money from our meager treasury on things like elections, instead of spending that money to research and create a formidable respectable republic that can't be abused by the military. It is sad that we agreed to Western demands to have frequent elections, supposedly as a sign of democracy, when in fact they don't mean much given the fundamental lack of a state model that is robust. Each election cycle costs billions of shillings, money that could have been put to things that help advance the building of a strong African republic. For example, in Uganda if our leadership was really interested and believed that having a national language like Swahili or Luganda was nation-building, why can't they propose the canceling of an election cycle and put all that money in teaching all our people the national language? This vital nation-building exercise cannot take more than five years, and it would have better dividends than an election full of bribery and stealing. To me such a worthwhile national project should merit the reconciliation between government and opposition to work on one objective.

I strongly believe that if we Africans understood our history objectively and how disadvantaged we are, there is no way someone would think that the solution to our problems is in one group fighting and killing another. How shocked I was to see black people in South African killing other black people from other parts of the continent in the recent xenophobic attacks. And what is worse is that the police and the political establishment did not do enough to stop this. In fact, you heard politicians and cultural leaders siding with the public and letting the mayhem go on unpunished. If this can happen in the most advanced country on the continent, one whose constitution has been billed as the most liberal in the world (even more than that of America), doesn't this mean that there is something really wrong with the way we Africans have organized our countries, blindly cutting and pasting from Europe or America?

There has to be a way that we can build a society that is harmonious and welcoming to all Africans and all humans. Such a society would embody the spirit I feel when I talk to traditional peoples. Why can't that spirit be transferred to the national level?

Many people say Africa has no culture – meaning there isn't a long history of written tradition. Of course, they forget the ancient civilizations like Egypt, but to an extent they have a point. The Egyptian civilization rose and fell. The modern civilization rose, and has not fallen. In this modern civilization, the same assertion cannot be made about the Arabs, the Chinese, the Indians, the Japanese and the Koreans. Do you know why? It is because they have an indigenous writing tradition within the modern era. Why can't our leaders realise that this is the fundamental reason for our low standing in the face of other peoples. If we could channel all our national energies toward ensuring that there is a writing culture among all our peoples, for sure we would take our rightful place in this modern civilization. It is no small thing that the term "pre-history" refers to things that happened before the written accounts.

When I went to France in 2006 I visited the Notre Dame Cathedral, which is one of the most magnificent man-made buildings I have ever visited. This marvelous building is more 800 years old and there is no structure in Uganda today that even comes close to its architecture and magnificence. Eight hundred years ago means it was built around 1200 AD. I tried to compare the France of 1200 and the Uganda of 1200 and there is nothing to compare. For one, we have no written account of the Uganda of 1200. Actually the country itself was not there, because the British had not yet called it Uganda. Also we don't have any structure that dates to that year, so I can confidently say that there was no structure of stone and marble that was around in Uganda at that time. If you consider that the Notre Dame building and hundreds of others like that were built by Europeans many years before they came and colonized Africa, don't you see that we had already been left behind in some aspect of this modern civilization? When you as an African can reach such an objective conclusion is when you can appreciate Frantz Fanon's words: "I have no wish to be the victim of the fraud of a black world. My life should not be devoted to drawing up the balance sheet of negro values ... There are in every part of the world men who search. I am not a prisoner of history. I should not seek [in history] for the meaning of my destiny. I should constantly remind myself that the real leap consists in introducing invention into existence." As Africans or Ugandans of today, we cannot look to written modern history to find our salvation or a golden age to refer to. However, by creating things in the present, we can reach the glory that we must.

The only way we can look to the past to get our bearing is if there is a way to consider the long lost ancient civilizations before the recorded ones. As I mentioned earlier, we don't have records of the civilizations before 10,000 BC. And I mentioned, it is very likely that for hundreds of thousands of years there were advanced civilizations in Africa and other parts of the world, but due to a catastrophe which many civilizations term "the great flood" or scientists refer to as the Ice Ages, it is plausible that all those ancient advanced civilizations perished, and with them any trace of their grandeur. So because there is no trace of that time, all we are left with is the modern Eurocentric recording of history, which puts Africa on the losing end.

That is why in my three books I am purposely putting less emphasis on history and more on creativity in my lifetime – which has a mere less than 100 years left. If I can create something before the next 100 years about which generations of future Africans can look back and say, "There was some human being named Emmanuel Kirunda who created this way of us looking at the world," it does not bother me a single bit whether the Uganda of 1200 AD was primitive compared to the France of 1200 AD. It is only if I write original ideas in my three books that I can stand toe to toe and compare and contrast myself with a European who has had the advantage of a glorious modern history in which his ancestors wrote dozens of books over thousands of years. And since to whom much is given, much is expected, I feel comfortable that I am not doing very badly given what history has served me. By this way of thinking, I have been able to heal myself of the inferiority complex and other psychological ills that the dominant Islamic and European civilizations unleashed on our collective humanity.

Without this vantage point or way of looking at the world, so that we can see the urgency of creation by us that is needed in this moment, I believe we Africans will never catch up. It is a fact that just like how our forefathers were dominated and left behind hundreds of years ago, if we let all the major creations today be done by Americans and Europeans (e.g. the ideas of nationhood, democratic institutions, religious thought, the internet, airplanes, computers, international organizations and economic theories), then in another couple of hundred years from now our grandchildren will yet again be at the rear end in terms of civilization. It is because of this realization that we have to rebuild our nations based on how original and ingenious we can be in our creativity. I mean creativity in all spheres of life, not just in music and dance. We have to be creative in religion, in politics, social organization, economic theory – basically creative firstly in the way we think. It is because of this reason that in my second book I gave the arrow of time not referencing historical events but rather the present time, and how the biggest creation of now (that is independent of the colonial history) should act as the most important date / event we reference as we go about re-orienting our thinking and organizing our society anew.

One of the issues I have witnessed in some African counties, for example our own, is how some traditional leaders or kings still want to be political agents. If we are to use the nation-state as the civilizing entity for people with a triple heritage, then it is essential that the traditional leaders stay with cultural roles only. If they venture into politics, all signs show that many citizens who are not indigenous to those areas are highly susceptible to being politically sidelined. In an actual sense, traditional leaders agitating for political roles lead to weakening the nation-building exercise. When you agitate for traditional leaders to have political powers, you are forgetting that the vast majority of our peoples come from small tribes who don't have traditional institutions, and this is a recipe for marginalizing them when they settle in areas with political traditional leaders.

So, just as the nation-state should be secular – not based on religion – so should it also be independent of tribal traditional rulers. The tribe did not civilize us and there is no sign that it will civilize us, so we have to choose and fight for the entity called "a nation-state" to be the civilizing force for all our aspirations and wishes. The black American civil rights leader and Pan African WEB Du Bois realized this fundamental issue when he said, "When a child is born in a tribe, the price of his growing up is giving up some of his freedom to the tribe. This he soon learns or he dies. When the tribe becomes a union of tribes [nation-state], the individual tribe surrenders some part of its freedom to the [nation-state]." He said this because he believed that, "If Africa unites, it will be because each nation, each tribe, gives up a part of its heritage for the good of the whole."

If you think this forfeiture of political power by our kings is too much for them to come to terms with, consider how much harder the change the Japanese Emperor had to go through was. Before 1945, the Japanese Emperor was considered God on Earth by the Japanese. In fact, most people could not even dare look at him, the way the Bible tells us that Moses on Mount Sinai could not dare look at the great God. Can you imagine how impossible it should have seemed for the victorious US to force the Japanese society to write it in their constitution and have the Emperor renounce his divinity in front of his subjects? Trust me, that has to be a million times harder than our so-called kings being humble enough to agree that they are cultural leaders of their peoples, and not political leaders of administrative areas. We all know the Japanese still revere their emperor unquestionably, but he has come down to be a human being like any of us, and the result is that you have a modern monarchy in Japan and a modern people living in the country. Nothing lost, only a paradigm shift in statehood.

Many of our tribes in Uganda or Africa, e.g. the Kikuyu in Kenya, had councils of elders or chiefs. We should recognize that that history and reality is authentic. Instead of blindly getting rid of cornerstones that are authentic to our state of being, we need to instead build on them. As Mazrui says, we need to realize at some point that the solution to Africa's war of culture does not lie in a mere geographical pronouncement; it must include a pronouncement that the ancestral is authentic. It might have been weak or disadvantaged, but it was authentically us. Knowing this but also being very mindful of the risk that traditional norms could cause our national building project, I propose in *The Fourth Republic* that instead of recreating a council of elders or chiefs – which is a static way of looking back at our traditions, we can upgrade it and go beyond what did not work. I propose a Council of Creators, which is the institution that brings together the young (who are worldly and can harness modernity and science) and the elders (who are the custodians of the continuity of our traditions). If you intimately consider the way our societal development was sabotaged, and weigh the various innovations I propose in *The Fourth Republic*, you will open your mind's eyes to see that the real politician that is worth our support should be one whose slogan loosely translates to DARE TO CREATE.